DAILY SCRIPTURE
guidebook

Spending time with Jesus every day is a nonnegotiable for me. *Daily Scripture Guidebook* is one of my go-to daily devotionals for reading the Bible in a year.

Zach Windahl, author of *The Bible, Simplified*

If you've ever wished for a Bible tour guide, Tim Wildsmith is your guy. By setting the pace and pointing out important context and themes along the way, his *Daily Scripture Guidebook* is the friend you need for your Bible-in-a-year journey.

Amanda Bible Williams, cofounder, She Reads Truth; general editor of *She Reads Truth Bible*

This guidebook makes reading through the entire Bible feel not just doable—but deeply meaningful. A wonderful tool for anyone ready to grow in their faith.

Raechel Myers, cofounder, She Reads Truth; general editor of *She Reads Truth Bible*

This guidebook is more than just a Bible reading plan—it's a daily invitation to encounter the voice of God. Tim Wildsmith has created a resource that is both deeply practical and spiritually rich, helping people walk through Scripture with clarity and consistency. I love that this plan begins with Jesus and keeps you anchored in the story of redemption from day one. If you've ever struggled to read the Bible daily, this will be a faithful and encouraging companion on the journey.

Darren Whitehead, lead pastor, Church of the City; author of *The Digital Fast*

Tim is doing pioneering work for this generation. He is helping folks understand "all things Bible." On his remarkable YouTube program, he has explained how Bibles are made and the variety of English translations. Now Tim goes to the heart of the matter. He will help you read and study what's inside the Book. In *Daily Scripture Guidebook* Tim provides an accessible paint-by-numbers approach for you to read through and engage with Scripture. This is more than a "check the box" reading program. This is a guide and a plan for you to learn about the Author of Life. From one "Bible nerd" to another, I simply love what Tim is doing.

Michael Easley, pastor; former president, Moody Bible Institute

As a pastor, I'm often asked how to engage the Bible in a meaningful, consistent way. Tim Wildsmith's *Daily Scripture Guidebook* is exactly the resource people are looking for. It's accessible, thoughtfully curated, and invites reflection without overwhelming the reader. This guidebook offers a gentle rhythm for daily engagement that nurtures both understanding and spiritual growth. Whether someone is just beginning their journey with Scripture or looking to deepen their practice, Wildsmith has created something truly valuable.

Sean Palmer, teaching pastor, Ecclesia Houston; preaching coach; and author of *Unarmed Empire*

Daily Scripture Guidebook is a refreshing and powerful tool to build a daily Bible reading habit. You can start any day of the year, and the plan's mix of Old Testament, New Testament, Psalms, and Proverbs keeps each day fresh and engaging. I especially appreciate how it pairs with the *Daily Scripture Bible* for easy navigation. Tim's weekly commentary adds rich context and life-giving encouragement to help you apply God's Word to daily life.

Ellen Krause, coauthor of *The EASY Bible Study Method*; cocreator, Coffee and Bible Time

The truth revealed in Scripture never changes, but sometimes we need to change how we read and reflect on Scripture. Tim Wildsmith's guidebook is like a breath of fresh air for serious followers of Jesus who are looking for a new and engaging way to read the Bible. The suggested readings offered in this book from the Old Testament, New Testament, and Psalms and Proverbs are a perfect mix of passages to stay grounded in biblical history and spend time with Jesus every day. Tim is a helpful guide for those who want to live in the story the Bible is telling!

Derek Vreeland, pastor; author of *Centering Jesus*

DAILY SCRIPTURE *guidebook*

A 52-Week Journey
Through the Bible

TIM WILDSMITH

ZONDERVAN
REFLECTIVE

ZONDERVAN REFLECTIVE

Daily Scripture Guidebook
Copyright © 2025 by Tim Wildsmith

Published by Zondervan, 3950 Sparks Drive SE, Suite 101, Grand Rapids, MI 49546, USA.
Zondervan is a registered trademark of The Zondervan Corporation, L.L.C., a wholly owned
subsidiary of HarperCollins Christian Publishing, Inc.

Requests for information should be addressed to customercare@harpercollins.com.

Zondervan titles may be purchased in bulk for educational, business, fundraising, or sales
promotional use. For information, please email SpecialMarkets@Zondervan.com.

ISBN 978-0-310-17515-5 (softcover)
ISBN 978-0-310-17516-2 (ebook)

HarperCollins Publishers, Macken House, 39/40 Mayor Street Upper,
Dublin 1, D01 C9W8, Ireland (https://www.harpercollins.com)

Cover design: Becca Wildsmith
Cover art: © Ace Bss716/Shutterstock; Becca Wildsmith
Interior design: Name goes here

Printed in the United States of America

25 26 27 28 29 LBC 6 5 4 3 2

CONTENTS

INTRODUCTION

Welcome to the *Daily Scripture Guidebook*. This book is designed to be both a guide and companion as you read through the entire Bible in one year. It's divided into fifty-two chapters, and in each one you'll find a reading schedule for the week (complete with checkboxes so you can track your progress), insights about the portions of Scripture you'll be reading, and some space to write down your reflections. My suggestion is that you read each chapter at the beginning of the week because my insights are designed to help you navigate the readings. In this introduction, I'll offer a few tips that will help you get the most out of this journey through the Bible.

The Reading Plan

There are a ton of great Bible reading plans out there, and I have followed several over the years. The plan we're going to follow comes from the *Daily Scripture* Bible, available in multiple Bible translations. This reading plan is unique because each day includes a reading from the Old Testament, the New Testament, and a psalm or a proverb. Let me share a few reasons why I like this plan.

IT KEEPS THINGS FRESH.

Anyone who has ever tried to read the Bible straight through from Genesis to Revelation knows there are several places where it can get . . . difficult. I often joke that Leviticus is the place where many readers doing read-the-Bible-in-a-year plans get off track or stop altogether. Don't get me wrong. I think Leviticus is an important book. But it's nowhere near as compelling or easy to read as Genesis, Exodus, and many other books of the Bible. I know many people have given up on their Bible reading plan simply because Leviticus is such a struggle to get through. But the *Daily Scripture* reading plan includes readings from three different places every day, which will help keep you from getting bogged down in some of the more challenging spots.

You get to spend time with Jesus every day.

The New Testament comprises less than 25 percent of the Bible. This means that if you read straight through from Genesis to Revelation, you have to read for nine months before you get to the gospel of Matthew and are able to spend time with Jesus (yes, I know that the Old Testament is filled with references to Jesus, but his presence in the New Testament is more direct). This plan includes the New Testament from day 1, so you will interact with Jesus and his first followers every day for an entire year.

You will develop a daily rhythm of reading the Bible.

Some plans give you days off, which can be a good thing for certain people (if that's you, make sure you check out the following list of tips). But the *Daily Scripture* reading plan is just that: daily. It encourages you to read your Bible every single day. My hope is that after following this plan for a year, you will have developed a new daily rhythm of reading the Bible. When our lives are rooted in the Word of God, we become more and more like the people God created us to be.

You can follow this plan in your favorite Bible simply by placing a ribbon or bookmark in each section: Old Testament, New

Testament, Psalms, and Proverbs. Doing this will allow you to quickly pick up where you left off the day before. But if you want to avoid all that jumping around, check out the *Daily Scripture* Bibles from Zondervan. These Bibles are not in traditional order, but instead follow the unique order of this reading plan.

One important thing to know is that this reading plan is not date specific, which means you don't have to start on January 1. You can begin whenever you're ready, and the plan will guide you in a complete read-through of the Bible over the next 365 days.

Six Tips for Completing the Journey

I have successfully read through the Bible in a year several times, but I've also tried and failed on multiple attempts. So before you begin your yearlong journey through the Bible, here are a few tips I have learned (through success and failure) to help you make the most of the experience. These first three tips are more practical in nature. The next three are all about making this year through the Bible a truly meaningful and transformative experience.

Tip 1—Stick to the plan.

The biggest reason many people fail to successfully read the Bible in a year is simply because they don't stick to their plan. I find that once I miss a few days and fall behind, I get so discouraged that I just give up. The best way to avoid this is by making this reading plan a priority in your daily schedule. Most people should be able to read all three sections of the reading plan in about ten to fifteen minutes each day. If you do miss a day, then catch up the next day by reading two days of the plan. And if you know it's going to be consistently difficult to read on a certain day of the week, then modify the plan so that you double up on the day before or after.

Tip 2—Find a Bible that's right for you.

I am convinced that you will want to spend more time reading the Bible when you find one you truly love. Start by choosing a translation of the Bible (check out my book *Bible Translations for Everyone* if you need help figuring out which one is right for you). Then look for an edition of that translation that draws you in. Most major translations are available in a variety of formats (study Bibles, journaling Bibles, premium Bibles, large print Bibles, etc.). Trust me, when you find a Bible that combines the right translation and the right format for you, you won't want to put it down.

Tip 3—Read at the same time and place every day.

Consistency is important when developing new habits, so choose a time and place to do your Bible reading each day. Many people do it first thing in the morning. Others opt for right before bed (this never works for me because I get too sleepy before I'm done with my reading). I have one friend who reads his Bible each day on his lunch break. I highly recommend you choose a place where you can read without distraction. I have a small room at the front of my home where the morning light is lovely, and it has become my peaceful place to read and study the Bible, usually with a cup of good coffee close by. Make this a consistent rhythm in your life and it will quickly become something you look forward to every day.

Tip 4—Engage with the text.

Don't just *read* the Bible; engage with the text in a deeper way. Write down questions that come to mind while you're reading, and then go look up the answers after you finish your reading for the day. Highlight or underline key words or phrases that stand out to you. Each week pick one verse to memorize (this level of engagement will require a bit more time every day, but I think you'll find it to be worth it). Use the space provided in this book for daily reflection to consider what you learned from the readings and how you can apply it to your life.

Tip 5—Invite someone to join you.

The only thing better than reading the Bible in a year is doing it with someone you love. Invite a friend or family member to join you on this journey through the Bible. This will naturally create some accountability to stick to the plan. It will also give you someone to share your thoughts and questions with.

Tip 6—Remember to pray.

Yes, this plan is about reading the Bible in a year. But the time we spend reading the Bible should go hand in hand with prayer. Perhaps you want to pray *before* you read every day. Pray for your loved ones, offer some gratitude to God, and invite him to speak to you through the texts you're about to read. Or maybe you want to pause *after* your daily reading to ask God to help you apply what you've read. An even better idea: Do both! Imagine the kind of impact this could have if you not only read the Bible every day for a year but also took the time to dwell in God's presence through prayer.

It's Time to Begin

God has a way of meeting us through his Word in incredible and often unexpected ways. My prayer is that this book will be a helpful resource as you read through the Bible in the days, weeks, and months ahead. I hope you enjoy the journey.

> Your word is a lamp for my feet,
> a light on my path. (Ps. 119:105)

WEEK 1

Daily Readings

	Old Testament	New Testament	Psalms / Proverbs	
Day 1	Genesis 1:1–2:17	Matthew 1:1–25	Psalm 1:1–6	☐
Day 2	Genesis 2:18–4:16	Matthew 2:1–18	Psalm 2:1–12	☐
Day 3	Genesis 4:17–6:22	Matthew 2:19–3:17	Psalm 3:1–8	☐
Day 4	Genesis 7:1–9:17	Matthew 4:1–22	Proverbs 1:1–7	☐
Day 5	Genesis 9:18–11:9	Matthew 4:23–5:20	Psalm 4:1–8	☐
Day 6	Genesis 11:10–13:18	Matthew 5:21–42	Psalm 5:1–12	☐
Day 7	Genesis 14:1–16:16	Matthew 5:43–6:24	Psalm 6:1–10	☐

Old Testament

This week's Old Testament readings take us through the first sixteen chapters of Genesis. A lot happens here as the story of God and the people of Israel unfolds, but I'd like to draw your attention to the opening chapter.

Genesis 1 tells us seven times that when God looked on the world as he was creating it, he saw that it was good. The final verse of the chapter even says it was *very* good.

> God saw all that he had made, and it was very good. And there was evening, and there was morning—the sixth day. (Gen. 1:31)

What do you think God is trying to tell us?

One of the most important takeaways from this opening chapter of the Bible is that God created something good. That goodness is the foundation of all creation. The beginning of this story—our story—is good. And we need to remember that, because the pages ahead are filled with countless stories that are *not* good. The Bible is so full of sadness and loss and death that it can be overwhelming for many readers. Not only that, but when we look up from these pages and examine the world around us, it too can be full of great sorrow.

If all of this was created to be good, then what went wrong?

Keep reading. In a couple of chapters, sin enters the story. The sinfulness of humanity is going to interrupt God's good and perfect creation.

But when you complete this journey of reading through the Bible, you'll see that sin and sadness and death do not get the final word. When all is said and done, God makes all things new and returns them to the way they were right here in the garden at the beginning. The end of the story is also *very* good.

So when you feel overwhelmed, don't lose heart. Remember that this is a good story. Maybe you will want to flip back here to the opening pages every now and then to be reminded of that. God created something good, and the story is not over until he makes it good again.

New Testament

Our New Testament readings this week are in the first six chapters of Matthew. Many biblical scholars agree that Matthew was written to a primarily Jewish audience, and one of the major themes of this account of the life of Jesus is his status as the long-awaited Messiah. Matthew repeatedly highlights how Jesus fulfills different prophecies from the Hebrew Bible, and in these first few chapters you will notice several distinct connections to the Old Testament.

One example of this is the opening genealogy in Matthew 1. Not only does this genealogy create a clear connection between Jesus and King David, but it also traces the lineage of Jesus back to Abraham, the great patriarch of the Israelite people. This differs from a similar genealogy in the gospel of Luke, which goes all the way back to Adam.

Why do you think these two genealogies are different? Can you think of any reasons why Matthew and Luke would begin their genealogies of Jesus with two different people? Make a mental note, because I'll offer some insights on Luke's genealogy in week 12.

Another key moment that would have immediately reminded Matthew's first readers of the Old Testament is in chapter 2, when King Herod secretly plans to have Jesus killed. This is one of many similarities between Jesus and Moses highlighted in the gospel of Matthew (see how many more you can find along the way). The epic Sermon on the Mount in chapter 5 is the first of five distinct teaching sections recorded by Matthew, which parallels the first five books of the Old Testament called the Torah. I love it when Scripture echoes Scripture.

You're going to be reading Matthew for the next six weeks while also reading through Genesis and Exodus, and I encourage you to make note of anything in Matthew that seems to connect with what you read in the Old Testament. It's likely that Matthew intentionally made these connections to help his readers understand that what God was doing through Jesus was the continuation and fulfillment of what the Bible has been about from the very beginning.

Psalms and Proverbs

The book of Psalms is a collection of 150 ancient Hebrew poems, songs, and prayers written by a variety of authors (seventy-three of the Psalms are attributed to King David). There are several different types: psalms of praise, psalms of lament, psalms of thanksgiving, royal psalms, and didactic psalms. From ancient times to today, the psalms have been used both publicly and privately for worship, prayer, and reflection. I encourage you to read the psalms slowly and, if possible, more than once. The more familiar you become with them, the more you will be able to feel their rhythm.

Proverbs is filled with hundreds of short, clever sayings designed to impart wisdom on those who read them. Because there are thirty-one chapters, many people choose to read through the entire book every month (chapter 1 on the first day of the month, chapter 2 on the second day of the month, and so on). Our reading plan has us returning to Proverbs every four days to read just a few verses at a time. So, once again, take it slow and allow yourself to think about what these verses can teach you about living a life of wisdom.

Reflections

Write down a few reflections on this week's readings.

Day 1: Genesis 1:1–2:17; Matthew 1:1–25; Psalm 1:1–6

Day 2: Genesis 2:18–4:16; Matthew 2:1–18; Psalm 2:1–12

Day 3: Genesis 4:17–6:22; Matthew 2:19–3:17; Psalm 3:1–8

Day 4: Genesis 7:1–9:17; Matthew 4:1–22; Proverbs 1:1–7

Day 5: Genesis 9:18–11:9; Matthew 4:23–5:20; Psalm 4:1–8

Day 6: Genesis 11:10–13:18; Matthew 5:21–42; Psalm 5:1–12

Day 7: Genesis 14:1–16:16; Matthew 5:43–6:24; Psalm 6:1–10

_____

_____

_____

_____

_____

_____

WEEK 2

	Old Testament	New Testament	Psalms / Proverbs	
Day 8	Genesis 17:1–18:33	Matthew 6:25–7:23	Proverbs 1:8–19	☐
Day 9	Genesis 19:1–20:18	Matthew 7:24–8:22	Psalm 7:1–9	☐
Day 10	Genesis 21:1–23:20	Matthew 8:23–9:13	Psalm 7:10–17	☐
Day 11	Genesis 24:1–67	Matthew 9:14–38	Psalm 8:1–9	☐
Day 12	Genesis 25:1–26:35	Matthew 10:1–31	Proverbs 1:20–33	☐
Day 13	Genesis 27:1–28:22	Matthew 10:32–11:15	Psalm 9:1–6	☐
Day 14	Genesis 29:1–30:43	Matthew 11:16–30	Psalm 9:7–12	☐

Old Testament

Last week we were introduced to Abram at the end of Genesis 11. He is one of the most important figures in the Bible because it's his covenant with God that establishes what will become the people of Israel. Genesis 1–11 was the origin story of humanity, but with Abram we begin to explore the special relationship between God and his chosen people.

This week we arrive at an important moment in Genesis 17, where God reaffirms this covenant and, while doing so, changes Abram's name to Abraham. This change is ever so small, but it represents something massive: Abram means "exalted father," but Abraham means "father of multitudes."

> No longer will you be called Abram; your name will be Abraham, for I have made you a father of many nations. I will make you very fruitful; I will make nations of you, and kings will come

from you. I will establish my covenant as an everlasting covenant between me and you and your descendants after you for the generations to come, to be your God and the God of your descendants after you. (Gen. 17:5–7)

Not only does God promise to give Abraham a great family that will outnumber the stars in the sky (Gen. 15:5), but he also promises to be their God forever and to bless them and bless the whole world through them (Gen. 12:2–3). Abraham's new name becomes synonymous with God's promise, and that's why his name is repeated throughout the Bible by other great figures such as Moses, David, Isaiah, the apostle Paul, and even Jesus. They don't just talk about "Father Abraham" because he's their ancestor; they talk about him because he represents the special covenant they have with God.

Much of what we read about in the Bible revolves around this relationship between God and his people. As you'll see, the people of Israel struggle to hold up their end of the covenant. The pages ahead are filled with wild, twisting stories where they continually screw up. But God remains faithful to his promises even when they fail. That's good news for them, and it's good news for you and me too.

New Testament

The gospel of Matthew includes many incredible teaching moments from Jesus. Some of them come in large sections (like the Sermon on the Mount in chapters 5–7), but others occur in small moments along the way. One of my favorite minor moments is found in these three verses:

Come to me, all you who are weary and burdened, and I will give you rest. Take my yoke upon you and learn from me, for I am gentle and humble in heart, and you will find rest for your souls. For my yoke is easy and my burden is light. (Matt. 11:28–30)

Jesus uses the word *rest* twice in these three verses, and both times it is accompanied by a command. In the first verse, he says to all who are weary: "Come to me . . . and I will give you rest."

When you want to rest, what do you turn to? Is it sleeping, reading, eating a good meal, watching TV? Or do you find rest in Jesus?

Don't miss the context of what's happening here. This is first-century Israel, where the Jewish people Jesus was speaking to were under the heavy restrictions of the Mosaic law. Plus, they were living under the watchful eye of the Roman Empire. It is this challenging environment in which Jesus is offering rest. He's offering them a better way, but they must come to him. *They have to trust him.*

In the next verse, Jesus explains *how* to get that rest: "Take my yoke upon you and learn from me." But what does it mean to take on the yoke of Christ?

The most common image of a yoke is one where two animals are linked together to bear the weight of something. So this is an invitation to link up with Jesus. And the truth is that we can't take on his yoke unless we first take off our own. He is inviting us to lay our burdens down. Or perhaps it's more accurate to say that as we take on his yoke, he takes on ours. This is really hard for some of us because we like to be in control. But we find rest for our souls by surrendering everything to Jesus and trusting him. That's what it means to live easy and light.

Psalms and Proverbs

Psalm 8 explores the majesty of God. It's so good that many hymns and worship songs still use King David's ancient words to help us sing praises to God thousands of years later. If you have time this week, read Psalm 8 more than once. Read it slowly and notice how David's worship of God leads him to reflection.

> When I consider your heavens,
>> the work of your fingers,
> the moon and the stars,
>> which you have set in place,
> what is mankind that you are mindful of them,
>> human beings that you care for them? (Ps. 8:3–4)

David's awe of God and creation leads him to reflect on just how astonishing it is that God cares about people. The fact that this majestic God loves us and invites us to participate in the work of his *very good* creation is truly remarkable.

Let that sink in.

The creator of the universe loves you.

Reflections

Write down a few reflections on this week's readings.

Day 8: Genesis 17:1–18:33; Matthew 6:25–7:23; Proverbs 1:8–19

_____

_____

_____

_____

_____

Day 9: Genesis 19:1–20:18; Matthew 7:24–8:22; Psalm 7:1–9

Day 10: Genesis 21:1–23:20; Matthew 8:23–9:13; Psalm 7:10–17

Day 11: Genesis 24:1–67; Matthew 9:14–38; Psalm 8:1–9

Day 12: Genesis 25:1–26:35; Matthew 10:1–31; Proverbs 1:20–33

Day 13: Genesis 27:1–28:22; Matthew 10:32–11:15; Psalm 9:1–6

Day 14: Genesis 29:1–30:43; Matthew 11:16–30; Psalm 9:7–12

Week 3

Daily Readings

	Old Testament	New Testament	Psalms / Proverbs	
Day 15	Genesis 31:1–55	Matthew 12:1–21	Psalm 9:13–20	☐
Day 16	Genesis 32:1–33:20	Matthew 12:22–45	Proverbs 2:1–11	☐
Day 17	Genesis 34:1–35:29	Matthew 12:46–13:17	Psalm 10:1–11	☐
Day 18	Genesis 36:1–37:36	Matthew 13:18–35	Psalm 10:12–18	☐
Day 19	Genesis 38:1–39:23	Matthew 13:36–58	Psalm 11:1–7	☐
Day 20	Genesis 40:1–41:40	Matthew 14:1–21	Proverbs 2:12–22	☐
Day 21	Genesis 41:41–42:38	Matthew 14:22–15:9	Psalm 12:1–8	☐

Old Testament

Our Old Testament readings this week pick up in the middle of Jacob's story, and in Genesis 32 we find a pivotal and peculiar scene where Jacob wrestles with God. The setting is dark—literally at night—and mysterious. Jacob finds himself alone on the banks of the Jabbok River (a branch of the Jordan), where a shadowy figure attacks him.

> So Jacob was left alone, and a man wrestled with him till daybreak. When the man saw that he could not overpower him, he touched the socket of Jacob's hip so that his hip was wrenched as he wrestled with the man. Then the man said, "Let me go, for it is daybreak."
>
> But Jacob replied, "I will not let you go unless you bless me." (Gen. 32:24–26)

The figure responds by asking Jacob what his name is. Remember, this is the same Jacob who stole his brother Esau's blessing from their father, Isaac. Jacob's name is synonymous with this deceptive act, so by saying his own name, he is forced to admit who he really is.

And then something remarkable happens.

The shadowy figure changes Jacob's name. And it's not just any name. His name is changed to Israel. He becomes the name-sake of God's chosen people. This is what redemption looks like. Jacob was a deceiver constantly on the run from who God had called him to be. He fought God, literally and figuratively, for a blessing that was only temporary. But God had something better planned for his life. He gave him a new name and a new destiny. He gave him a blessing that would last forever.

If you ever feel like you're running from who God created you to be, return to this passage. Read it again and again. Be reminded that God fights for you, even when it's you he has to fight.

New Testament

This week's New Testament readings give us snapshots of Jesus's life, including some amazing miracles, parables, and his teaching on the Sabbath. Matthew 12 opens with a face-off between Jesus and the Pharisees, who take issue with the fact that the disciples were disobeying the Sabbath laws of the Torah. Notice how Jesus tries to show them that their legalistic views are missing something. The Pharisees are so focused on the "letter of the law" that they can't see what the law was truly intended for. Immediately after this encounter, Jesus goes into the synagogue and heals someone. His ability to heal is affirmation of his teachings about the Sabbath, but this entire episode causes the Pharisees to despise him even more. Why do you think the Pharisees were so bothered by the good things Jesus did?

Chapter 13 is the third of five extended teaching "discourses" in Matthew. Bible commentaries call this the Parabolic Discourse because Jesus teaches about the kingdom of God through parables, which are short stories that illustrate a deeper truth. Jesus uses things familiar to the people of his day—farming, baking, fishing, etc.—to give them clues about what God is up to all around them. In some cases, as with the parable of the sower, Jesus offers an explanation of what the parable means. In others, we are invited to interpret for ourselves. Which ones do you find most compelling?

In chapter 14 we learn the sad fate of John the Baptist, and then Jesus performs two of his most incredible miracles when he feeds five thousand people (with only five loaves of bread and two fish) and walks on water. Things are clearly escalating, and Matthew wants us to feel the tension. When you read these passages, imagine yourself as a bystander. How would you feel if you witnessed Jesus saying and doing these things? What would you say to him?

Psalms and Proverbs

Proverbs is filled with short, simple sayings intended to impart wisdom to readers, but wisdom is not a simple thing, and it's not easy to attain. A lot of people equate wisdom to knowledge, but it's more than that (we probably all know people who are awfully smart yet lack wisdom). Wisdom is a combination of knowledge, experience, and good judgment. Wisdom is something we have to pursue and work at. Proverbs 2:4 tells us to search for wisdom in the same way that we might search for hidden treasure.

That sounds like a lot of work. Is it worth it?

Keep reading.

The pursuit of wisdom leads to knowledge and understanding (v. 6), success (v. 7), protection (v. 8), discretion (v. 11), and righteousness (v. 20). Wisdom also protects us from all sorts of bad things (vv. 12–19).

So yes, the pursuit of wisdom is a lot of work, but if you want to truly live the good life, it's worth the effort.

Reflections

Write down a few reflections on this week's readings.

Day 15: Genesis 31:1–55; Matthew 12:1–21; Psalm 9:13–20

Day 16: Genesis 32:1–33:20; Matthew 12:22–45; Proverbs 2:1–11

Day 17: Genesis 34:1–35:29; Matthew 12:46–13:17; Psalm 10:1–11

Day 18: Genesis 36:1–37:36; Matthew 13:18–35; Psalm 10:12–18

Day 19: Genesis 38:1–39:23; Matthew 13:36–58; Psalm 11:1–7

Day 20: Genesis 40:1–41:40; Matthew 14:1–21; Proverbs 2:12–22

Day 21: Genesis 41:41–42:38; Matthew 14:22–15:9; Psalm 12:1–8

WEEK 4

	Old Testament	New Testament	Psalms / Proverbs	
Day 22	Genesis 43:1–44:34	Matthew 15:10–39	Psalm 13:1–6	
Day 23	Genesis 45:1–47:12	Matthew 16:1–20	Psalm 14:1–7	
Day 24	Genesis 47:13–48:22	Matthew 16:21–17:13	Proverbs 3:1–10	
Day 25	Genesis 49:1–50:26	Matthew 17:14–18:9	Psalm 15:1–5	
Day 26	Exodus 1:1–3:22	Matthew 18:10–35	Psalm 16:1–11	
Day 27	Exodus 4:1–6:12	Matthew 19:1–15	Psalm 17:1–5	
Day 28	Exodus 6:13–8:32	Matthew 19:16–30	Proverbs 3:11–20	

Old Testament

Genesis concludes with the dramatic story of Joseph and his brothers. It is certainly fitting that the sons of Jacob—the infamous birthright swindler—had their own issues as siblings. Yet God uses the injustice Joseph's own brothers inflicted on him as a pathway to redemption. After being elevated to a position of great leadership in Egypt, Joseph rescues his family from severe famine. And as Genesis comes to a close, we can see just how committed God is to the covenant he established with Abraham.

It feels like a happy ending, doesn't it?

Not so fast.

Unless this is your first time reading the Bible, you know that the story is about to get wild. When we turn the page from Genesis to Exodus, we're jumping forward several generations in the history of the people of Israel. The descendants of Abraham, Isaac, and Jacob flourished in the safe haven of Egypt, but their numbers grew so large that the Egyptians began to fear them, and we learn in Exodus 1 that the Israelites were forced into slavery.

This new book is off to a dismal start for the people of God, but then Moses enters the story. He's an unlikely hero, but we are about to see God transform him into an incredible leader.

There's a lot going on in Exodus, and for good reason. This is arguably the most important part of the Old Testament because it forms the very foundation of the Israelites' understanding of their covenant relationship with God. This defining moment in Exodus will be mentioned repeatedly throughout the Bible. As you reflect on your daily readings this week, consider how what God does for his people would have impacted future generations of Israelites, and how those same things impact you.

New Testament

A few years ago I traveled to Israel as a chaplain for a group of about thirty university students. At each stop along the way, our guide would give us the lay of the land and share some historical context, and then it was my job to open the Bible and offer devotional insights that connected with our location. One of the most powerful moments of that trip happened at Banias, a place on the northern edge of the country with a small cave at the base of a steep cliff surrounded by streams. In ancient times this area was known as Caesarea Philippi, and Matthew tells us it was here that Jesus had the following exchange with his disciples:

> When Jesus came to the region of Caesarea Philippi, he asked his disciples, "Who do people say the Son of Man is?"
>
> They replied, "Some say John the Baptist; others say Elijah; and still others, Jeremiah or one of the prophets."

"But what about you?" he asked. "Who do you say I am?"

Simon Peter answered, "You are the Messiah, the Son of the living God."

Jesus replied, "Blessed are you, Simon son of Jonah, for this was not revealed to you by flesh and blood, but by my Father in heaven. And I tell you that you are Peter, and on this rock I will build my church, and the gates of Hades will not overcome it." (Matt. 16:13–18)

At first glance it doesn't seem like the setting of Caesarea Philippi is significant to the story. But what I learned from our guide was that this location was closely associated with a Greek god named Pan, and Pan's worshipers believed that this cave was a gateway to the underworld.

As I stood there and read the passage, I realized that Jesus brought his disciples to this place on purpose. Here at a rocky cliff known as the gateway to hell, Peter proclaims that Jesus is the Messiah. And Jesus responds by telling Peter (a name that means "the rock") that he will be the foundation of the church and that the very gates of hell—I like to imagine Jesus pointing at the cave when he said this—will not be able to overcome it.

This is a powerful text, but it is even more powerful when you realize where it took place. There are many places in our world that are truly hell on earth. Jesus did not avoid these places. He took his followers into them and proclaimed the truth.

Psalms and Proverbs

I once heard someone describe psalms as ancient songs of praise and thanksgiving to God. It's true that the psalms are the hymnbook of the Hebrew Bible, but have you noticed that they're not all positive and upbeat? In fact, one of the most common types of psalms are those of lament.

Think about that for a moment.

The ancient hymnbook of our faith is filled with prayers, poems, and songs bursting with anguish and anger. In many of them, you can almost see the writer shaking their fist at God.

One of my favorites is Psalm 13, which David wrote during a troubling moment when he was likely on the run for his life. The first two verses are heavy and intense.

> How long, LORD? Will you forget me forever?
>> How long will you hide your face from me?
> How long must I wrestle with my thoughts
>> and day after day have sorrow in my heart?
>> How long will my enemy triumph over me? (Ps. 13:1–2)

Have you ever wanted to look at God and say, "How long, Lord?" Yeah, me too.

And I find it comforting to know that crying out to God like this is demonstrated in the Psalms. It's okay for us to feel overwhelmed. It's even okay for us to question what God is up to when our lives don't seem to make any sense. In the next two verses, David boldly demands an answer from God. But then something beautiful happens. In the closing two verses, he seems to take a deep breath, and his sorrow turns into joy.

> But I trust in your unfailing love;
>> my heart rejoices in your salvation.
> I will sing the LORD's praise,
>> for he has been good to me. (Ps. 13:5–6)

This pattern is repeated many times in the psalms of lament. Crying out to God is okay, but we also need to be reminded that God has been and will continue to be faithful. No matter what we face, his love never fails.

Reflections

Write down a few reflections on this week's readings.

Day 22: Genesis 43:1–44:34; Matthew 15:10–39; Psalm 13:1–6

Day 23: Genesis 45:1–47:12; Matthew 16:1–20; Psalm 14:1–7

Day 24: Genesis 47:13–48:22; Matthew 16:21–17:13; Proverbs 3:1–10

Day 25: Genesis 49:1–50:26; Matthew 17:14–18:9; Psalm 15:1–5

Day 26: Exodus 1:1–3:22; Matthew 18:10–35; Psalm 16:1–11

Day 27: Exodus 4:1–6:12; Matthew 19:1–15; Psalm 17:1–5

Day 28: Exodus 6:13–8:32; Matthew 19:16–30; Proverbs 3:11–20

WEEK 5

	Old Testament	New Testament	Psalms / Proverbs	
Day 29	Exodus 9:1–10:29	Matthew 20:1–19	Psalm 17:6–12	☐
Day 30	Exodus 11:1–12:51	Matthew 20:20–34	Psalm 17:13–15	☐
Day 31	Exodus 13:1–14:31	Matthew 21:1–17	Psalm 18:1–6	☐
Day 32	Exodus 15:1–16:36	Matthew 21:18–32	Proverbs 3:21–35	☐
Day 33	Exodus 17:1–18:27	Matthew 21:33–22:14	Psalm 18:7–15	☐
Day 34	Exodus 19:1–20:26	Matthew 22:15–46	Psalm 18:16–24	☐
Day 35	Exodus 21:1–22:31	Matthew 23:1–39	Psalm 18:25–36	☐

Old Testament

Our readings in Exodus this week are enthralling. The story picks up detailing the plagues of Egypt and the hard heart of Pharaoh, followed by the climactic first Passover and the death of the first-born, which compels Pharaoh to finally let the Israelites go. Next we'll read about the crossing of the Red Sea, God's provision for his people in the desert wilderness, their arrival at Mount Sinai, and the giving of the Ten Commandments.

Buried in the middle of this dramatic portion of Scripture is something I don't want you to miss—the first song in the Bible. It's easy to overlook when so many other epic things are happening, but in Exodus 15, just after the crossing of the Red Sea, Moses and the Israelites raise up a song of praise to God.

I confess that this song makes me uncomfortable because much of it is filled with imagery of the drowning of Pharaoh and his armies. How are we to reconcile what Jesus says about loving our enemies with the way Exodus 15 celebrates their destruction? One thing I notice is that even though this song serves as a celebration of the defeat of the Egyptians, it's really about God's power and deliverance. It's about salvation. Moses and the people of Israel witness God's miraculous rescue, and their response is worship.

> The LORD is my strength and my defense;
>> he has become my salvation.
> He is my God, and I will praise him,
>> my father's God, and I will exalt him. (Ex. 15:2)

This is the first song in the Bible. In Revelation 15 we find the last song in the Bible, where John tells us it's "the song of God's servant Moses and of the Lamb" (Rev. 15:3). It's not identical to the song from Exodus (in Revelation we find no references to the defeat of the Egyptians), but the overall theme is very much the same. It's a song about the greatness of God.

> **WORD STUDY:** When you read the word *salvation* in Exodus 15:2, the Hebrew word being translated is *yeshua*. The ancient Greek translation of this word is *Iesous*, which is where we get the name Jesus. Right in the middle of the incredible Exodus story we find the first song in the Bible, and hidden within this song we find a glimmer of the hope and salvation that is to come in Jesus.

New Testament

If you could listen to only one song for the rest of your life, what would it be? I don't know about you, but I *hate* questions like that. I can never pick just one. I'm more of a Top 5 list kind of guy.

In Matthew 22 the Pharisees ask Jesus a similar question. They don't want to know his favorite song, but they do want to know his favorite commandment. Jesus quickly answers the question by quoting two passages from Deuteronomy and Leviticus.

> Jesus replied: "'Love the Lord your God with all your heart and with all your soul and with all your mind.' This is the first and greatest commandment. And the second is like it: 'Love your neighbor as yourself.' All the Law and the Prophets hang on these two commandments." (Matt. 22:37–40)

This response has become a catchphrase of sorts for Christians: "Love God, Love People." But that's an extreme oversimplification of what Jesus means. He says the most important thing is to love God, but he qualifies that statement by saying we must do so with all our hearts, souls, and minds. That is a deep and profound kind of love. What does it look like for you to love God with all your heart, all your soul, and all your mind?

And Jesus doesn't stop there. He tells us to love our neighbors. In Luke 10 we will read about a similar encounter where someone asks Jesus to define *neighbor*. In response, Jesus tells the parable of the good Samaritan. In this parable, bandits attack a Jewish man while he's traveling. Robbed, beaten, and left for dead, he is ignored by two Jewish religious leaders. But a Samaritan— someone the Jews hated—came along and felt compassion for the wounded man. He helped him.

So Jesus answers the question "Who is my neighbor?" with a story about a man who showed extravagant compassion for someone he disagreed with. That's what he means when he says, "Love your neighbor as yourself." What does it look like for you to truly love people, even those you disagree with?

Remember when I brought up wisdom? Wrestling with questions like these and applying them to our lives takes wisdom—living out the answers is tough and necessary. I find myself coming back to these verses again and again to refocus on loving God with everything I have and loving my neighbor as myself.

Psalms and Proverbs

It's fitting that we'll spend quite a bit of time this week in Psalm 18, where David sings to the Lord in much the same way that Moses and the Israelites sang their first song in Exodus 15. The preface to Psalm 18 tells us that David "sang to the Lord the words of this song when the Lord delivered him from the hand of all his enemies and from the hand of Saul." At fifty verses, this is the fourth longest psalm in the Bible, and David takes his time to fully express his love to God.

If you have time, I encourage you to read all of Psalm 18 in one sitting the first time. After that, follow the reading plan and focus on the smaller sections of it. I find that this psalm makes a powerful statement as a whole and has many little moments within it that I need to dwell on more intently. Every time I read Psalm 18, I see something new.

Reflections

Write down a few reflections on this week's readings.

Day 29: Exodus 9:1–10:29; Matthew 20:1–19; Psalm 17:6–12

Day 30: Exodus 11:1–12:51; Matthew 20:20–34; Psalm 17:13–15

Day 31: Exodus 13:1–14:31; Matthew 21:1–17; Psalm 18:1–6

Day 32: Exodus 15:1–16:36; Matthew 21:18–32; Proverbs 3:21–35

Day 33: Exodus 17:1–18:27; Matthew 21:33–22:14; Psalm 18:7–15

Day 34: Exodus 19:1–20:26; Matthew 22:15–46; Psalm 18:16–24

_____

_____

_____

_____

_____

_____

Day 35: Exodus 21:1–22:31; Matthew 23:1–39; Psalm 18:25–36

_____

_____

_____

_____

_____

_____

Week 6

Daily Readings

	Old Testament	New Testament	Psalms / Proverbs	
Day 36	Exodus 23:1–24:18	Matthew 24:1–31	Proverbs 4:1–9	☐
Day 37	Exodus 25:1–26:37	Matthew 24:32–25:13	Psalm 18:37–42	☐
Day 38	Exodus 27:1–28:43	Matthew 25:14–46	Psalm 18:43–50	☐
Day 39	Exodus 29:1–30:38	Matthew 26:1–30	Psalm 19:1–6	☐
Day 40	Exodus 31:1–33:6	Matthew 26:31–46	Proverbs 4:10–19	☐
Day 41	Exodus 33:7–34:35	Matthew 26:47–68	Psalm 19:7–14	☐
Day 42	Exodus 35:1–36:38	Matthew 26:69–27:10	Psalm 20:1–9	☐

Old Testament

The second half of Exodus is a string of interconnected events at Sinai. The most infamous portion of these passages is the story of the golden calf in chapters 32–34. But the last time I read through the Bible, something stood out to me—the golden calf saga is sandwiched between two extended sections about the tabernacle. In chapters 25–31, God gives Moses detailed plans for a portable worship structure where God will dwell among his people. It describes everything inside, as well as how the priests must dress. Using nearly identical wording as chapters 25–31, chapters 35–40 describe the construction of the tabernacle.

When people think about Exodus, these tabernacle descriptions probably aren't what come to mind first. Yet eleven chapters of the book focus on them.

Why do you think that is?

I think God is serious about dwelling among his people. These detailed plans show us that God is intentional and exceedingly creative when it comes to being with us. It's easy to get bogged down in passages like this that are filled with long lists of materials and measurements, especially when everything is repeated just a few chapters later. But when you read these passages, think about how much God cares about being with his people. And if you're a creative person, these passages of Scripture about the tabernacle may become some of your favorites. What's being described here is beautiful, and in chapters 31 and 35, two men named Bezalel and Oholiab are recognized for their great skills as artisans. God even says that Bezalel's artistic abilities come from being filled by the Spirit (Ex. 31:3). How awesome is that!

New Testament

Things escalate near the end of the gospel of Matthew. Chapter 26 is seventy-five verses long and describes several key moments, including Judas agreeing to betray Jesus, the disciples and Jesus partaking in the Last Supper, Jesus praying in the Garden of Gethsemane before being arrested, and Jesus facing an inquisition by the high priest Caiaphas and the whole Sanhedrin.

But the final seven verses of Matthew 26 focus on Peter. After sneaking up to the courtyard of the high priest to watch Jesus be questioned, three bystanders notice Peter and confront him about being with Jesus. Mere hours after telling Jesus that he would die before disowning him, Peter denies even knowing him. Notice that his denials become increasingly hostile.

1st denial: "'I don't know what you're talking about,' he said" (v. 70).

2nd denial: "He denied it again, with an oath: 'I don't know the man!'" (v. 72).

3rd denial: "Then he began to call down curses, and he swore to them, 'I don't know the man!'" (v. 74).

It's a stunning betrayal.

And yet, if you and I are honest with ourselves, we know we're capable of doing the exact same thing. Just like Peter, we find ourselves in moments every day where we can choose to be identified with Jesus, or we can deny him with our words and actions. My prayer for myself and for you is that we will always have the courage to say we are with Jesus.

Psalms and Proverbs

David describes the heavens declaring the glory of God in the first six verses of Psalm 19. I particularly love what he says in the middle two verses:

> They have no speech, they use no words;
>> no sound is heard from them.
> Yet their voice goes out into all the earth,
>> their words to the ends of the world. (Ps. 19:3–4)

The beauty and wonder of creation speak volumes about God without saying a single word. What a stunning mental image.

But then in verses 7–14, the focus abruptly shifts to the law of the Lord.

Word Study: David uses the divine name of God in Hebrew—rendered in English as "the Lord"—exactly seven times in these verses. This four-letter name, YHWH, is known as the Tetragrammaton and is often pronounced "Yahweh," although Jews typically do not say the name aloud out of reverence.

At first glance, these two halves of Psalm 19 may seem disconnected. Some scholars believe they were originally two separate psalms that were later joined together. That may very well be the case, but when you look closely, they fit together quite well.

The key to their connection is the way David talks about the law. Notice that he does not speak about it in rigid, forceful, or legalistic terms. Instead, he describes it as perfect, trustworthy, right, radiant, and pure. It's more precious than gold and sweeter than honey. David doesn't see the law of the Lord as a burden. He sees it as a gift. When you think about it that way, the law sounds a lot like creation. Both are beautifully intricate, and both give us a reason to be filled with awe and joy.

Reflections

Write down a few reflections on this week's readings.

Day 36: Exodus 23:1–24:18; Matthew 24:1–31; Proverbs 4:1–9

Day 37: Exodus 25:1–26:37; Matthew 24:32–25:13; Psalm 18:37–42

Day 38: Exodus 27:1–28:43; Matthew 25:14–46; Psalm 18:43–50

Day 39: Exodus 29:1–30:38; Matthew 26:1–30; Psalm 19:1–6

Day 40: Exodus 31:1–33:6; Matthew 26:31–46; Proverbs 4:10–19

Day 41: Exodus 33:7–34:35; Matthew 26:47–68; Psalm 19:7–14

Day 42: Exodus 35:1–36:38; Matthew 26:69–27:10; Psalm 20:1–9

Week 7

Daily Readings

	Old Testament	New Testament	Psalms / Proverbs	
Day 43	Exodus 37:1–38:31	Matthew 27:11–44	Psalm 21:1–7	☐
Day 44	Exodus 39:1–40:38	Matthew 27:45–66	Proverbs 4:20–27	☐
Day 45	Leviticus 1:1–3:17	Matthew 28:1–20	Psalm 21:8–13	☐
Day 46	Leviticus 4:1–5:13	Mark 1:1–28	Psalm 22:1–11	☐
Day 47	Leviticus 5:14–7:10	Mark 1:29–2:17	Psalm 22:12–21	☐
Day 48	Leviticus 7:11–8:36	Mark 2:18–3:30	Proverbs 5:1–14	☐
Day 49	Leviticus 9:1–10:20	Mark 3:31–4:29	Psalm 22:22–31	☐

Old Testament

This week brings us to the end of Exodus. As you read about the completion of the tabernacle and it being filled with the glory of the Lord, take a few moments to consider everything that has occurred in this epic book. Can you see why this was such an important book for the people of Israel?

What a powerful story of God's faithfulness.

And now we come to Leviticus.

Leviticus is the place where many people struggle to follow traditional Bible reading plans, and I think the main reason for this is that the text of Scripture makes a dramatic shift. Exodus is full of moments so exciting that several movies have been made about it. Leviticus, on the other hand, is filled with chapter after chapter of repetitive descriptions of offerings, sacrifices, and purity laws. It's safe to say that no one in Hollywood is working on a Leviticus movie.

But that doesn't mean Leviticus is irrelevant. Quite the opposite, in fact.

Leviticus picks up right where Exodus left off. God calls to Moses from the newly completed tabernacle and lists out the rules and regulations for several types of offerings. We have already seen that the people of Israel have a sin problem that separates them from God. What we find in Leviticus is God's way of reconciliation. God is holy and people are not. If they want to be with God, they must abide by these regulations to purify themselves from sin.

Many scholars believe that the placement of Leviticus at the center of the Torah (it's the third of the five books) is a nod to its importance. In the last chapter of Exodus, Moses can't enter the tabernacle. But in the first chapter of Numbers, he is inside the tent of meeting with the Lord. What happens in between is Leviticus. Its very placement in the Torah symbolizes the importance of its content, as the regulations are the key to enabling people to dwell in the presence of God.

New Testament

It's also a week of transition in our New Testament readings as we finish Matthew and begin Mark. The climactic final two chapters of Matthew are equally brutal and beautiful. Take your time and make a note of what you're feeling as you read through the death and resurrection of Jesus, and don't miss the unique conclusion in Matthew's final five verses, where Jesus gives the Great Commission.

> Therefore go and make disciples of all nations, baptizing them in the name of the Father and of the Son and of the Holy Spirit, and teaching them to obey everything I have commanded you. And surely I am with you always, to the very end of the age. (Matt. 28:19–20)

In this passage Jesus tells the disciples to do four things: go, make disciples, baptize, and teach. Since he starts with "go," that feels like the primary command, but that's not the case.

Let's take a little dive into Greek grammar here. The word translated here as "go" has the exact same ending (or suffix) as the words "baptizing" and "teaching." You grammar nerds will know that these are called participles (the *-ing* ending gives it away). For you less nerdy readers, a participle is a word formed from a verb and used as an adjective or noun. What all of this means is that the imperative verb of this sentence is not "go" but "make disciples."

This is important because if we read these verses with *go* as the imperative verb, we may compartmentalize these verses into something that is only about missionaries or mission trips, activities that involve going for an evangelistic purpose. But Jesus is not asking his disciples to go on a mission trip; he's asking them to pursue a new way of life. The focus is not the going; it's the making of disciples.

What does this look like? These participles—"Baptizing" and "teaching"—tell us.

It means people will hear the good news about Jesus, and they will believe and respond in baptism. But it doesn't stop there, does it? Jesus then commands his disciples to teach these new followers "to obey everything I have commanded you" (v. 20). Jesus's life and ministry were filled with teachings about how to live in light of the reality of the kingdom of God being near. He's saying here that making disciples is not just about conversions but also about helping people build his rhythms into their lives.

This sounds like a tall task, especially when you consider that he tells them to make disciples of *all nations*. But don't miss the very last line of the gospel of Matthew: "And surely I am with you always, to the very end of the age" (Matt. 28:20).

Jesus promises to be with them.

The Great Commission may be challenging, but with Jesus, all things are possible.

Psalms and Proverbs

Right in the middle of this week's readings from Proverbs is a simple yet profound verse.

> Above all else, guard your heart,
>> for everything you do flows from it. (Prov. 4:23)

Quite a bit of wisdom is found in Proverbs, yet here we are told to do one thing *above all else*. That's a strong statement. And that one thing is to guard our hearts.

I often hear this phrase used in the context of romantic relationships.

"Guard your heart," someone says to another, "so you don't get hurt."

That is certainly good advice when it comes to romance, but in Proverbs the heart represents more than just feelings. According to this verse, it's the very wellspring of life. Our hearts are like the source of a stream—who we are and everything we do flows from them. This is why we need to protect them.

What do you want your life to overflow with?

What are you doing to guard your heart?

Reflections

Write down a few reflections on this week's readings.

Day 43: Exodus 37:1–38:31; Matthew 27:11–44; Psalm 21:1–7

Day 44: Exodus 39:1–40:38; Matthew 27:45–66; Proverbs 4:20–27

Day 45: Leviticus 1:1–3:17; Matthew 28:1–20; Psalm 21:8–13

Day 46: Leviticus 4:1–5:13; Mark 1:1–28; Psalm 22:1–11

Day 47: Leviticus 5:14–7:10; Mark 1:29–2:17; Psalm 22:12–21

Day 48: Leviticus 7:11–8:36; Mark 2:18–3:30; Proverbs 5:1–14

Day 49: Leviticus 9:1–10:20; Mark 3:31–4:29; Psalm 22:22–31

WEEK 8

	Old Testament	New Testament	Psalms / Proverbs	
Day 50	Leviticus 11:1–12:8	Mark 4:30–5:20	Psalm 23:1–6	
Day 51	Leviticus 13:1–59	Mark 5:21–6:6a	Psalm 24:1–10	
Day 52	Leviticus 14:1–57	Mark 6:6b–29	Proverbs 5:15–23	
Day 53	Leviticus 15:1–16:34	Mark 6:30–56	Psalm 25:1–7	
Day 54	Leviticus 17:1–18:30	Mark 7:1–30	Psalm 25:8–15	
Day 55	Leviticus 19:1–20:27	Mark 7:31–8:13	Psalm 25:16–22	
Day 56	Leviticus 21:1–22:33	Mark 8:14–9:1	Proverbs 6:1–11	

Old Testament

The first sixteen chapters of Leviticus are dedicated to offerings, sacrifices, and rituals performed by the priests. In chapter 17 the focus shifts to rules about everyday life that all the people of Israel are to obey. It's not just the priests who are expected to be holy, but all the people. This section is often called the Holiness Code because it focuses on ritual and moral purity.

> **Word Study:** The Hebrew word *qodesh* that is used throughout Leviticus and translated in English as "holy" has a depth of meaning that includes being set apart, and the Lord repeatedly tells the people to do things differently than the neighboring people groups around them.

You are to be holy to me because I, the LORD, am holy, and I have set you apart from the nations to be my own. (Lev. 20:26)

The Holiness Code covers a wide range of topics, including marriage, sex, worship, farming, eating, animals, and life in community. Some of these laws are still relevant for us today (telling the truth, loving others, showing respect to elders, avoiding idolatry), while others aren't nearly as applicable to our everyday lives as they were to those of the ancient Israelites (animal sacrifices, dietary restriction, purification rituals). As you read these chapters, remember what we talked about last week: The requirements laid out in Leviticus are God's way of reconciliation. He is holy and people are not. These exhaustive regulations about everyday life were what was required for people to be in right relationship with God.

Let the weight of that sink in.

I know I could never live up to all of this. Could you?

Thankfully, we aren't the ancient Israelites. We are still called to be holy and set apart, but to be in right relationship with God, the only thing required of us is faith in his Son. Jesus fulfilled these very laws through his death and resurrection. Leviticus reminds us of how broken and sinful we are, but it also allows us to see just how much Jesus has done for us.

New Testament

Unlike the gospels written by Matthew and Luke, Mark does not begin with the birth of Jesus and ease us into the story of his life and ministry. It dives right in with his baptism, his temptation by Satan in the wilderness, his calling of the disciples, and the beginning of his ministry of preaching and healing. And that's all in the first chapter! By the time we come to the end of chapter 4, the story is well under way, and Jesus has been telling parables about the kingdom of God.

Then something dramatic happens. In Mark 4:35–41, Jesus and the disciples find themselves caught in a powerful storm on the Sea of Galilee.

What would you have done if you were on that boat with Jesus and the disciples? The Sea of Galilee is about seven hundred feet below sea level, and it is surrounded by large hills, so these storms can be sudden and severe. Remember that many of these guys were fishermen, and they were used to being on this very body of water. So the fact that they were terrified tells us this storm was serious.

And what was Jesus doing in the middle of this furious storm? He was sleeping!

Have you ever been in one of life's storms and felt like God was sleeping? Have you ever asked him, "Do you even care about me, God?" The disciples did just that, and Jesus woke up and miraculously calmed the storm. But what he did immediately afterward is perhaps even more important: Jesus questioned the disciples about their faith. This is Mark's way of inviting anyone reading this story to consider their own lack of faith when they face storms in their lives.

The disciples' fear of the storm overwhelmed them so much that it made them question whether Jesus even cared about them. If, during a storm, the guys who lived and worked alongside Jesus could lose sight of who he was, then it stands to reason that we can too.

Is your fear stronger than your faith?

This story ends with another unanswered question: The disciples ask, "Who is this?" (v. 41). Again, Mark invites his readers to answer it for themselves.

How we answer the question "Who is this?" about Jesus has a direct impact on what we do when we face storms in our own lives. Do we choose fear or faith? That depends on who we think Jesus really is.

So I ask you: Who is this? Who is Jesus to you?

He is the one who calms the storms. He is the one who speaks peace into our fear-filled lives. He is the one worthy of a faith stronger than our greatest fears.

Psalms and Proverbs

Psalm 23 is arguably the most popular psalm of all time. It's only six verses long, but it says a lot about God's character and love for his people. In the first four verses David calls the Lord his shepherd, which is fitting because he was once a shepherd himself. He knows what it means to care for and protect sheep. Now David is a king, and as he dwells on all the ways God has cared for him, the image of a shepherd comes to mind. The first three verses are serene and picturesque, but then we come to one of the most memorable verses in the Bible.

> Even though I walk
> through the darkest valley,
> I will fear no evil,
> for you are with me;
> your rod and your staff,
> they comfort me. (Ps. 23:4)

The contours of the landscape in Israel can be quite severe. When I visited Bethlehem several years ago, I remember thinking it would have been a treacherous place to be a shepherd because of all the crags in the hillside that sheep could easily fall into. I imagine David writing this psalm with those very hillsides in mind. He does not use the word *trust* in these verses, but he clearly trusts God to protect him.

How have you seen God care for you like a shepherd cares for their sheep?

Reflections

Write down a few reflections on this week's readings.

Day 50: Leviticus 11:1–12:8; Mark 4:30–5:20; Psalm 23:1–6

Day 51: Leviticus 13:1–59; Mark 5:21–6:6a; Psalm 24:1–10

Day 52: Leviticus 14:1–57; Mark 6:6b–29; Proverbs 5:15–23

Day 53: Leviticus 15:1–16:34; Mark 6:30–56; Psalm 25:1–7

Day 54: Leviticus 17:1–18:30; Mark 7:1–30; Psalm 25:8–15

Day 55: Leviticus 19:1–20:27; Mark 7:31–8:13; Psalm 25:16–22

Day 56: Leviticus 21:1–22:33; Mark 8:14–9:1; Proverbs 6:1–11

WEEK 9

Daily Readings

	Old Testament	New Testament	Psalms / Proverbs
Day 57	Leviticus 23:1–24:23	Mark 9:2–32	Psalm 26:1–12
Day 58	Leviticus 25:1–26:13	Mark 9:33–10:12	Psalm 27:1–6
Day 59	Leviticus 26:14–27:34	Mark 10:13–31	Psalm 27:7–14
Day 60	Numbers 1:1–2:9	Mark 10:32–52	Proverbs 6:12–19
Day 61	Numbers 2:10–3:51	Mark 11:1–25	Psalm 28:1–9
Day 62	Numbers 4:1–5:10	Mark 11:27–12:12	Psalm 29:1–11
Day 63	Numbers 5:11–6:27	Mark 12:13–27	Psalm 30:1–7

Old Testament

As we turn the page from Leviticus to Numbers, we find Moses inside the tent of meeting, which is still in the Sinai desert. God tells him to take a census of the Israelites (thus the title Numbers), and we learn that the number of those at least twenty years old and able to serve in the army was 603,550 (1:45–46), which means that the total number of Israelites—including the Levites, women, children, and others unable to serve in the army—far exceeded this number.

After an extended stay at Mount Sinai, it is time for the people of Israel to make their way to the promised land. In Numbers 2, God gives instructions to Moses and Aaron about how the tribes are to be arranged in their camps. With the tabernacle at the center, three tribes camp in each direction (north, south, east, and west). This structure is symbolic not only because the Lord and the tabernacle are at the center but also because the arrangement of the tribes forms the shape of a cross. Yes, even here in the pages of Numbers, we find a hint of Jesus.

This week's readings are filled with names and numbers, but also a handful of powerful moments occur between God and the people of Israel. Don't miss the priestly blessing that God instructs Aaron and the Levites to pray over the people in chapter 6. It is one of the most beautiful passages in the Torah.

> The LORD bless you
> and keep you;
> the LORD make his face shine on you
> and be gracious to you;
> the LORD turn his face toward you
> and give you peace. (Num. 6:24–26)

New Testament

One of the things I love most about the Gospels is all the interactions Jesus has with the people he crosses paths with. What may seem like small, random encounters are actually critical moments that Matthew, Mark, Luke, and John use to teach us important truths about Jesus. This week we read one of my personal favorites in Mark 10:46–52, when Jesus meets a blind beggar named Bartimaeus in the city of Jericho. This story has quite a bit of depth and nuance, with much to say about faith, discipleship, healing, and the very power of Jesus. And it comes to us in a rather simple story of a blind man asking Jesus to help him see.

After crying out to Jesus and refusing to be quiet when those around him shushed him, Bartimaeus got his moment. Jesus stopped and called for him. And then this happened:

Throwing his cloak aside, he jumped to his feet and came to Jesus. (Mark 10:50)

Something crucial in this verse often gets overlooked.

Do you see what it is?

Look at those first four words. Why do you think Mark mentions that Bartimaeus threw his cloak aside?

One interpretation is that it was just to show how excited Bartimaeus was, meaning he was so happy that he forgot his cloak. But I think it's more important than that. Think about it. This cloak was likely one of the only possessions Bartimaeus had. He was a beggar, so he would spread this cloak out on the ground to collect the loose change and the scraps of food that people gave him. In the heat of the day and the cool of the night, he would use it to protect himself. This cloak was his livelihood, and he just threw it aside.

I think Mark wants to show us how much faith Bartimaeus had in Jesus. He didn't forget his cloak. He tossed it aside because he believed he wasn't going to need it anymore. He was so confident that Jesus was going to heal him that he left it behind.

What is your cloak?

Maybe it's something physical, or maybe it's something beneath the surface—pain, fear, guilt, jealousy, pride, insecurity, anger. Sometimes these things become such a huge part of our identity that we struggle to let them go. How often do we press into Jesus while still clinging to our cloaks? Bartimaeus gives us a beautiful glimpse of what it looks like to surrender to Jesus and trust him completely.

Psalms and Proverbs

In the middle of Proverbs 6 is a list of things God hates. Such strong language deserves our attention:

There are six things the LORD hates,
  seven that are detestable to him:
    haughty eyes,
    a lying tongue,
    hands that shed innocent blood,
    a heart that devises wicked schemes,
    feet that are quick to rush into evil,
    a false witness who pours out lies
    and a person who stirs up conflict in the
      community. (Prov. 6:16–19)

The way the first line uses a number followed by another number (six and seven) is a literary device ancient writers used. Some scholars think it's nothing more than a stylistic flourish used to grab attention; others think it implies that the last item in the list is the key that unlocks the true meaning and brings them all together.

Let's see how that plays out in these verses.

Is the seventh and final item in this list ("a person who stirs up conflict in the community") connected to the previous six?

It certainly is.

The first five things mentioned in these verses have to do with the human body—eyes, tongue, hands, heart, and feet—and each is correlated with a different sin. The sixth ("a false witness who pours out lies") shifts us closer to the whole person while remaining focused on the sin of lying. But the ending shows us what happens when all these things come together as one. These body parts form a person, and each sin connected with a body part has a negative impact on that person's community. The reason God hates pride ("haughty eyes"), lying, and violence is because they lead to something he detests even more: broken community.

Reflections

Write down a few reflections on this week's readings.

Day 57: Leviticus 23:1–24:23; Mark 9:2–32; Psalm 26:1–12

Day 58: Leviticus 25:1–26:13; Mark 9:33–10:12; Psalm 27:1–6

Day 59: Leviticus 26:14–27:34; Mark 10:13–31; Psalm 27:7–14

Day 60: Numbers 1:1–2:9; Mark 10:32–52; Proverbs 6:12–19

Day 61: Numbers 2:10–3:51; Mark 11:1–25; Psalm 28:1–9

Day 62: Numbers 4:1–5:10; Mark 11:27–12:12; Psalm 29:1–11

Day 63: Numbers 5:11–6:27; Mark 12:13–27; Psalm 30:1–7

WEEK 10

Daily Readings

	Old Testament	New Testament	Psalms / Proverbs	
Day 64	Numbers 7:1–65	Mark 12:28–44	Proverbs 6:20–29	☐
Day 65	Numbers 7:66–9:14	Mark 13:1–31	Psalm 30:8–12	☐
Day 66	Numbers 9:15–11:3	Mark 13:32–14:16	Psalm 31:1–8	☐
Day 67	Numbers 11:4–13:25	Mark 14:17–42	Psalm 31:9–18	☐
Day 68	Numbers 13:26–14:45	Mark 14:43–72	Proverbs 6:30–35	☐
Day 69	Numbers 15:1–16:35	Mark 15:1–32	Psalm 31:19–24	☐
Day 70	Numbers 16:36–18:32	Mark 15:33–47	Psalm 32:1–11	☐

Old Testament

In Numbers 10, the people of Israel set out from Sinai and make their way toward the promised land. We've been waiting for this moment since the second half of Exodus, and it's finally time to get this show on the road (literally).

But it doesn't take long before they are complaining again. They don't like traveling through the desert. They don't like the food that God has provided for them. They don't like the way Moses is leading them (even his brother and sister oppose him). They even have the audacity to say they were better off in Egypt, where they were slaves!

God has been so patient with these people, and he is trying to bless them with the land he promised their ancestor, Abraham, generations earlier. But they can't see the bigger picture because they are so focused on their own momentary discomfort. Every time I read these chapters, I just shake my head. These people are so frustrating.

And then I realize I am one of them.

Life is a journey, and just like the Israelites, I often lose sight of the destination. I forget that God has a plan. I complain because I'm uncomfortable or unsatisfied with how the journey is going. Can you relate?

When we find ourselves wandering in the desert, it's easy to forget that we're on our way to the promised land. But the desert is not the destination. It's just part of the journey. And if we keep that in mind, it will help us stay the course and trust the one who guides us.

New Testament

Mark is the shortest of the four gospels, and as you've probably noticed, it moves rather quickly through the story. The Greek word *euthus*, which is often translated as "immediately" or "at once," can be found more than forty times in Mark. Yet when we get to chapter 14, which is seventy-two verses long, the story noticeably slows down. Mark's writing becomes more deliberate and focused. He wants his readers to pay close attention as he carefully recounts a series of interconnected scenes in the final hours of Jesus's life.

The first two scenes take place around tables. At the home of Simon the Leper in Bethany, an unidentified woman pours out a jar of incredibly expensive perfume on Jesus. When some of those gathered at the table criticize her, Jesus rebukes them and connects what she has done to the ancient custom of anointing the body of a deceased person prior to burial. He is obviously not dead, but we are getting close to that crucial moment. Two days later, Jesus and his disciples gather in the upper room of a home in Jerusalem. Once again, Jesus's death is foreshadowed when he institutes the Lord's Supper.

The remainder of chapter 14 unfolds outdoors, first in the Garden of Gethsemane and then in the courtyard of the high priest. I find the garden scene heartbreaking, particularly when Jesus becomes overwhelmed as the reality of his impending death sinks in. His closest friends can't even stay awake to keep watch, and then one of his own disciples betrays him. It feels like we're suddenly in the wrong story and everything is out of control, but I think Mark does this deliberately to show us how intense these moments were.

After Jesus is arrested, a wild scene ensues where many false accusations are made against him, yet he remains silent until the high priest directly asks if he is the Messiah. One of the themes of Mark's gospel is the question of who Jesus really is (often referred to as the Messianic Secret). Here we finally get the answer from Jesus himself:

> "I am," said Jesus. "And you will see the Son of Man sitting at the right hand of the Mighty One and coming on the clouds of heaven." (Mark 14:62)

I think the reason Mark takes his time with each of these moments is because he wants his readers to slow down and immerse themselves in the story. As you read these passages this week, imagine yourself as one of the people gathered around the table with Jesus. Picture yourself seated along the edge of the courtyard. What would you have said or done? How would you have reacted to what Jesus said and did in these moments?

Psalms and Proverbs

When was the last time you confessed your sins to God? Is it a regular rhythm in your prayer life, or is it something you do only occasionally (or rarely)? In Psalm 32, David reminds us just how important confession is. The first two verses of this psalm celebrate the good news that our sins are forgiven and that God does not count them against us, but then David turns his focus to confession.

> When I kept silent,
>   my bones wasted away
>   through my groaning all day long.
> For day and night
>   your hand was heavy on me;
> my strength was sapped
>   as in the heat of summer.
>
> Then I acknowledged my sin to you
>   and did not cover up my iniquity.
> I said, "I will confess
>   my transgressions to the LORD."
> And you forgave
>   the guilt of my sin. (Ps. 32:3–5)

As I'm writing this, it's a hot summer day, and because of the extreme temperatures, I am avoiding several outdoor projects that need to be taken care of around my home. Needless to say, I know exactly what David means when he talks about his strength being "sapped as in the heat of summer." That exhaustion is what sin does to us. It saps our strength and weighs us down.

But thankfully, we don't have to live like that. David draws a direct line between confession and forgiveness. If being silent and not confessing our sins is harmful to us, then the exact opposite is true as well. Confession frees us from that oppressive heat and lifts the burden of sin from our shoulders.

Reflections

Write down a few reflections on this week's readings.

Day 64: Numbers 7:1–65; Mark 12:28–44; Proverbs 6:20–29

Day 65: Numbers 7:66–9:14; Mark 13:1–31; Psalm 30:8–12

Day 66: Numbers 9:15–11:3; Mark 13:32–14:16; Psalm 31:1–8

Day 67: Numbers 11:4–13:25; Mark 14:17–42; Psalm 31:9–18

Day 68: Numbers 13:26–14:45; Mark 14:43–72; Proverbs 6:30–35

Day 69: Numbers 15:1–16:35; Mark 15:1–32; Psalm 31:19–24

Day 70: Numbers 16:36–18:32; Mark 15:33–47; Psalm 32:1–11

WEEK 11

Daily Readings

	Old Testament	New Testament	Psalms / Proverbs	
Day 71	Numbers 19:1–21:3	Mark 16:1–20	Psalm 33:1–11	
Day 72	Numbers 21:4–22:20	Luke 1:1–25	Proverbs 7:1–5	
Day 73	Numbers 22:21–23:26	Luke 1:26–38	Psalm 33:12–22	
Day 74	Numbers 23:27–26:11	Luke 1:39–56	Psalm 34:1–10	
Day 75	Numbers 26:12–27:11	Luke 1:57–80	Psalm 34:11–22	
Day 76	Numbers 27:12–29:11	Luke 2:1–20	Proverbs 7:6–20	
Day 77	Numbers 29:12–31:24	Luke 2:21–40	Psalm 35:1–10	

Old Testament

This week's Old Testament readings have us following the Israelites from the Desert of Paran to the plains of Moab as they move closer and closer to the promised land. There are miracles, battles, another census, and even a talking donkey (yes, really). But I think the most compelling chapter we'll read this week is Numbers 20, which opens and closes with the deaths of Miriam and Aaron, respectively. The sister and brother of Moses have been his closest companions throughout these years in the desert, and their deaths signify the end of an important era in the history of God's people.

Sandwiched between the deaths of Miriam and Aaron is a story that has always troubled me. It starts with the people of Israel once again complaining about being stuck in the wilderness without sufficient food or water. Moses and Aaron turn to God, who offers to miraculously provide water for the people.

The LORD said to Moses, "Take the staff, and you and your brother Aaron gather the assembly together. Speak to that rock before their eyes and it will pour out its water. You will bring water out of the rock for the community so they and their livestock can drink." (Num. 20:7–8)

If this sounds familiar, that's because something similar happened many years earlier in Exodus 17. The key difference is that in Exodus God told Moses to strike the rock, but here in Numbers he tells Moses to *speak* to the rock.

But Moses does not obey God.

Then Moses raised his arm and struck the rock twice with his staff. Water gushed out, and the community and their livestock drank.

But the LORD said to Moses and Aaron, "Because you did not trust in me enough to honor me as holy in the sight of the Israelites, you will not bring this community into the land I give them." (Num. 20:11–12)

I've always wondered why this small blunder by Moses prevented him from seeing the promised land. That seems pretty harsh, doesn't it? But verse 12 shows us that it wasn't *what* Moses did but *why* he did it that offended God. Striking the rock showed that he did not trust and honor the Lord. This is a good reminder for us that obedience is much more about our hearts than our actions. If we truly trust and honor God, that will be reflected in how we live.

New Testament

The ending of Mark and the beginning of Luke give us unique insight into the composition and transmission of the Gospels. Most major translations have a note in the middle of Mark 16 that reads something like this: "The earliest manuscripts and some other ancient witnesses do not have verses 9–20."

What's going on here?

There are thousands of ancient Greek copies of the New Testament, ranging from small papyrus fragments with just a few verses to complete collections of all twenty-seven books. In two of the oldest and most trusted and reliable complete manuscripts, the gospel of Mark ends after verse 8. But in others it continues through verse 20. Biblical scholars consider these differences as they translate the Bible, and notes like this help us see the transparency of the process and give us confidence as readers that the Bibles we read from today are incredibly trustworthy.

Luke's introduction is unique among the Gospels because the writer speaks directly to his readers to assure them that he has "carefully investigated everything" and "decided to write an orderly account" (Luke 1:3). This is a good reminder that the biblical writers were real people who had their own agency and perspective. We can see these nuances clearly in the differences among the four gospels.

When some people think about how the Bible was written, they imagine God taking over a human's brain and body and writing for them. But that's not what biblical inspiration looks like. God inspired real people to write from their real experiences. We see this in the introduction to Luke as well as in countless other places in the Bible. Of course, these people were appointed by God and inspired by the Holy Spirit to write, but they also brought *themselves* fully to the task. This is why it's important that we consider the literary and historical contexts of each book of the Bible (something a great Study Bible can help with) to fully understand what God wants to teach us through them.

Psalms and Proverbs

Psalm 34:1–10 is all about worship and thanksgiving, with David singing the praises of God. After verse 10, David shifts the focus to teaching. He beckons his readers to listen closely and choose righteousness over evil.

This may feel like two different songs jammed together as one, but I think their connection is intentional. The first half repeatedly mentions God delivering his people from their troubles and fears. In the second half, we read the following:

> The eyes of the LORD are on the righteous,
>> and his ears are attentive to their cry;
> but the face of the LORD is against those who do evil,
>> to blot out their name from the earth.
>>> (Ps. 34:15–16)

Do you see the connection?

The reason God delivers his people is because he watches over those who choose righteousness. He hears their cries for help *because* they are righteous. We often want the first half of this psalm—God's protection and provision—without committing to the righteous way of life described in the second half. But David sees them as two sides of the same coin. Like David, we too can sing this same song of praise if we choose the way of righteousness.

Reflections

Write down a few reflections on this week's readings.

Day 71: Numbers 19:1–21:3; Mark 16:1–20; Psalm 33:1–11

Day 72: Numbers 21:4–22:20; Luke 1:1–25; Proverbs 7:1–5

Day 73: Numbers 22:21–23:26; Luke 1:26–38; Psalm 33:12–22

Day 74: Numbers 23:27–26:11; Luke 1:39–56; Psalm 34:1–10

Day 75: Numbers 26:12–27:11; Luke 1:57–80; Psalm 34:11–22

Day 76: Numbers 27:12–29:11; Luke 2:1–20; Proverbs 7:6–20

Day 77: Numbers 29:12–31:24; Luke 2:21–40; Psalm 35:1–10

WEEK 12

Daily Readings

	Old Testament	New Testament	Psalms / Proverbs	
Day 78	Numbers 31:25–32:42	Luke 2:41–52	Psalm 35:11–18	
Day 79	Numbers 33:1–34:29	Luke 3:1–22	Psalm 35:19–28	
Day 80	Numbers 35:1–36:13	Luke 3:23–4:13	Proverbs 7:21–27	
Day 81	Deuteronomy 1:1–2:23	Luke 4:14–37	Psalm 36:1–12	
Day 82	Deut. 2:24–4:14	Luke 4:38–5:16	Psalm 37:1–9	
Day 83	Deut. 4:15–5:33	Luke 5:17–32	Psalm 37:10–20	
Day 84	Deuteronomy 6:1–8:20	Luke 5:33–6:11	Proverbs 8:1–11	

Old Testament

This week we will begin the fifth and final book of the Torah, Deuteronomy.

> **WORD STUDY:** The title Deuteronomy is derived from Greek and means "second law" or "repeated law."

Deuteronomy is presented as a speech Moses gives to the Israelites in which he reiterates many of the same laws from Exodus (including the Ten Commandments) and urges them to give themselves fully to the Lord. You may already know one of the highlights of this speech found in chapter 6:

Hear, O Israel: The LORD our God, the LORD is one. Love the LORD your God with all your heart and with all your soul and with all your strength. (Deut. 6:4–5)

This passage is known as the Shema, which in Hebrew means "to hear," and it's one of the most important prayers in the Bible. For centuries, faithful Jews have prayed the words of the Shema every morning and every evening. It's this prayer that Jesus quotes in the Gospels when asked to name the most important commandment, after which he adds a line about loving your neighbor as yourself (Mark 12:29–31).

Let's consider the context of this prayer. Moses has just recapped Israel's rebellion against the Lord and their years of wandering in the wilderness. The next generation is about to go into the promised land, where they will meet people from other nations who worship false gods. The Israelites have a long history of turning their backs on God, and they are about to have more opportunities to do so. Moses clearly sees the hurdles in front of them, and he's begging them to listen. He reminds them that they serve the one true God and that loving him requires their whole selves.

I often start my day by praying Jesus's updated version of the Shema. I see it as a way of connecting myself to the historic roots of my faith, but more importantly, it is a way of anchoring myself to the truth of who God is in a world that often tempts me to give my heart, soul, and strength to other things. He is the one true God, and he alone is worthy of our love.

New Testament

All the way back in Week 1, I mentioned that the genealogy of Jesus in the gospel of Matthew differs from the one found in the gospel of Luke, and here we are. Matthew traces the lineage of Jesus back to Abraham, but Luke goes even further, all the way back to Adam.

Why is that?

It's because they were written with different audiences in mind. Matthew wrote to an audience that was primarily Jewish, and we can see that in the way he retells the story of Jesus's life and ministry. He repeatedly references Moses and other heroes of the Jewish faith. He continually shows how Jesus fulfills different prophecies from the Hebrew Bible. Matthew wanted his fellow Jews to come to faith in Jesus, so it makes sense that his genealogy of Jesus stops at Abraham, because he was the great patriarch of the Jewish people.

Luke, on the other hand, wrote primarily to Gentiles (non-Jews). We know that Luke was a companion of the apostle Paul, who was passionate about sharing the good news of Jesus with everyone, not just the Jews. Where Matthew presents Jesus as the long-awaited Jewish Messiah, Luke shows him to be the Son of God who brings salvation to all people. Naturally, when it is Luke's turn to write down the genealogy of Jesus, he goes all the way back to Adam. It's a subtle yet important nod to the fact that Jesus is not just the savior the Jews have been waiting for; he is the savior the whole world has been waiting for.

Psalms and Proverbs

Think about a time when you were outdoors and saw something that took your breath away. Maybe you were on a hike in the mountains or stargazing on a pitch-black night. I've experienced sunrises in the deserts of Arizona that brought me to tears and sunsets in the hills of Spain that gave me chills. What is the most beautiful thing you have ever seen in nature, and how did it make you feel?

In these moments, I think of David's ode to God in Psalm 36, particularly verses 5–7:

> Your love, Lord, reaches to the heavens,
>   your faithfulness to the skies.

Your righteousness is like the highest mountains,
> your justice like the great deep.

You, LORD, preserve both people and animals.
How priceless is your unfailing love, O God!
> People take refuge in the shadow of your wings.
>> (Ps. 36:5–7)

Read that again and let it sink in.

God's love and faithfulness and righteousness and justice are bigger and wider than we can ever imagine. When you think of the most beautiful and epic thing you have ever seen, it is still only a glimpse of who God is and how much he loves you.

Reflections

Write down a few reflections on this week's readings.

Day 78: Numbers 31:25–32:42; Luke 2:41–52; Psalm 35:11–18

_____

_____

_____

_____

_____

Day 79: Numbers 33:1–34:29; Luke 3:1–22; Psalm 35:19–28

_____

_____

_____

_____

_____

Day 80: Numbers 35:1–36:13; Luke 3:23–4:13; Proverbs 7:21–27

Day 81: Deuteronomy 1:1–2:23; Luke 4:14–37; Psalm 36:1–12

Day 82: Deuteronomy 2:24–4:14; Luke 4:38–5:16; Psalm 37:1–9

Day 83: Deuteronomy 4:15–5:33; Luke 5:17–32; Psalm 37:10–20

Day 84: Deuteronomy 6:1–8:20; Luke 5:33–6:11; Proverbs 8:1–11

_____

_____

_____

_____

_____

_____

WEEK 13

	Old Testament	New Testament	Psalms / Proverbs	
Day 85	Deut. 9:1–10:22	Luke 6:12–36	Psalm 37:21–31	☐
Day 86	Deut. 11:1–12:32	Luke 6:37–7:10	Psalm 37:32–40	☐
Day 87	Deut. 13:1–14:29	Luke 7:11–35	Psalm 38:1–12	☐
Day 88	Deut. 15:1–16:20	Luke 7:36–50	Proverbs 8:12–21	☐
Day 89	Deut. 16:21–18:22	Luke 8:1–18	Psalm 38:13–22	☐
Day 90	Deut. 19:1–20:20	Luke 8:19–39	Psalm 39:1–13	☐
Day 91	Deut. 21:1–22:30	Luke 8:40–9:9	Psalm 40:1–8	☐

Old Testament

We are reading fourteen chapters from Deuteronomy this week, including chapter after chapter of important laws that God wants the people of Israel to diligently obey. One of the commands repeated time and time again in these chapters (and throughout the entire Torah) is that they must not worship other gods. The Lord makes it abundantly clear that they are to worship him and him alone.

Why does God keep bringing this up?

Part of the answer is practical. The Israelites are about to go into the promised land, and they will encounter many new people groups. These nations worship other gods, not the one true God of Israel. The Lord is preparing them for the temptations they will face and setting clear expectations for how he expects them to behave. And he says it over and over again because they have proven themselves to be weak and easily manipulated.

It's easy to read these chapters and convince ourselves that this mandate doesn't apply to us all that much. But just because we don't live in an ancient culture doesn't mean we are not constantly tempted to worship other gods. The gods of today may not have funny names and cultic rituals, but they still tempt us. I'm talking about gods like money, power, success, celebrity, sex, and materialism. Everywhere we go, we are bombarded with opportunities to worship these false gods. Just like the Israelites, we are weak and easily manipulated. Just like the Israelites, we easily turn our backs on the one true God.

As you read Deuteronomy, make a note of every time other gods are mentioned, and ask yourself if you're guilty of worshiping any false idols. Which ones entice you most? How can you guard yourself from the temptation to worship anything other than the Lord?

New Testament

Several years ago my wife and I built a house. Well, *we* didn't build it; we hired someone to build it for us. Early in the process, we went to visit the site of our new home and discovered a completed foundation. As we stood there looking at the structure that our home would be built on, I was reminded of Jesus's parable about the wise and foolish builders (Luke 6:46–49). At first glance, this parable seems rather simple. There are two houses. One has a solid foundation; the other does not. When a flood strikes, the house on the solid foundation is fine, but the other is destroyed.

But how do we know if our life's foundation is the good one or the bad one?

Thankfully, Jesus makes it clear in the opening verses of this parable.

As for everyone who comes to me and hears my words and puts them into practice, I will show you what they are like.

They are like a man building a house, who dug down deep and laid the foundation on rock. When a flood came, the torrent struck that house but could not shake it, because it was well built. (Luke 6:47–48)

You see, this is the very last passage in what is often called the Sermon on the Plain in Luke 6. Similar to (but less famous than) the Sermon on the Mount in the gospel of Matthew, the Sermon on the Plain is filled with Jesus's teachings on how to live. And he concludes with this analogy of two foundations, saying that if we live according to his teachings, our lives won't collapse when the storms hit. But if we don't follow his teachings, we're in trouble.

It's amazing how this passage connects with the Lord's repeated command in Deuteronomy. God incessantly warned Israel not to worship other gods, emphasizing loyalty and faithfulness to him. The Sermon on the Plain passage suggests that living by Jesus's teachings not only strengthens our lives but also ensures that our worship and devotion remain directed toward the one true God. So examine your life. Compare it to how Jesus teaches us to live. Find your weak spots and invite God to make repairs so that your foundation is secure.

Psalms and Proverbs

How often do you think about death? Some people obsess over it; others try not to think about it at all. Either way, death is something each of us must reconcile with, and in a powerful moment in the middle of Psalm 39, David gives us a healthy perspective on death.

> Show me, LORD, my life's end
>   and the number of my days;
>   let me know how fleeting my life is.

> You have made my days a mere handbreadth;
>> the span of my years is as nothing before you.
> Everyone is but a breath,
>> even those who seem secure. (Ps. 39:4–5)

Here David asks the Lord to show him how fleeting life is, but he's not doing it out of some morbid preoccupation. He wants to be reminded that life is short so he can focus on what really matters, which is God. Death is not something we should hyperfocus on, and it's also not something we should avoid thinking about. It is a reality we all face, and we should ask God to give us clarity about that so we can make the most of the time we have.

Reflections

Write down a few reflections on this week's readings.

Day 85: Deuteronomy 9:1–10:22; Luke 6:12–36; Psalm 37:21–31

Day 86: Deuteronomy 11:1–12:32; Luke 6:37–7:10; Psalm 37:32–40

Day 87: Deuteronomy 13:1–14:29; Luke 7:11–35; Psalm 38:1–12

_____

_____

_____

_____

_____

Day 88: Deuteronomy 15:1–16:20; Luke 7:36–50; Proverbs 8:12–21

_____

_____

_____

_____

_____

Day 89: Deuteronomy 16:21–18:22; Luke 8:1–18; Psalm 38:13–22

_____

_____

_____

_____

_____

Day 90: Deuteronomy 19:1–20:20; Luke 8:19–39; Psalm 39:1–13

_____

_____

_____

_____

_____

Day 91: Deuteronomy 21:1–22:30; Luke 8:40–9:9; Psalm 40:1–8

WEEK 14

Daily Readings

	Old Testament	New Testament	Psalms / Proverbs	
Day 92	Deut. 23:1–25:19	Luke 9:10–27	Proverbs 8:22–31	☐
Day 93	Deut. 26:1–28:14	Luke 9:28–56	Psalm 40:9–17	☐
Day 94	Deuteronomy 28:15–68	Luke 9:57–10:24	Psalm 41:1–6	☐
Day 95	Deut. 29:1–30:10	Luke 10:25–11:4	Psalm 41:7–13	☐
Day 96	Deut. 30:11–31:29	Luke 11:5–32	Proverbs 8:32–36	☐
Day 97	Deut. 31:30–32:52	Luke 11:33–54	Psalm 42:1–6a	☐
Day 98	Deut. 33:1–34:12	Luke 12:1–34	Psalm 42:6b–11	☐

Old Testament

In this momentous week in our reading plan, we will finish Deuteronomy—the fifth and final book of the Torah—and say goodbye to Moses, who has been with us for the past ten weeks. Let's reflect on all that has happened in the life of Moses:

- being placed as an infant in a basket on the Nile River
- being raised as a prince in Egypt
- going on the run after murdering an Egyptian
- meeting God in the form of a burning bush
- facing Pharoah in a showdown marked by the ten plagues
- leading the people of Israel out of slavery in Egypt
- parting the Red Sea
- overseeing construction of the tabernacle so God could dwell among the people

- leading the Israelites through the wilderness toward the promised land

Moses has lived through so much, and now at the end of his life, he makes one final speech to the people of Israel. The speech stretches across several chapters. It includes a renewal of the covenant, the naming of Joshua as his successor, a public reading of the law, an epic song, and blessings spoken over each of the twelve tribes. One of the highlights of this speech is found in Deuteronomy 30:11–20, where Moses tells the people that they have two choices: life and prosperity or death and destruction. His encouragement is simple: Choose life.

The greatest hero of the Bible (so far) is about to take his last breaths at the end of a remarkable life, and all he wants is for his people to remain faithful to God by obeying his commands and loving him with all their hearts. This is what it means to choose life, and even though our world is much different from the world of the ancient Israelites, we have the same choice.

Will you choose life?

New Testament

Of the many meals described in the Bible, Jesus's feeding of the five thousand would have made a great headline: "Jesus Feeds 5,000!" This story is so legendary that many of us have the details of the miracle memorized: five loaves, two fish, twelve baskets, and over five thousand people.

But what if I told you that the miracle is only part of the story?

As you read Luke 9:10–17, notice that we don't get any specifics about the miracle itself. Luke doesn't seem concerned with *how* Jesus turned five loaves and two fish into enough food (and then some) for thousands of people. If how Jesus did this is not the point of the story, then what is?

It's about the who, what, when, and where.

Who got to participate in this meal?

Everybody. Jesus did not ask for credentials. He didn't make sure that everyone there believed the right things and had no sin in their lives. And that's because the table of Jesus is open to everyone. He wants to build bigger tables, not smaller ones.

What did Jesus serve at this meal?

Whatever the disciples had. In this case, it was five loaves and two fish. If we're willing to offer God whatever we have, he'll say, "I can work with that." And when it's all said and done, we'll have more than we started with.

When did this meal take place?

At an inconvenient time. Jesus and the disciples were trying to get away. The crowds interrupted that plan, but Jesus welcomed them anyway. With Jesus, there is no "right time" for a meal. His table is always open.

Where did this meal take place?

Right where they were. The text tells us they were in a "remote place" somewhere near Bethsaida. Jesus didn't tell the disciples to go find the right place. They had a meal right then and there.

Do you see how all of this is shaping up?

Whoever, whatever, whenever, wherever—Jesus is doing something miraculous all around us. And he wants us to be part of it.

Psalms and Proverbs

We have two readings from Proverbs 8 this week, a chapter in which wisdom speaks directly to the reader. In verses 22–31, wisdom describes being present at the dawn of creation as God formed the earth:

> "The Lord brought me forth as the first of his works,
>> before his deeds of old;
> I was formed long ages ago,
>> at the very beginning, when the world came to be.
> When there were no watery depths, I was given birth,
>> when there were no springs overflowing with water;
> before the mountains were settled in place,
>> before the hills, I was given birth,
> before he made the world or its fields
>> or any of the dust of the earth. (Prov. 8:22–26)

In many ways, this passage reminds me of the opening lines of the gospel of John (which we'll begin reading in Week 17) where Jesus is called "the Word" who was "with God in the beginning" (John 1:1–2). Being present at creation establishes a sense of authority and power, which is a natural way for us to think about Jesus, but we don't often think about wisdom in the same way. We tend to see wisdom as an admirable personality trait, not a powerful force that was present at the dawn of creation. But Proverbs helps us see that the true nature of wisdom is deeper and more important than just a characteristic we ascribe to our elders. It is a source of life.

> For those who find me find life
>> and receive favor from the Lord. (Prov. 8:35)

Reflections

Write down a few reflections on this week's readings.

Day 92: Deuteronomy 23:1–25:19; Luke 9:10–27; Proverbs 8:22–31

Day 93: Deuteronomy 26:1–28:14; Luke 9:28–56; Psalm 40:9–17

Day 94: Deuteronomy 28:15–68; Luke 9:57–10:24; Psalm 41:1–6

Day 95: Deuteronomy 29:1–30:10; Luke 10:25–11:4; Psalm 41:7–13

Day 96: Deuteronomy 30:11–31:29; Luke 11:5–32; Proverbs 8:32–36

Day 97: Deuteronomy 31:30–32:52; Luke 11:33–54; Psalm 42:1–6a

Day 98: Deuteronomy 33:1–34:12; Luke 12:1–34; Psalm 42:6b–11

WEEK 15

	Old Testament	New Testament	Psalms / Proverbs	
Day 99	Joshua 1:1–2:24	Luke 12:35–59	Psalm 43:1–5	▪
Day 100	Joshua 3:1–5:12	Luke 13:1–30	Proverbs 9:1–12	▪
Day 101	Joshua 5:13–7:26	Luke 13:31–14:14	Psalm 44:1–12	▪
Day 102	Joshua 8:1–9:15	Luke 14:15–35	Psalm 44:13–26	▪
Day 103	Joshua 9:16–10:43	Luke 15:1–32	Psalm 45:1–9	▪
Day 104	Joshua 11:1–12:24	Luke 16:1–18	Proverbs 9:13–18	▪
Day 105	Joshua 13:1–14:15	Luke 16:19–17:10	Psalm 45:10–17	▪

Old Testament

The book of Joshua picks up right where Deuteronomy left off. Moses has died, and now God is going to empower Joshua to "be strong and courageous" (1:6–7) as he leads the people of Israel into the promised land. Joshua's first order of business is to send spies into Jericho to scope things out. The Torah has taught us to expect the worst from the foreigners living in this land, yet the first one we encounter (a prostitute named Rahab) risks her own life to protect the spies and professes faith in God, saying, "The LORD your God is God in heaven above and on the earth below" (2:11). Rahab's story foreshadows that the kingdom of God will one day include all people.

Upon hearing the spies' report that Jericho is ripe for the taking, Joshua leads the Israelites to the edge of the Jordan River. In a scene reminiscent of the parting of the Red Sea, as soon as the feet of the priests carrying the ark of the covenant touch the edge of the water, the river stops flowing and the Israelites cross on dry ground. Notice that the river backs up to a town called Adam and is cut off all the way to the Dead Sea (3:16). Perhaps this is a coincidence, but the symbolism is powerful. What God is doing in this moment goes all the way back to Adam and will not finish until the very end. Maybe it's because we're also reading the gospel of Luke right now (with its focus on Jesus as the salvation of all people), but it's hard not to think that this passage about the Israelites crossing the Jordan is a signpost pointing to the much larger plan of salvation that culminates in Jesus.

Joshua 6–12 details many years of battles between the Israelites and various Canaanite people groups. This is one of the most violent sections of the Bible, and it can be uncomfortable to read. It's possible that these accounts use some hyperbole, as warring nations at this time often overstated their successes and downplayed their losses. Several of the people groups that are "totally destroyed" by Joshua and the Israelites are still around in later chapters. But we need to recognize that these passages have something to say about God's justice on human evil. The Canaanites were, by and large, a morally wicked people who worshiped false gods and participated in horrific cultic practices like child sacrifice. These chapters, while uncomfortable, remind us that God will not tolerate evil forever. He is the God of mercy, but he is also the God of justice.

New Testament

In Luke 15, Jesus tells a trio of parables about things that get lost: a sheep, a coin, and a son. The parable of the lost son (often called the prodigal son) is one of my favorite passages of Scripture. We tend to focus on the younger son when we read this parable, but please don't miss what happens with the older son in the final eight verses. After returning home from working in his father's fields, the older son sees the party that is being thrown for his brother and becomes irate. He refuses to go in, so his father goes out and begs him to join the party.

The cultural context of this moment is important to understand.

A distinguished father would have never disgraced himself by leaving the party, let alone *begging* his own son to join them. More than likely, if one of the servants said, "Sir, your older son is back from the fields, but he is refusing to come in," the father would have either forced him to join the party or said, "Fine, let him stay out there."

But this father is different. He goes out to both sons. He invites both of them to come home. These two sons are more alike than they may seem.

Do you see the parallel Jesus is drawing between the two sons? The older son did not abandon his father like his younger brother did. He followed the rules. He was responsible. He behaved as a good son should. But Jesus makes it clear that the older son's actions were self-serving rather than driven by genuine love for his father. In this sense, both sons placed themselves above their father. They did it in different ways, but both of them were prodigals.

Do you see yourself in the younger son? Have you abandoned God in search of fulfillment from something else? Do you need to come home and find rest? It doesn't matter what you've done. God's love for you is boundless. As soon as you turn home, you'll see that he is running to meet you.

Or do you see yourself in the older son? Have you done everything right and followed all the rules yet found yourself on the outside looking in? The father is extending his invitation to you as well. Will you join the party?

Psalms and Proverbs

You may have noticed last week that Psalm 42 has a heading that says, "Book 2." That's because Psalms is divided into five sections, or books, as a nod to the five books of the Torah. Book 2 contains Psalms 42–72 and is often called the Elohistic Psalter because the primary Hebrew name for God used in these psalms is Elohim. In the other books, the most common name for God is Yahweh. When reading your Bible, you can tell which name is being used based on the translation: Elohim usually appears as "God," while Yahweh is commonly translated as "the LORD."

You may also notice that several of the psalms in Book 2 are attributed to the sons of Korah. We learn in 1 Chronicles that David put these men in charge of the music at the tabernacle. So the sons of Korah were the worship leaders for the people of Israel, and a handful of their original songs made it into the Bible.

As you read these opening psalms in Book 2, make a note of anything that feels different from the psalms you have read up to this point. It's often those subtle differences that allow us to find new meaning and insight in Scripture.

Reflections

Write down a few reflections on this week's readings.

Day 99: Joshua 1:1–2:24; Luke 12:35–59; Psalm 43:1–5

Day 100: Joshua 3:1–5:12; Luke 13:1–30; Proverbs 9:1–12

Day 101: Joshua 5:13–7:26; Luke 13:31–14:14; Psalm 44:1–12

Day 102: Joshua 8:1–9:15; Luke 14:15–35; Psalm 44:13–26

Day 103: Joshua 9:16–10:43; Luke 15:1–32; Psalm 45:1–9

Day 104: Joshua 11:1–12:24; Luke 16:1–18; Proverbs 9:13–18

Day 105: Joshua 13:1–14:15; Luke 16:19–17:10; Psalm 45:10–17

Week 16

Daily Readings

	Old Testament	New Testament	Psalms / Proverbs	
Day 106	Joshua 15:1–16:10	Luke 17:11–37	Psalm 46:1–11	
Day 107	Joshua 17:1–18:28	Luke 18:1–30	Psalm 47:1–9	
Day 108	Joshua 19:1–21:19	Luke 18:31–19:10	Proverbs 10:1–10	
Day 109	Joshua 21:20–22:34	Luke 19:11–44	Psalm 48:1–8	
Day 110	Joshua 23:1–24:33	Luke 19:45–20:26	Psalm 48:9–14	
Day 111	Judges 1:1–2:5	Luke 20:27–21:4	Psalm 49:1–20	
Day 112	Judges 2:6–3:31	Luke 21:5–38	Proverbs 10:11–20	

Old Testament

As you read last week, the first half of Joshua focuses on the rise of a new leader and the battles fought by the Israelites to secure the promised land. In the second half, the focus turns to how this newly acquired land will be divided among the twelve tribes of Israel. Ten chapters (Joshua 13–22) are devoted to the division of the land, and let's face it, this is not the most enthralling section of the Bible.

Did it really have to be this long?

Couldn't they have just summarized these details in a few verses?

Of course they could have, but that would not have done justice to what is taking place here. Think about how many times the covenant between God and the people of Israel has been mentioned so far in the Old Testament. At every turn in this story, the covenant has been renewed. The Israelites have recommitted themselves to love and obey the Lord, and in return, he has promised to be their God and to provide them with their own land in which their descendants can flourish for generations. Remember what God said to Abraham:

> I will establish my covenant as an everlasting covenant between me and you and your descendants after you for the generations to come, to be your God and the God of your descendants after you. The whole land of Canaan, where you now reside as a foreigner, I will give as an everlasting possession to you and your descendants after you; and I will be their God. (Gen. 17:7–8)

These chapters in Joshua may be dull, but they show us that God fulfilled his promise to Abraham. It's this promise that Joshua reminds the Israelites about in his farewell speech in chapter 23. And in his final act, Joshua gathers all the tribes of Israel together to once again renew the covenant with God. He reminds them of God's faithfulness, and he implores them to remain faithful as well. As you finish the book of Joshua, remember that it's not just about battles and bloodshed. In these pages we are reminded that God will do what he says. When he makes a promise, he will deliver.

New Testament

Every time I read Luke 19, a catchy little song I learned as a child in Sunday School pops into my head:

> *Zacchaeus was a wee little man*
> *And a wee little man was he*
> *He climbed up in a sycamore tree*
> *For the Lord he wanted to see*
>
> *And as the Savior passed that way*
> *He looked up in the tree*

And he said, Zacchaeus you come down
For I'm going to your house today

I often wonder if the popularity of this children's song has negatively impacted the powerful message found in the story of Zacchaeus. Not only does the song leave out that Zacchaeus was a tax collector (which is important), but it also only gets us through the first five verses of this passage. There are five more verses, and the second half of this story is incredibly important and powerful.

Zacchaeus excitedly welcomes Jesus to his home while the crowd mutters their disapproval. Tax collectors were despised in these days, usually because they were dishonest and cheated people to benefit themselves. That Jesus is going to the home of such a sinner tells us that he cares for the lost and broken.

And suddenly we see the astonishing effect Jesus has on people. Zacchaeus pledges to give half of his possessions to the poor and promises to pay back anyone he's cheated four times the amount.

So you see, there's more to this story than that little song lets on. Yes, Zacchaeus was a short man who climbed a tree to see Jesus. And yes, Jesus noticed him up in that tree and invited himself to Zacchaeus's home. But this is a redemption story about a sinner whose life was forever changed when he met Jesus. No matter who you are or what you've done, Jesus wants to invite himself into your life. Will you welcome him?

Psalms and Proverbs

In previous weeks, we read Proverbs 1–9, which includes several extended passages that read like lessons from a father to a son. There are also a handful of poems from the personified voice of Wisdom. You might notice a shift this week in Proverbs 10, which tells us that we have now come to "the proverbs of Solomon." For the next twenty chapters (through Proverbs 29), we will find hundreds of wise sayings—mostly two-line verses—attributed to King Solomon, the son of David. These proverbs cover a wide range of topics from every facet of life, but the focus is still the pursuit of wisdom. Solomon wants his readers to discover the good life that is found when we fear the Lord and live with righteousness.

As you read the proverbs of Solomon, I encourage you to note the ones that are particularly meaningful or insightful to you. Highlight or underline them in your Bible. Write them down and leave them somewhere you'll see them throughout the week. For example, as I read Proverbs 10, I noticed that Solomon mentions our mouths multiple times. It's a reminder that what I say is a reflection of my heart, and I want my words to be a "fountain of life" (10:11) to those around me.

Reflections

Write down a few reflections on this week's readings.

Day 106: Joshua 15:1–16:10; Luke 17:11–37; Psalm 46:1–11

Day 107: Joshua 17:1–18:28; Luke 18:1–30; Psalm 47:1–9

Day 108: Joshua 19:1–21:19; Luke 18:31–19:10; Proverbs 10:1–10

Day 109: Joshua 21:20–22:34; Luke 19:11–44; Psalm 48:1–8

Day 110: Joshua 23:1–24:33; Luke 19:45–20:26; Psalm 48:9–14

Day 111: Judges 1:1–2:5; Luke 20:27–21:4; Psalm 49:1–20

Day 112: Judges 2:6–3:31; Luke 21:5–38; Proverbs 10:11–20

WEEK 17

Old Testament

The book of Judges recounts the next phase of Israel's leadership, in which they are led by a succession of twelve warrior leaders, also known as judges. If you're wondering why the Israelites need warriors for leaders when we just read about their conquests over the Canaanites throughout the book of Joshua, the answer is found in the first two chapters of Judges. There we learn that the generation after Joshua has not remained faithful to the Lord. The people have forgotten all that he has done for them. They have neglected the covenant. They have intermingled with the people of Canaan and adopted their crooked morals. They have even begun to worship other gods.

As a consequence of their unfaithfulness, God no longer protects the Israelites from the nations around them, but he raises up judges to lead them. Judges 3–16 tells us the stories of Othniel, Ehud, Shamgar, Deborah, Gideon, Tola, Jair, Jephthah, Ibzan, Elon, Abdon, and Samson. Don't miss an important recurring line throughout these chapters:

The Israelites did evil in the eyes of the LORD.

This phrase is repeated over and over. God gives the people a judge who saves them from certain defeat at the hands of one of their enemies, and the next thing you know, the Israelites have turned their backs on God again.

I teach a university class called Understanding the Bible, and every time I get to Judges, I walk up to the whiteboard and draw a massive downward spiral. That's what I see happening to the Israelites here in Judges. They are stuck in a pattern of self-destruction that they can't escape. It's a shocking turn considering all that we've seen God do for these people since their days of slavery in Egypt, and yet somehow I'm not surprised. Perhaps it's because I know how quickly I can turn my own back on God when things seem to be going my way.

God has every right to give up on the Israelites, but once again he remains faithful. Their story certainly gets bleak along the way, but as we'll see next week, hope is on the horizon.

New Testament

How many times have you taken the Lord's Supper? Some churches observe this sacrament only once a month; others partake every week. Regardless of how often you come to the table, does it ever make you think about Passover? I often forget that this was a Passover meal for Jesus and his disciples, which we read about this week in Luke 22.

Passover was and is a major Jewish holiday that commemorates God's deliverance of his people from slavery in Egypt. Pharaoh was stubborn, so God sent a series of plagues, and the final one was the death of the firstborn males in all of Egypt. The Jews followed instructions to wipe the blood of a lamb on their doorposts, and when the angel of death *passed over* their homes, their children were spared. But everywhere else in Egypt, the firstborn were killed. After this, Pharaoh relented and let God's people go.

From that moment on, the Jewish people have celebrated the Passover meal. It is their way of remembering God's faithfulness. That's what Jesus and his friends are doing on this night in Luke 22, just before he is about to be arrested and crucified. They are remembering. They are looking back.

But then Jesus invites them to look forward.

This Passover meal takes a turn as Jesus twice mentions the coming arrival of the kingdom of God, which at this point he has been teaching about for three years. Intriguingly, he says he won't eat this meal again until "it finds fulfillment in the kingdom of God" (v. 16). The implication of Jesus's words is that the Lord's Supper anticipates the future feast of the Messiah. He hasn't done the work of the Messiah yet, but he's about to. And that work—his death and resurrection—will unleash the kingdom of God until he returns to make all things new.

So Jesus refocuses their attention to this glorious future of the Messiah, and then he breaks the bread and passes the cup and says, "Do this in remembrance of me. . . . This is the new covenant" (vv. 19–20). In a holy moment when faithful Jews are gathering to look back and remember God's covenant promises and the faithfulness and redemption he showed them in Egypt, Jesus says there is a new covenant. There is a new redemption. Jesus is shifting their perspective, and he's shifting ours as well. Whenever we come to the table, we need to remember what God did at Passover, but we also need to remember what Jesus did at Calvary.

Psalms and Proverbs

Psalm 51 is a powerful prayer of repentance written by King David after the prophet Nathan confronted him for committing adultery with Bathsheba and having her husband killed (we won't get to that part of the Old Testament in our reading plan for another few weeks, but you can find the story in 2 Samuel 11–12).

The Psalms are the prayer book of our faith, and even though most of us aren't guilty of the same sins that David committed, his prayer of repentance in Psalm 51 offers us a template for how we can approach God with our own sins:

- He confesses his sin.
- He pleads for God's mercy and forgiveness.
- He asks God to cleanse him.
- He recommits himself to faithfulness.
- He promises to help other sinners repent as well.

I have a bit of a love-hate relationship with this psalm. I love that I can pray these words when I have sinned against God, but I hate that I have to pray them so often. But the good news is that the more I pray Psalm 51, the more I feel God's grace and mercy in my life.

Reflections

Write down a few reflections on this week's readings.

Day 113: Judges 4:1–5:31; Luke 22:1–38; Psalm 50:1–15

Day 114: Judges 6:1–7:8a; Luke 22:39–62; Psalm 50:16–23

Day 115: Judges 7:8b–8:35; Luke 22:63–23:25; Psalm 51:1–9

Day 116: Judges 9:1–57; Luke 23:26–56; Proverbs 10:21–30

Day 117: Judges 10:1–11:40; Luke 24:1–35; Psalm 51:10–19

Day 118: Judges 12:1–13:25; Luke 24:36–53; Psalm 52:1–9

Day 119: Judges 14:1–15:20; John 1:1–28; Psalm 53:1–6

WEEK 18

Daily Readings

	Old Testament	New Testament	Psalms / Proverbs	
Day 120	Judges 16:1–17:13	John 1:29–51	Proverbs 10:31–11:8	☐
Day 121	Judges 18:1–19:30	John 2:1–25	Psalm 54:1–7	☐
Day 122	Judges 20:1–21:25	John 3:1–21	Psalm 55:1–11	☐
Day 123	Ruth 1:1–2:23	John 3:22–36	Psalm 55:12–23	☐
Day 124	Ruth 3:1–4:22	John 4:1–26	Proverbs 11:9–18	☐
Day 125	1 Samuel 1:1–2:26	John 4:27–42	Psalm 56:1–13	☐
Day 126	1 Samuel 2:27–4:22	John 4:43–5:15	Psalm 57:1–6	☐

Old Testament

The book of Judges ends with a short postscript: "In those days Israel had no king; everyone did as they saw fit" (Judg. 21:25). It's here that the books of 1 and 2 Samuel (followed by 1 and 2 Kings) pick up the story and tell us about the era of Israel's monarchy. But there is a short book in our reading plan sandwiched between Judges and 1 Samuel. The book of Ruth is a beautiful story that serves as an interlude in this broader narrative.

One thing I want you to notice as you read Ruth is that God does not play an active role in this story. Unlike everything else we have read up to this point in the Old Testament, God does not talk to the people in this story or serve as the central figure moving the plot forward.

Does that mean God is not present in Ruth?

Absolutely not.

We see God's faithfulness and providence woven throughout

this story. There are eighty-five verses in Ruth, and the Hebrew words for "redeem" or "redeemer" are mentioned over twenty times. It seems that this little story is trying to tell us something about redemption.

The key to truly understanding the powerful redemption story in Ruth is found in the closing verses, where we learn that Ruth is the great-grandmother of King David. That's why the book of Ruth is located between Judges and 1 Samuel. This is the origin story of Israel's greatest king.

When this book was written, David was the greatest king in the history of Israel. But what you and I know now (that they did not know back then) is that an even greater king was coming in David's line. He is an eternal king, and his name is Jesus. The incredible story of redemption found in Ruth sets the stage for the greatest redemption story ever told. In that story, my friends, we *all* get to be redeemed. So as you read about God's faithfulness to Naomi and Ruth, know that this is but a glimpse of his faithfulness to us. This redemption story is our redemption story.

New Testament

At the end of last week, we began reading the gospel of John, which is the fourth and final account of Jesus's life and ministry. Many readers rightly notice a different tone in John than in the other gospels. Matthew, Mark, and Luke are commonly called the Synoptic Gospels (the word *synoptic* means that something has the same general synopsis) because they share a basic outline and many of the same stories. John includes a few of the same stories as the other gospels but incorporates several that are found only in John. There are also fewer parables in John than in the other gospels, and we find significantly more attention given to Jerusalem, as well as more metaphorical and spiritual language.

I find it helpful to think of John as the philosophical gospel.

From the opening line's emphasis on the preexistence of Christ ("In the beginning was the Word, and the Word was with God, and the Word was God.") to the seven "I am" statements made by Jesus throughout the book, one of the major themes of John is a philosophical exploration of Jesus as the incarnate Son of God. We find a great example in this week's readings during an encounter between Jesus and a Pharisee named Nicodemus.

> Now there was a Pharisee, a man named Nicodemus who was a member of the Jewish ruling council. He came to Jesus at night and said, "Rabbi, we know that you are a teacher who has come from God. For no one could perform the signs you are doing if God were not with him."
>
> Jesus replied, "Very truly I tell you, no one can see the kingdom of God unless they are born again."
>
> "How can someone be born when they are old?" Nicodemus asked. "Surely they cannot enter a second time into their mother's womb to be born!" (John 3:1–4)

Nicodemus hears Jesus say "born again," and he interprets it literally. But Jesus is speaking metaphorically and spiritually, and his response to Nicodemus highlights his status as the Son of God (Don't miss that this passage includes one of the most famous verses in the Bible, John 3:16.). Keep this philosophical perspective in mind as you read John. It may help you see things more clearly than Nicodemus could.

Psalms and Proverbs

Each of the psalms we are reading this week were written by David when he was on the run from his enemies. As you might expect, they include quite a few pleas for God's mercy and deliverance.

David doesn't hesitate to ask the Lord to wipe out his enemies. But what stands out as I read these psalms is how much worship David offers to God in these moments.

> I will sacrifice a freewill offering to you;
>> I will praise your name, Lord, for it is good. (Ps. 54:6)

> In God, whose word I praise,
>> in the Lord, whose word I praise—
> in God I trust and am not afraid.
>> What can man do to me? (Ps. 56:10–11)

> Be exalted, O God, above the heavens;
>> let your glory be over all the earth. (Ps. 57:5)

When I'm struggling, my first instinct is not to worship God. In difficult times, I'm more of a whiner than a worshiper. Yet here David is, on the run for his life from enemies desperate to kill him, yet he's singing God's praises. What a great reminder that God is worthy of worship no matter what circumstances we face.

Reflections

Write down a few reflections on this week's readings.

Day 120: Judges 16:1–17:13; John 1:29–51; Proverbs 10:31–11:8

Day 121: Judges 18:1–19:30; John 2:1–25; Psalm 54:1–7

Day 122: Judges 20:1–21:25; John 3:1–21; Psalm 55:1–11

Day 123: Ruth 1:1–2:23; John 3:22–36; Psalm 55:12–23

Day 124: Ruth 3:1–4:22; John 4:1–26; Proverbs 11:9–18

Day 125: 1 Samuel 1:1–2:26; John 4:27–42; Psalm 56:1–13

Day 126: 1 Samuel 2:27–4:22; John 4:43–5:15; Psalm 57:1–6

WEEK 19

Old Testament

After a brief interlude with the book of Ruth, the Old Testament picks up where Judges left off. Starting in 1 Samuel, we will read four books in a row that chronicle a new phase of leadership for the people of Israel, in which God raises up kings to rule over them. Originally, the book of Samuel and the book of Kings were single volumes, but they had to be divided when the Hebrew Bible was translated into Greek in the second century BC (a translation called the Septuagint) because they couldn't fit onto one scroll.

The first seven chapters of 1 Samuel are dedicated to its namesake. Not only was Samuel the last judge to lead Israel, but he was also a prophet and a priest. His remarkable origin story (which we read last week) positioned him as Israel's new leader at a time when the Philistines were wreaking havoc on them. Samuel leads the Israelites to an unlikely victory and a time of extended peace. But just when things start looking up, chapter 8 reveals that Samuel's sons are not worthy successors to their father, but instead "they turned aside after dishonest gain and accepted bribes and perverted justice" (1 Sam. 8:3b).

In a callback to the phrase repeated multiple times in the final chapters of Judges ("In those days Israel had no king; everyone did as they saw fit."), the elders of Israel see the wickedness of Samuel's sons and demand that Samuel anoint a king to lead them. What follows is a remarkable exchange between Samuel and the Lord.

> But when they said, "Give us a king to lead us," this displeased Samuel; so he prayed to the Lord. And the Lord told him: "Listen to all that the people are saying to you; it is not you they have rejected, but they have rejected me as their king. As they have done from the day I brought them up out of Egypt until this day, forsaking me and serving other gods, so they are doing to you."
> (1 Sam. 8:6–8)

You see, the Israelites' desire for a king is just another rejection of God. They look at the world around them and convince themselves that they need to be like everyone else (sound familiar?). But the truth is that the only king they need is God. Remember this moment as the story of Israel's monarchy unfolds in our readings over the next several weeks. God tries to warn them, but they won't listen. And it's going to lead to disaster.

New Testament

There's an interesting moment in our final New Testament reading this week, and depending on which translation you're reading from, it may be difficult to spot. Most major translations have either an in-text note or a footnote at the very end of John 7. My NIV Bible has a bracketed note in the middle of the column of scriptural text that reads like this:

[The earliest manuscripts and many other ancient witnesses do not have John 7:53–8:11. A few manuscripts include these verses, wholly or in part, after John 7:36, John 21:25, Luke 21:38 or Luke 24:53.]

The passage in question is about a woman caught in adultery, and it is one of several places in the New Testament where there is variance among the ancient Greek manuscripts. As this note indicates, some of the earliest manuscripts of John do not contain this passage. Many later manuscripts do include it, but in different places. These notes are a way for the translators to be transparent about the history of the biblical text we read today.

You might be wondering how many different ancient manuscripts there are and how we can trust that the Bibles we read today are accurate. Rest at ease. Biblical scholars have been studying these texts for centuries and compiling the best possible versions of them (a process called textual criticism). I have studied this at length, and I can vouch for the trustworthiness of our Bibles (if this topic interests you, I talk about it in detail in my book called *Bible Translations for Everyone*).

The text itself fits well within the overarching themes of the Gospels. A group of religious leaders called Pharisees bring a woman caught in adultery to Jesus. The laws of the Torah say she should be stoned to death, and they want to test Jesus to see what he will do. They seek violence, but he responds with grace, saying, "Let any one of you who is without sin be the first to throw a stone at her" (John 8:7).

This is a simple yet profound example of what Jesus did time and time again when he took the ancient laws of the Hebrew Bible and infused them with new levels of love and mercy. He redefines what the Law is all about. But at the same time, Jesus does not ignore sin. At the very end, he tells the woman to leave her life of sin. Jesus takes sin seriously. But the good news for all of us sinners is that he takes grace seriously too.

Psalms and Proverbs

Sometimes the Bible makes me laugh, and this week I found myself chuckling during one of our readings from Proverbs.

> Like a gold ring in a pig's snout
> > is a beautiful woman who shows no discretion.
> (Prov. 11:22)

The thought of a pig with a gold ring through its nose is more than humorous; it's ridiculous. No one would waste something that precious on a pig. But we know that the book of Proverbs is designed to impart wisdom on its readers. So what wisdom can be found in this amusing and bizarre mental image?

It's easy to think that this proverb is comparing a beautiful woman without discretion to a pig, but that's not the case. If you look closely, you'll see that the beautiful woman comes first in the second line, putting her in parallel with the gold ring in the first line. So the point of this proverb is that in the same way a gold ring is wasted on a pig, outer beauty is wasted on someone who does not have discretion.

WORD STUDY: The Hebrew word translated as "discretion" in this verse is used elsewhere in the Old Testament to describe judgment, reason, and wise counsel. Who we are on the inside—our character—is more important than what we look like on the outside.

Reflections

Write down a few reflections on this week's readings.

Day 127: 1 Samuel 5:1–7:17; John 5:16–30; Psalm 57:7–11

Day 128: 1 Samuel 8:1–10:8; John 5:31–47; Proverbs 11:19–28

Day 129: 1 Samuel 10:9–12:25; John 6:1–24; Psalm 58:1–11

Day 130: 1 Samuel 13:1–14:23; John 6:25–59; Psalm 59:1–8

Day 131: 1 Samuel 14:24–15:35; John 6:60–7:13; Psalm 59:9–17

Day 132: 1 Samuel 16:1–17:37; John 7:14–44; Proverbs 11:29–12:7

Day 133: 1 Samuel 17:38–18:30; John 7:45–8:11; Psalm 60:1–4

WEEK 20

	Old Testament	New Testament	Psalms / Proverbs	
Day 134	1 Samuel 19:1–20:42	John 8:12–30	Psalm 60:5–12	□
Day 135	1 Samuel 21:1–23:29	John 8:31–59	Psalm 61:1–8	□
Day 136	1 Samuel 24:1–25:44	John 9:1–34	Proverbs 12:8–17	□
Day 137	1 Samuel 26:1–28:25	John 9:35–10:21	Psalm 62:1–12	□
Day 138	1 Samuel 29:1–31:13	John 10:22–42	Psalm 63:1–11	□
Day 139	2 Samuel 1:1–2:7	John 11:1–44	Psalm 64:1–10	□
Day 140	2 Samuel 2:8–3:21	John 11:45–12:11	Proverbs 12:18–27	□

Old Testament

After Samuel anoints Saul as the first king of Israel in 1 Samuel 9, Saul's story plays out over the remainder of 1 Samuel. Saul is portrayed as someone who has incredible potential, and the early days of his reign are quite successful. But trouble moves in when—despite repeated warnings from Samuel—Saul proves to be so dishonest and prideful that the Lord rejects him as king of Israel.

In chapter 16 we're introduced to a boy named David. After killing the giant Philistine, Goliath, David gains recognition as a fierce warrior. Saul is threatened by David's success and becomes increasingly obsessed with having David killed. The second half of 1 Samuel is filled with incidents between Saul and David as the former's life and reign come to an end while the latter prepares for his time to come. The final chapters are particularly sad when you consider how Saul's story began.

This is a good opportunity for us to consider ways in which we might resemble Saul in our own attitudes and actions. His life should be a flashing warning sign for each of us. You might be thinking, "But I've never tried to murder one of my enemies!" Me neither, but I have mistreated people because of my own pride. And I've certainly become obsessed with things that don't really matter because of my own irrational fears. If we don't want our weaknesses to consume us as Saul's consumed him, then it's important that we recognize what they are, confess them to God, and ask him to help us pursue a more righteous way of living.

New Testament

The powerful story of the death and resurrection of Lazarus is found in John 11, and right in the middle of that passage is a fascinating interaction between Martha and Jesus (vv. 17–27). Martha's brother Lazarus is dead. When Jesus arrives, he comforts her by saying, "Your brother will rise again." Martha's response is appropriate for a faithful Jew of her day: "I know he will rise again in the resurrection at the last day" (John 11:24).

She's referencing a standard Jewish teaching of that time (based on Daniel 12:2 and other Old Testament passages) that all of God's people from past generations would be resurrected and given new bodies in the new creation. Martha thinks Jesus is just being "that guy" who says something cheesy and spiritual at a funeral to try to make her feel better, but look at what he says next: "Jesus said to her, 'I am the resurrection and the life. The one who believes in me will live, even though they die; and whoever lives by believing in me will never die. Do you believe this?'" (John 11:25–26).

Jesus is essentially saying to Martha, "You believe there is a great and glorious day of resurrection coming at the end of the age, when all believers will be raised bodily from the grave.

You're right, but here's the mystery: I am the arrival of that day." Resurrection is not just a theological idea; it is a person, and his name is Jesus. After making this incredible assertion, Jesus asks Martha if she believes. Her response is a full-fledged confession of faith in Jesus as Lord and Savior. Martha understands what Jesus is saying, and she believes.

This question is also asked of us. Do you believe that Jesus is the resurrection and the life? If so, confess your faith to him right here and right now.

Psalms and Proverbs

Imagine you are isolated in the desert without water. The heat is blistering, and the longer you're out there, the more desperate you become to find a drink. This vivid mental image is exactly what David uses to describe his devotion to God in the opening stanza of Psalm 63.

> You, God, are my God,
>> earnestly I seek you;
> I thirst for you,
>> my whole being longs for you,
> in a dry and parched land
>> where there is no water. (Ps. 63:1)

David spent quite a bit of time on the run and in fear for his own safety. Reading about the intense trials of his life in 1–2 Samuel helps us make sense of the deep emotion we find in the many psalms David penned. We know from the final three verses of this psalm that David is struggling with his enemies (this was likely written during the time of Absalom's conspiracy against David that we'll read about in 2 Samuel), which makes his confidence in God all the more remarkable.

I think the key to David's ability to remain devoted to God during troubling times is based on his past experiences with God. When he struggles in the present, he looks to the past. Throughout the psalms, David repeatedly mentions that God has been good to him, almost as if he needs to remind himself.

Perhaps we should follow David's example.

When you find yourself in times of trouble, think back to all the moments of God's goodness and faithfulness to you. Let those moments be the ones that spur you on to keep worshiping and trusting God when you're struggling.

Reflections

Write down a few reflections on this week's readings.

Day 134: 1 Samuel 19:1–20:42; John 8:12–30; Psalm 60:5–12

_____

_____

_____

_____

_____

Day 135: 1 Samuel 21:1–23:29; John 8:31–59; Psalm 61:1–8

_____

_____

_____

_____

_____

_____

Day 136: 1 Samuel 24:1–25:44; John 9:1–34; Proverbs 12:8–17

Day 137: 1 Samuel 26:1–28:25; John 9:35–10:21; Psalm 62:1–12

Day 138: 1 Samuel 29:1–31:13; John 10:22–42; Psalm 63:1–11

Day 139: 2 Samuel 1:1–2:7; John 11:1–44; Psalm 64:1–10

Day 140: 2 Samuel 2:8–3:21; John 11:45–12:11; Proverbs 12:18–27

Week 21

Daily Readings

	Old Testament	New Testament	Psalms / Proverbs	
Day 141	2 Samuel 3:22–5:5	John 12:12–36	Psalm 65:1–13	☐
Day 142	2 Samuel 5:6–6:23	John 12:37–13:17	Psalm 66:1–12	☐
Day 143	2 Samuel 7:1–8:18	John 13:18–38	Psalm 66:13–20	☐
Day 144	2 Samuel 9:1–10:19	John 14:1–31	Proverbs 12:28–13:9	☐
Day 145	2 Samuel 11:1–12:31	John 15:1–16:4	Psalm 67:1–7	☐
Day 146	2 Samuel 13:1–39	John 16:5–17:5	Psalm 68:1–6	☐
Day 147	2 Samuel 14:1–15:12	John 17:6–26	Psalm 68:7–14	☐

Old Testament

2 Samuel opens with David learning of Saul's death, followed by a series of chapters detailing the struggle for power between David and the remaining members of Saul's family and military. After several years of battles and schemes, the game of thrones ends in victory for David, who seizes the city of Jerusalem—which is also called Zion—and makes it his capital (2 Sam. 5:6–16).

If you were to visit Jerusalem today, just south of the Temple Mount you would find an archaeological site known as the City of David. This is where David settled after conquering Jerusalem. When I visited this site several years ago, I climbed to the top and looked out over the Kidron Valley, and I saw hundreds of homes rising up from the adjacent hillside. My mind immediately went to one of the chapters from our readings this week, and I turned to my tour guide and said, "Is this where David saw Bathsheba taking a bath?" She gave me a sly grin and then gathered the rest of our group together and asked someone to read 2 Samuel 11.

Up to this point, David has proven to be a man of great character. The past few chapters have included celebrations of his many victories over the nations surrounding Israel as well as his kindness and mercy toward the descendants of Saul. The Lord even made a new covenant with David, promising a future, eternal king from his line of descendants (yes, Jesus was of the line of David). But then, in the course of just one chapter, David becomes an adulterer and a murderer.

It's hard to be surprised at this point, isn't it? We have seen, time and time again, that God's people are weak and prone to sin.

But unlike with Saul, whose pride got the best of him, when Nathan confronts David in 2 Samuel 12, he confesses his sin against God and repents. David is not perfect. He has deep flaws. But we see by this response that his heart is good. David's humility and repentance are met with God's grace. There are still consequences for his sinful actions, but he is allowed to remain king. What a great reminder that when we repent, God is faithful to forgive our sins and restore us.

New Testament

A significant shift happens in John 13, which is the beginning of what is known as the Upper Room Discourse. Chapters 1–12 feature action-packed stories about Jesus that serve to reveal who he was. Those twelve chapters move quickly and cover several years of Jesus's ministry. But everything *slows down* in chapter 13. The next five chapters (13–17) all take place over the course of one night. John is inviting his readers to slow down and take a closer look.

It was just before the Passover Festival. Jesus knew that the hour had come for him to leave this world and go to the Father.

Having loved his own who were in the world, he loved them to the end. (John 13:1)

Passover is an important Jewish festival that serves as a key theme in the gospel of John. Passover is alluded to when Jesus is called the Lamb in John 1:29, it's Passover in chapter 2 when Jesus cleanses the temple and speaks of it being rebuilt, and it's Passover in chapter 6 when Jesus feeds the five thousand.

So here we are at Passover once again, but this time Jesus knows it is a critical moment that marks the beginning of the end. His arrest, beating, crucifixion, and resurrection are all about to happen.

So what does he do?

He washes his disciples' feet.

Have you ever washed someone's feet? It's gross. Yet here we have the savior of the world humbling himself and doing something a servant would do. It's easy to miss the significance of this moment, and Jesus even asks the disciples if they understand what it means (v. 12).

> "You call me 'Teacher' and 'Lord,' and rightly so, for that is what I am. Now that I, your Lord and Teacher, have washed your feet, you also should wash one another's feet. I have set you an example that you should do as I have done for you." (John 13:13–15)

Notice that "Teacher" and "Lord" go hand in hand. Jesus does not separate them. Many people call Jesus a great teacher without making him Lord of their lives. And some of us have made Jesus our Lord and Savior without making him our teacher. We want his grace and love. We want salvation. We want heaven. But we don't want to live the way he taught us to live. In this moment, Jesus slows down to teach his disciples to follow him through acts of humility and service to others. When we make Jesus our Lord, we must also live according to his teachings.

Psalms and Proverbs

In the midst of a series of psalms of praise written by King David, the seven verses of Psalm 67 rise up as a call for all people to worship the Lord. But they also have a unique literary structure. See if you can spot it.

> May God be gracious to us and bless us
> > and make his face shine on us—
> so that your ways may be known on earth,
> > your salvation among all nations.
>
> May the peoples praise you, God;
> > may all the peoples praise you.
> May the nations be glad and sing for joy,
> > for you rule the peoples with equity
> > and guide the nations of the earth.
> May the peoples praise you, God;
> > may all the peoples praise you.
>
> The land yields its harvest;
> > God, our God, blesses us.
> May God bless us still,
> > so that all the ends of the earth will fear him.
> > (Ps. 67:1–7)

If you look closely, you can see a common literary device writers of the Bible used called a chiasm, in which words and phrases are repeated in reverse order. The pairs of verses that open and close this psalm (1–2 and 6–7) speak of God's blessings that extend throughout the earth. Verses 3 and 5 are identical, calling on all people to praise God. That leaves verse 4 at the center of this psalm, offering us the key to the entire thing: We worship God because he is our just ruler and guide. When we put it all together, Psalm 67 teaches us that God is worthy of our worship, and when we praise him, he blesses us in return.

Reflections

Write down a few reflections on this week's readings.

Day 141: 2 Samuel 3:22–5:5; John 12:12–36; Psalm 65:1–13

_____

_____

_____

_____

_____

Day 142: 2 Samuel 5:6–6:23; John 12:37–13:17; Psalm 66:1–12

_____

_____

_____

_____

_____

Day 143: 2 Samuel 7:1–8:18; John 13:18–38; Psalm 66:13–20

_____

_____

_____

_____

_____

Day 144: 2 Samuel 9:1–10:19; John 14:1–31; Proverbs 12:28–13:9

Day 145: 2 Samuel 11:1–12:31; John 15:1–16:4; Psalm 67:1–7

Day 146: 2 Samuel 13:1–39; John 16:5–17:5; Psalm 68:1–6

Day 147: 2 Samuel 14:1–15:12; John 17:6–26; Psalm 68:7–14

WEEK 22

Daily Readings

	Old Testament	New Testament	Psalms / Proverbs	
Day 148	2 Samuel 15:13–16:14	John 18:1–24	Proverbs 13:10–19	
Day 149	2 Samuel 16:15–18:18	John 18:25–40	Psalm 68:15–20	
Day 150	2 Samuel 18:19–19:43	John 19:1–27	Psalm 68:21–27	
Day 151	2 Samuel 20:1–21:22	John 19:28–20:9	Psalm 68:28–35	
Day 152	2 Samuel 22:1–23:7	John 20:10–31	Proverbs 13:20–14:4	
Day 153	2 Samuel 23:8–24:25	John 21:1–25	Psalm 69:1–12	
Day 154	1 Kings 1:1–2:12	Acts 1:1–22	Psalm 69:13–28	

Old Testament

The second half of 2 Samuel is filled with twists and turns as David's power-hungry son, Absalom, rebels against him and David is forced to flee for his life yet again. Many of David's most gut-wrenching psalms were written during this time. When the dust finally settles, Absalom is dead, and David is back on the throne in Jerusalem. But his life is filled with great sadness. When you read these passages this week, it might make sense why we tend to focus on David's origin story. His rise to power is much more exciting and uplifting than his final days.

There is, however, a glimmer of hope.

In chapter 22 David looks back on his life, and even with all the pain and sadness he has experienced, he can't help but lift up a song of praise to the Lord.

The LORD is my rock, my fortress and my deliverer;

> my God is my rock, in whom I take refuge,
> > my shield and the horn of my salvation.
> He is my stronghold, my refuge and my savior—
> > from violent people you save me. . . .

> Therefore I will praise you, Lord, among the nations;
> > I will sing the praises of your name.
> > > (2 Sam. 22:2–3, 50)

This song is almost identical to the one found in Psalm 18, but it's placement here at the end of 2 Samuel complements the song we read from Hannah in the opening pages of 1 Samuel. This means that the entire saga we've read over the past few weeks in 1–2 Samuel—which was originally one unified work—is bookended by songs of praise and thanksgiving to God. This epic story tells us about a vital era in the history of the people of Israel. But the text itself reminds us that everything starts and ends with the greatness of the Lord. He alone is worthy of praise.

New Testament

In John 20 we learn that after Jesus was crucified, the disciples went into hiding. Imagine for a moment that you are one of them. You've spent the last three years of your life with this guy, and it's been a wild ride. And just about the time you're starting to connect the dots—to figure out who he really is— the whole thing falls apart. The last week of your life has been unimaginable. Your friend has been arrested, beaten, and exe- cuted. And now you've just learned his body is missing. You're afraid for your own life and the lives of everyone close to you. This is easily the most anxious, stressful, and fearful day of your entire life.

But then Jesus shows up.

You watched him die, but now he's standing right in front of you.

And what does he say?

"Peace be with you."

> **WORD STUDY:** We often think of peace as the absence of conflict. But the Hebrew word Jesus would have used for peace is *shalom*. This is an important word in the Bible, and when it's used, it refers not only to the absence of conflict but also to the presence of restoration and wholeness.

This is not your average peace. It's something deeper and wider. Jesus shows up for his friends in the scariest moment of their lives, and he speaks this restorative peace over them. And it works!

> After he said this, he showed them his hands and side. The disciples were overjoyed when they saw the Lord. (John 20:20)

Now stop imaging that you're one of the disciples and just be you for a moment. Have you ever been restless or anxious or filled with fear? We often look to other things when we need peace in our lives, but nothing can compare to the peace Jesus offers. Ask him to give you that peace right now.

Psalms and Proverbs

I have found it's best to read Proverbs slowly. With so many two-line phrases stacked on top of one another (many of which jump back and forth between topics), engaging with them in a meaningful way is nearly impossible when I read too quickly. When I see a passage from Proverbs in our reading plan, I try to give myself a few extra minutes to slow down and read more carefully. This week, my "slow reading" of Proverbs 13 led me to dwell on one verse in particular.

> Whoever disregards discipline comes to poverty and
>   shame,
>   but whoever heeds correction is honored.
>   (Prov. 13:18)

I don't know many people who enjoy discipline or correction. On the contrary, most people do whatever they can to avoid it. That's because when we are being disciplined, it means we are in the wrong. We don't want to be wrong; we want to be right. This leads to a sense of resentment (at least for me) toward anyone who seeks to correct us. Yet the wisdom of this ancient proverb reminds us that this type of resentment only leads to trouble.

The opposite of resentment is gratitude. Not only should we be willing to accept that we aren't always going to be in the right, but we should also be grateful for those moments when discipline or correction can help us get back on track.

Reflections

Write down a few reflections on this week's readings.

Day 148: 2 Samuel 15:13–16:14; John 18:1–24; Proverbs 13:10–19

Day 149: 2 Samuel 16:15–18:18; John 18:25–40; Psalm 68:15–20

Day 150: 2 Samuel 18:19–19:43; John 19:1–27; Psalm 68:21–27

Day 151: 2 Samuel 20:1–21:22; John 19:28–20:9; Psalm 68:28–35

Day 152: 2 Samuel 22:1–23:7; John 20:10–31; Proverbs 13:20–14:4

Day 153: 2 Samuel 23:8–24:25; John 21:1–25; Psalm 69:1–12

Day 154: 1 Kings 1:1–2:12; Acts 1:1–22; Psalm 69:13–28

WEEK 23

Daily Readings

	Old Testament	New Testament	Psalms / Proverbs	
Day 155	1 Kings 2:13–3:15	Acts 1:23–2:21	Psalm 69:29–36	
Day 156	1 Kings 3:16–5:18	Acts 2:22–47	Proverbs 14:5–14	
Day 157	1 Kings 6:1–7:22	Acts 3:1–26	Psalm 70:1–5	
Day 158	1 Kings 7:23–8:21	Acts 4:1–22	Psalm 71:1–8	
Day 159	1 Kings 8:22–9:9	Acts 4:23–5:11	Psalm 71:9–18	
Day 160	1 Kings 9:10–11:13	Acts 5:12–42	Proverbs 14:15–24	
Day 161	1 Kings 11:14–12:24	Acts 6:1–7:19	Psalm 71:19–24	

Old Testament

In 1–2 Samuel, we read through about 150 years of history, but in 1–2 Kings (which also began as one longer work that was later divided into two because it couldn't fit onto one scroll) we move quickly through 400 years. It all begins with the reign of Solomon, son of David and Bathsheba. Solomon is typically remembered for three things: wisdom, the construction of the temple, and his many wives. All three of these are found in our readings this week.

Solomon gets off to a strong start. He loves God and shows enough humility to ask for a discerning heart instead of a long life, wealth, or victory over his enemies. The Lord honors this request and gives Solomon an abundance of wisdom. His kingdom experiences a level of peace that the Israelites have never known before. With no wars to be fought, Solomon turns his attention to fulfilling his father David's dream of building a permanent temple for the Lord.

Don't miss the significance of the temple. Just as the Lord dwelled in the tabernacle during Moses's time, he now resides in the temple. This will be the central location of the life and faith of the Jewish people. From here on out, everything will revolve around the temple.

Solomon's story takes up only the first eleven chapters of 1 Kings (four of which focus on the construction and dedication of the temple). For ten chapters, everything goes great. But in chapter 11, it all falls apart. Solomon marries hundreds of women from the nations outside Israel, and despite repeated warnings from the Lord, he breaks the first commandment and begins worshiping the gods of his wives. Before the chapter ends, Solomon is dead and his kingdom is in disarray.

When I read Solomon's story, I can't help but wonder what could have been if only he had remained devoted to the Lord. The people of Israel have reached new heights thanks to his wisdom and leadership, but one of history's greatest downward spirals is about to start. Solomon's story serves as a reminder that we must always remain faithful to God, even when things are going well.

New Testament

After the conclusion of the four gospels, we come to Acts, one of my favorite books in the Bible. Also written by Luke (think of it as the second half of his gospel), Acts tells the riveting story of the first Christ followers as they formed what would become the early church. Luke writes with a sophisticated literary style that is highly organized and intentionally structured, and he has a flair for the dramatic. In these pages you'll read of arrests, riots, narrow escapes, trials, and even a shipwreck. He gives special attention to geography, so I strongly suggest reading Luke with a biblical map nearby. And he loves speeches (Acts has thirty-two of them).

In the opening chapter of Acts, the resurrected Jesus meets

with his disciples, teaching about the kingdom of God and promising that the Holy Spirit will empower them to go and be his messengers in the world. In chapter 2 the disciples gather to celebrate Pentecost, a huge agricultural festival that drew tens of thousands of Jews to Jerusalem from all over the known world.

And that's when the Holy Spirit shows up.

It's a peculiar scene where the Spirit empowers the disciples to speak in other languages. And sure enough, all the other Jews gathered in Jerusalem for Pentecost can understand them. The locations mentioned in Acts 2:9–11 correspond to modern-day Iran, Babylon, Turkey, North Africa, and Italy.

If you were a first-century Jew reading this account from Luke about people gathered from all over the known world and speaking different languages, one specific Old Testament story would have flashed through your mind: the Tower of Babel. Luke is masterfully alluding to the scene from Genesis 11 when everyone was confused by the different languages being spoken. But here at Pentecost, the exact opposite happens: clarity. And what is this clarity all about? What were they talking about in all those languages?

The wonders of God.

At this point Peter stands up and preaches his first sermon. He quotes three Old Testament texts that talk about the Messiah (Joel 2, Psalm 16, and Psalm 110), and he explains how Jesus is the fulfillment of these passages. It's a powerful message that compels three thousand people to follow Jesus. And this is only the beginning.

Psalms and Proverbs

Pay attention when words are repeated in Hebrew poetry. The word *refuge* is used more than forty times in Psalms, and David uses it three times in Psalm 71.

What comes to mind when you think about refuge?

For some reason, the immediate mental image I have is of a

makeshift shelter deep within a forest where someone could take cover during a storm. It's a place of safety and warmth.

David says that's how he feels about God. When trouble comes (and now that we've read through David's entire story, we know he faced quite a bit of trouble), he turns to the Lord for shelter and protection. When his enemies are after him, his hiding place is not a location but God himself. This requires a great deal of trust.

Where do you turn in times of trouble? Where do you go to find refuge? Do you turn to God or to someone (or something) else?

I want God to be the first thing I think about when I hear the word *refuge*. I want to fully trust in who God is and what he has done for me so that I am able to find rest in him even during my darkest moments.

Reflections

Write down a few reflections on this week's readings.

Day 155: 1 Kings 2:13–3:15; Acts 1:23–2:21; Psalm 69:29–36

Day 156: 1 Kings 3:16–5:18; Acts 2:22–47; Proverbs 14:5–14

Day 157: 1 Kings 6:1–7:22; Acts 3:1–26; Psalm 70:1–5

Day 158: 1 Kings 7:23–8:21; Acts 4:1–22; Psalm 71:1–8

Day 159: 1 Kings 8:22–9:9; Acts 4:23–5:11; Psalm 71:9–18

Day 160: 1 Kings 9:10–11:13; Acts 5:12–42; Proverbs 14:15–24

Day 161: 1 Kings 11:14–12:24; Acts 6:1–7:19; Psalm 71:19–24

WEEK 24

Old Testament

Solomon is succeeded by his son Rehoboam. But one of Solomon's officials, Jeroboam, leads the northern tribes of Israel to reject Rehoboam as king. The kingdom splits, with Jeroboam as the first king in the north (which retains the name Israel) and Rehoboam as the king in the south (which is called Judah). The rest of 1–2 Kings will jump back and forth between the reigns of the kings that follow, with a total of twenty from the north and twenty from the south. You'll notice that the text tells us if the king "did what was right in the eyes of the LORD" or "did evil in the eyes of the LORD." When all is said and done, only eight of the forty kings (each of them in the southern kingdom of Judah) honored and obeyed God.

In the middle of this dismal narrative about the divided kingdom and its many wicked leaders, 1 Kings introduces Elijah, one of the greatest prophets in the Bible (we read about him this week in 1 Kings 17–19 and 2 Kings 1–2). The Lord gives Elijah the difficult task of confronting Ahab, Israel's most sinister king. This leads to an intense showdown between Elijah and the prophets of Baal (a false god the Israelites worshiped during this time) on Mount Carmel. This scene likely springs to mind first when people think of Elijah, but I'd like to draw your attention to the following chapter, when Elijah goes into hiding in a cave on Mount Horeb.

> The Lord said, "Go out and stand on the mountain in the presence of the Lord, for the Lord is about to pass by."
> Then a great and powerful wind tore the mountains apart and shattered the rocks before the Lord, but the Lord was not in the wind. After the wind there was an earthquake, but the Lord was not in the earthquake. After the earthquake came a fire, but the Lord was not in the fire. And after the fire came a gentle whisper. When Elijah heard it, he pulled his cloak over his face and went out and stood at the mouth of the cave.
> Then a voice said to him, "What are you doing here, Elijah?"
> (1 Kings 19:11–13)

What an incredible moment! You would think that the Lord would appear to Elijah in a dramatic way, like the great wind or earthquake or fire. But instead, Elijah finds him in the gentle whisper. How often do we miss what God is doing in our lives because we want him to show up in a huge way? How often do we ignore his gentle whisper? When I think of Elijah, I'm reminded that God speaks to us in the quiet and still moments of life. May we listen closely and hear the voice of the Lord more clearly.

New Testament

In the opening chapter of Acts, Jesus tells the disciples that they will be his witnesses "in Jerusalem, and in all Judea and Samaria, and to the ends of the earth" (Acts 1:8). If you look closely, you'll notice that this is exactly how Luke structures the book. The first seven chapters take place in Jerusalem. Chapters 8–12 describe events in the regions of Judea and Samaria. Starting in Acts 13, we'll read about Paul's missionary journeys all over the Roman Empire, which reached the farthest corners of the known world at that time.

Our readings this week pick up in Jerusalem during Stephen's dramatic speech before the Sanhedrin, in which he recalls the history of the people of Israel and says that Jesus is the Messiah. A riot ensues, and Stephen is stoned to death by the angry mob. This incident causes followers of Jesus to flee from Jerusalem in fear, and they scatter throughout Judea and Samaria. But we are told immediately that they do not stop telling people about Jesus: "Those who had been scattered preached the word wherever they went" (Acts 8:4).

Don't miss this: Persecution leads to growth. The death of Stephen is horrific, but it is the inciting incident that pushes the good news of Jesus beyond Jerusalem. Within two chapters, we read the powerful story of Peter and the centurion named Cornelius, and suddenly this movement of Jewish believers in Jesus expands into the gentile world as well. Then the church finds a new base in Antioch (modern-day Antakya, Turkey), which becomes an outpost for even further expansion and is the place where the disciples are first called Christians.

God used something awful in the death of Stephen to spark something beautiful. Our first two New Testament readings this week are so discouraging, but by the end of the week, we have a multiethnic, international community of believers in Jesus. This movement is growing, and it's not going to slow down.

Psalms and Proverbs

Psalm 73 is the first of eleven psalms in a row written by a man named Asaph, who was a poet and musician from the tribe of Levi. He and his sons are mentioned throughout 1–2 Chronicles, and they served as worship leaders during the reigns of David and Solomon. The only other psalm attributed to Asaph outside these eleven is Psalm 50.

You may notice that Asaph's psalms feel a bit darker than many of the other psalms we've read, particularly those of David, which always seem to find hope even in the worst circumstances. Asaph writes of God's judgment on the people of Israel for their sins and includes prophetic language about their destruction.

> O God, why have you rejected us forever?
>> Why does your anger smolder against the sheep
>>> of your pasture?
> Remember the nation you purchased long ago,
>> the people of your inheritance, whom you
>>> redeemed—
>> Mount Zion, where you dwelt.
> Turn your steps toward these everlasting ruins,
>> all this destruction the enemy has brought on
>>> the sanctuary. (Ps. 74:1–3)

Despite the heavier tone of Asaph's psalms of lament, we see glimmers of hope and trust throughout. Where David shouts God's praises in the midst of his struggles, Asaph is more prone to whisper them. But as we saw in Elijah's story, whispers aren't always a bad thing. Sometimes a whisper is the only praise we have to offer.

Reflections

Write down a few reflections on this week's readings.

Day 162: 1 Kings 12:25–14:20; Acts 7:20–43; Psalm 72:1–20

Day 163: 1 Kings 14:21–16:7; Acts 7:44–8:3; Psalm 73:1–14

Day 164: 1 Kings 16:8–18:15; Acts 8:4–40; Proverbs 14:25–35

Day 165: 1 Kings 18:16–19:21; Acts 9:1–31; Psalm 73:15–28

Day 166: 1 Kings 20:1–21:29; Acts 9:32–10:23a; Psalm 74:1–9

Day 167: 1 Kings 22:1–53; Acts 10:23b–11:18; Psalm 74:10–17

Day 168: 2 Kings 1:1–2:25; Acts 11:19–12:19a; Proverbs 15:1–10

WEEK 25

	Old Testament	New Testament	Psalms / Proverbs	
Day 169	2 Kings 3:1–4:37	Acts 12:19b–13:12	Psalm 74:18–23	☐
Day 170	2 Kings 4:38–6:23	Acts 13:13–41	Psalm 75:1–10	☐
Day 171	2 Kings 6:24–8:15	Acts 13:42–14:7	Psalm 76:1–12	☐
Day 172	2 Kings 8:16–9:37	Acts 14:8–28	Proverbs 15:11–20	☐
Day 173	2 Kings 10:1–11:21	Acts 15:1–21	Psalm 77:1–9	☐
Day 174	2 Kings 12:1–14:22	Acts 15:22–41	Psalm 77:10–20	☐
Day 175	2 Kings 14:23–15:38	Acts 16:1–15	Psalm 78:1–8	☐

Old Testament

Our Old Testament readings this week are predominantly focused on Elisha, who is mentioned close to ninety times in these early chapters of 2 Kings. Elisha was a protégé of Elijah (yes, the similarity of their names can be confusing). He famously asked for a double portion of Elijah's spirit, and sure enough, we read about fourteen miracles Elisha performed in 2 Kings, compared with seven miracles Elijah performed.

> **WORD STUDY:** In Hebrew the name Elisha means "God is my salvation," and many of the miracles we read about this week involve Elisha rescuing people from death and disease. Even after his death, he continued to do miracles.

Elisha died and was buried.

Now Moabite raiders used to enter the country every spring. Once while some Israelites were burying a man, suddenly they saw a band of raiders; so they threw the man's body into Elisha's tomb. When the body touched Elisha's bones, the man came to life and stood up on his feet. (2 Kings 13:20–21)

Read Elisha's miracle stories closely. Do you notice anything familiar about them? Who do they remind you of?

Is it a coincidence that a prophet whose name means "God is my salvation" performed many of the same miracles that Jesus would later perform? The hand of God was clearly on Elisha, but even with twice as many miracles as his famous predecessor, he offers only but a glimpse of the miraculous salvation found in Jesus.

New Testament

In our readings this week, the unfolding story of the New Testament becomes laser focused on a man named Paul. After setting out on the first of three missionary journeys in Acts 13, Paul becomes the principal figure for the rest of the book, and the next thirteen books of the New Testament are letters Paul wrote during his ministry. Make no mistake, Jesus is still the primary focus of these texts. But Paul is the vessel through which the message about Jesus spreads. It's not a stretch to say that next to Jesus, the apostle Paul is the most important person in the history of Christianity.

So who was Paul?

Because we're going to spend a lot of time with him in the weeks and months ahead, we should know who we're dealing with.

Paul originally went by the name Saul. He was a Jew born outside of Israel in a place called Tarsus, which is in modern-day Turkey. This means he was a citizen of the Roman Empire who was fluent in Greek while also being devoutly Jewish. As a teenager Saul moved from Tarsus to Jerusalem to study the Torah under a leading Jewish scholar of the Sanhedrin named Gamaliel (who we read about in Acts 5).

As an adult, Saul became a leading Pharisee in Jerusalem known for violently persecuting followers of Jesus. The first mention of Saul in the Bible is during the stoning of Stephen in Acts 7, and chapter 8 says Saul approved of the mob killing him. In Acts 9:1 we're told that Saul was "breathing out murderous threats against the Lord's disciples" as he made his way to Damascus to hunt down Christians. But on the way, he had an incredible encounter with Jesus, and his life was forever changed. The great persecutor of Christians changed his name from Saul to Paul and became the leading Christian teacher and missionary of that time.

Paul's background uniquely positioned him for the task God had for him. His Jewish heritage and education under a leading Jewish scholar gave him the ability to interpret the life, death, and resurrection of Jesus from the theological framework of Judaism found in the Hebrew Scriptures. In his letters, he directly cites the Old Testament close to one hundred times, with countless indirect references. But his upbringing in Tarsus as a Roman citizen who was fluent in Greek positioned him to carry the message of Jesus into the non-Jewish world as well. He was the perfect person situated at the perfect moment in history to help the good news of Jesus spread far and wide like never before.

Psalms and Proverbs

This week we're reading only ten verses from Proverbs, but two of them offer deep wisdom on how to view wealth and abundance.

> Better a little with the fear of the LORD
> than great wealth with turmoil.

Better a small serving of vegetables with love
than a fattened calf with hatred.
(Prov. 15:16–17)

The word *better* at the beginning of each verse tells us there is about to be a comparison. Whatever is described in the first part of the verse is better than the alternative found in the second part of the verse. Notice it does not say that having little is better than having great wealth or that a small serving of vegetables is better than a fattened calf. That's not the whole point. The word *with* is found in each line as well. In the first verse, the fear of the Lord is better than turmoil. In the second verse, love is better than hatred.

These verses have multiple layers.

Is it possible to have wealth and abundance while also having the fear of the Lord and love? Of course it is. But more than two thousand verses in the Bible mention money and wealth, and many of them include warnings. That's because it is easy to become so obsessed with money that we lose sight of what really matters. We must always be aware of what comes *with* our wealth and abundance.

Reflections

Write down a few reflections on this week's readings.

Day 169: 2 Kings 3:1–4:37; Acts 12:19b–13:12; Psalm 74:18–23

_____

_____

_____

_____

_____

_____

Day 170: 2 Kings 4:38–6:23; Acts 13:13–41; Psalm 75:1–10

Day 171: 2 Kings 6:24–8:15; Acts 13:42–14:7; Psalm 76:1–12

Day 172: 2 Kings 8:16–9:37; Acts 14:8–28; Proverbs 15:11–20

Day 173: 2 Kings 10:1–11:21; Acts 15:1–21; Psalm 77:1–9

Day 174: 2 Kings 12:1–14:22; Acts 15:22–41; Psalm 77:10–20

Day 175: 2 Kings 14:23–15:38; Acts 16:1–15; Psalm 78:1–8

WEEK 26

Daily Readings

	Old Testament	New Testament	Psalms / Proverbs	
Day 176	2 Kings 16:1–17:41	Acts 16:16–40	Proverbs 15:21–30	
Day 177	2 Kings 18:1–19:13	Acts 17:1–21	Psalm 78:9–16	
Day 177	2 Kings 19:14–20:21	Acts 17:22–18:8	Psalm 78:17–31	
Day 179	2 Kings 21:1–22:20	Acts 18:9–19:13	Psalm 78:32–39	
Day 180	2 Kings 23:1–24:7	Acts 19:14–41	Proverbs 15:31–16:7	
Day 181	2 Kings 24:8–25:30	Acts 20:1–38	Psalm 78:40–55	
Day 182	1 Chronicles 1:1–2:17	Acts 21:1–26	Psalm 78:56–72	

Old Testament

As 2 Kings comes to a close, the Northern Kingdom (Israel) has been in a serious downward spiral thanks to their evil kings. In the opening verses of chapter 17, they are attacked by the Assyrian Empire. The capital city of Samaria falls, and all the Israelites in the north are deported from the promised land and forced to live in exile in Assyria. This took place in 722 BC.

The Southern Kingdom (Judah) remains intact, and we read the stories of heroic kings Hezekiah and Josiah this week in chapters 18–20 and 22–23, respectively. Despite the renewal of the covenant by Josiah, his successors turn their backs on God, and in the end, the fate of the south is also exile. It's not the Assyrians this time but the Babylonians. The final chapter of 2 Kings takes place in 587 BC, when King Nebuchadnezzar of Babylon attacks the city of Jerusalem with his entire army. Every important building is burned to the ground, including the royal palace and, worst of all, the temple. It's an utterly devastating conclusion.

Think back on everything we have read so far in this story about the people of Israel. Going all the way back to God's covenant with Abraham, it was always about them being the chosen people of God, who would make them more numerous than the stars and give them a land to call their own. The Israelites have been through so much, including slavery in Egypt, but this exile is the darkest moment in their history. The land that was theirs has been taken from them, and the very temple of the Lord has been destroyed.

Why would God allow this to happen?

I encourage you to carefully read 2 Kings 17:7–23, which tells us quite clearly that the exile was a consequence of Israel's sin. They did not honor the covenant they made with God. Instead of worshiping him alone and setting themselves apart from others, they worshiped other gods and adopted the practices of the nations around them. So God "thrust them from his presence" (2 Kings 24:20).

This is rock bottom for the Israelites. It cannot get any worse.

I want you to feel the tension and the sadness of this situation as you read it. This is heartbreaking and should remind us that we need to take God seriously. But I also want you to know that redemption is coming. God gets angry with his people, but he always remains faithful.

New Testament

This week's New Testament readings begin in Acts 16:16–40, but if you go back to verse 10, you'll see one of my favorite little nuances of the Bible.

> After Paul had seen the vision, we got ready at once to leave for Macedonia, concluding that God had called us to preach the gospel to them. (Acts 16:10)

Did you catch it?

It's easy to miss, but this is the first verse in which Luke uses the word "we" as the narrator in Acts. Many biblical scholars believe this was his way of indicating when and where he first joined up with Paul. Look closely, and you'll notice several more "we" verses in the chapters ahead.

Acts 16–20 recounts Paul's second and third missionary journeys, in Asia Minor and Greece. We see a pattern in Paul's approach. When he arrives in a new place, he goes first to the synagogue to explain and prove to the Jews that Jesus is the long-awaited Messiah they have been waiting for. He then goes into the city to preach the good news to the Gentiles (non-Jews), which was approved by the apostles and elders in Jerusalem (Acts 15).

We see Paul's brilliance on full display when he visits Athens (Acts 17:16–34), a city filled with idols and all kinds of pagan worship practices. After he visits with Jews in the synagogue and preaches to Gentiles in the city streets, word about him spreads. A group of Greek philosophers invites Paul to the Areopagus, also known as Mars Hill, to speak with the council members. In the sermon that follows, Paul contextualizes his message about Jesus for his audience. He quotes from some of their favorite philosophers (Epimenides and Aratus), and he points to an altar inscribed "TO AN UNKNOWN GOD" and tells them they have been unknowingly worshiping the one true God. As we saw last week, Paul's background as a Roman citizen who was fluent in Greek culture and customs allowed him to present the gospel in a way these people could comprehend.

What does it look like for us to do the same in our world today?

How can we help the people around us better understand the good news of Jesus?

Psalms and Proverbs

All of this week's readings from Psalms are in chapter 78, which at seventy-two verses is the second longest psalm. We're still in the middle of a series of psalms written by Asaph, but this one is more than twice as long as any of his others.

Why do think that is?

What does Asaph have so much to say about?

This psalm reads more like a sermon than a song. Asaph looks back across Israel's history and confronts the people with their wickedness. They have forgotten what God has done for them. They have neglected the covenant. They have worshiped other gods. They have spoken against God. They have sinned and sinned and sinned.

This psalm is so long because Israel's list of sins against God is so long.

Isn't it fitting that we're reading Psalm 78 in the same week that we're reading about the exile in 2 Kings? What Asaph describes here is exactly what led to Israel's downfall.

But don't miss the glimmers of hope he scatters in as well.

> Yet he was merciful;
>> he forgave their iniquities
>> and did not destroy them.
> Time after time he restrained his anger
>> and did not stir up his full wrath.
> He remembered that they were but flesh,
>> a passing breeze that does not return.
>> (Ps. 78:38–39)

Reflections

Write down a few reflections on this week's readings.

Day 176: 2 Kings 16:1–17:41; Acts 16:16–40; Proverbs 15:21–30

Day 177: 2 Kings 18:1–19:13; Acts 17:1–21; Psalm 78:9–16

Day 178: 2 Kings 19:14–20:21; Acts 17:22–18:8; Psalm 78:17–31

Day 179: 2 Kings 21:1–22:20; Acts 18:9–19:13; Psalm 78:32–39

Day 180: 2 Kings 23:1–24:7; Acts 19:14–41; Proverbs 15:31–16:7

Day 181: 2 Kings 24:8–25:30; Acts 20:1–38; Psalm 78:40–55

Day 182: 1 Chronicles 1:1–2:17; Acts 21:1–26; Psalm 78:56–72

WEEK 27

Daily Readings

	Old Testament	New Testament	Psalms / Proverbs	
Day 183	1 Chronicles 2:18–4:8	Acts 21:27–22:21	Psalm 79:1–13	
Day 184	1 Chronicles 4:9–5:26	Acts 22:22–23:11	Proverbs 16:8–17	
Day 185	1 Chronicles 6:1–81	Acts 23:12–35	Psalm 80:1–7	
Day 186	1 Chronicles 7:1–9:1a	Acts 24:1–27	Psalm 80:8–19	
Day 187	1 Chron. 9:1b–10:14	Acts 25:1–22	Psalm 81:1–7	
Day 188	1 Chron. 11:1–12:22	Acts 25:23–26:23	Proverbs 16:18–27	
Day 189	1 Chron. 12:23–14:17	Acts 26:24–27:12	Psalm 81:8–16	

Old Testament

2 Kings ends with the Israelites in exile and the city of Jerusalem destroyed. When we turn the page, we find ourselves in 1 Chronicles, which opens with a genealogy starting from Adam. It's as if the whole story of the Bible has started over. If this feels a bit odd, that's because 1–2 Chronicles did not follow 1–2 Kings in the original Hebrew Bible. This is one of several places where the book order of the Christian Old Testament does not follow the traditional Jewish order of the Hebrew Bible. The book of Chronicles (which was also divided in two when it was translated into Greek for the Septuagint) was originally the last book of the Hebrew Bible.

The Hebrew title of the book means "Events of the Days," and the book was written long after the exile as a concluding summary of the Scriptures and a record of the history of the Jewish people up to that point. The title we use—Chronicles—comes from Jerome, who translated the Bible into Latin in the late fourth century AD. In this legendary text called the Vulgate, Jerome called this book "a chronicle of sacred history."

Notice that the first word of Chronicles is *Adam*. Yes, it goes all the way back to the beginning. Over the course of the next nine chapters, we'll read the full story of the people of Israel—from Abraham all the way through David—in the form of family genealogies that focus on the royal line of David as well as the priesthood (descendants of Aaron). It's not the most riveting thing for us to read, but for its original Jewish readers, this was an epic look back at their ancestral history that helped them understand their identity.

After a brief mention of Saul in chapters 9–10, the focus of 1 Chronicles turns to the reign of King David in chapter 11. As you read this week and next, see if you notice anything different about this account of David's life and reign compared with what we read back in 2 Samuel. Write down anything that stands out to you, and I'll offer some insights next week.

New Testament

After the conclusion of his third missionary journey, Paul makes his way back to Jerusalem, and that's when things get messy. Many of the same zealous Jews that once joined Paul in persecuting Christians now have their sights set on him. In the six chapters of Acts we read this week, Paul is beaten multiple times, placed in prison, and repeatedly asked to explain himself to the authorities, including the Sanhedrin, multiple governors, and King Agrippa. As I read these passages, I can't help but think about the final hours of Jesus's life. Paul is experiencing many of the same trials Jesus went through, but he somehow manages to avoid getting handed over to be executed.

These chapters move quickly, but they account for several

years of Paul's life, and he is in prison almost the entire time. It's easy to see the downside of this. The most prolific missionary of the early church era—perhaps of all time—is unable to go out and spread the gospel for an extended period of time.

But that's not the whole story.

God uses this seemingly wasted time for good. Paul invokes his status as a Roman citizen to demand a trial before Caesar. The Roman governor Festus (Acts 25) grants this wish, and in our final reading this week, Paul is on his way to the capital of the Roman Empire. He's still a prisoner, but the gospel is about to spread to the most influential city in the world.

Not only that, but during this time in prison, Paul wrote letters to some of the church communities he established on his missionary journeys. Many of those prison letters—Ephesians, Philippians, Colossians, and Philemon—became part of the New Testament. Think about that. The very Bible we are reading through right now includes texts written during Paul's time in prison. He took what could have easily seemed like a setback and turned it into a new opportunity, and two thousand years later, we are still learning and growing because of it.

If I were Paul, I would have been tempted to give up. My instinct is to shut down when I face persecution. But just like God used Paul's struggles to advance the gospel, he can use our broken lives as well. Paul refused to give up, and that is a great reminder for us to do the same.

Psalms and Proverbs

Has stubbornness ever gotten you into trouble?

It sure has for me.

Just as the book of Chronicles looks back on the story of the Israelites, Psalm 81 is a reflective song of praise that simultaneously calls the people to remember God's faithfulness while also recognizing all the ways in which they have neglected the covenant and disobeyed him. In two simple and direct verses in the middle of this psalm, we find that the reason for Israel's troubles is stubbornness.

> But my people would not listen to me;
>> Israel would not submit to me.
> So I gave them over to their stubborn hearts
>> to follow their own devices. (Ps. 81:11–12)

God has been faithful to these people, and he has been clear about what he expects from them. The problem has always been that they are stubborn. They have chosen time and time again to turn their backs on God, and at a certain point, he decided to let them have it their way. As we've seen over the past few weeks, having it their way led them straight into destruction every single time.

But the final four verses of this psalm are God's promise to love and protect his people as long as they follow his ways. The choice is theirs, and it's ours as well. What does it look like for you to recommit yourself to obedience?

Reflections

Write down a few reflections on this week's readings.

Day 183: 1 Chronicles 2:18–4:8; Acts 21:27–22:21; Psalm 79:1–13

Day 184: 1 Chronicles 4:9–5:26; Acts 22:22–23:11; Proverbs 16:8–17

Day 185: 1 Chronicles 6:1–81; Acts 23:12–35; Psalm 80:1–7

Day 186: 1 Chronicles 7:1–9:1a; Acts 24:1–27; Psalm 80:8–19

Day 187: 1 Chronicles 9:1b–10:14; Acts 25:1–22; Psalm 81:1–7

Day 188: 1 Chron. 11:1–12:22; Acts 25:23–26:23; Proverbs 16:18–27

Day 189: 1 Chron. 12:23–14:17; Acts 26:24–27:12; Psalm 81:8–16

WEEK 28

Daily Readings

	Old Testament	New Testament	Psalms / Proverbs	
Day 190	1 Chron. 15:1–16:36	Acts 27:13–44	Psalm 82:1–8	
Day 191	1 Chron. 16:37–18:17	Acts 28:1–16	Psalm 83:1–18	
Day 192	1 Chronicles 19:1–22:1	Acts 28:17–31	Proverbs 16:28–17:4	
Day 193	1 Chron. 22:2–23:32	Romans 1:1–17	Psalm 84:1–7	
Day 194	1 Chron. 24:1–26:19	Romans 1:18–32	Psalm 84:8–12	
Day 195	1 Chron. 26:20–27:34	Romans 2:1–16	Psalm 85:1–7	
Day 196	1 Chron. 28:1–29:30	Romans 2:17–3:8	Proverbs 17:5–14	

Old Testament

Last week I asked you to compare how the book of Chronicles and the book of Samuel portray the life of David. This week we'll finish reading the rest of David's story for the second time, and it should become clear that Chronicles has omitted all the negative stories about Israel's most beloved king. David's adulterous affair with Bathsheba and the murder of her husband, Uriah, are nowhere to be found. His struggles with Saul aren't mentioned. Neither is his tormented relationship with his son Absalom. The worst moments of David's life have been left out.

Instead, 1 Chronicles portrays David as the ideal king. He is a victorious hero who leads mighty warriors into battle against the Philistines, Moabites, Arameans, Edomites, Ammonites, Amalekites, and many more. He is a heartfelt worshiper who has a deep and abiding relationship with the Lord. He ministers to his people and makes detailed preparations for the temple. 1 Chronicles proves to be a highlight reel of David's reign, but that's not because the writer was trying to sanitize David's story and fool us into thinking he was perfect. The text even mentions the book of Samuel—which we know is filled with stories of David's lesser moments—as a good record of David's life.

The key to understanding why Chronicles tells this story in this way is something I told you last week: This book was originally the conclusion of the Hebrew Bible (and still is for modern Jews). Its purpose is to summarize the entire Old Testament and, perhaps more importantly, to help readers anticipate what they can look forward to in the future. This retelling of David's story includes several allusions to a future messianic king who will establish God's eternal kingdom. As we'll see when we read the books of prophecy, this future savior becomes an important figure for the people of Israel in the years during and after the exile. It makes sense, then, that the final book of the Hebrew Bible would look back on Israel's story from the perspective of those waiting for a new king. And David, the greatest king from their past, offers them a glimpse of an even greater king that they hope for in the future.

New Testament

Acts concludes with Paul under house arrest in Rome, awaiting trial before Caesar. But the New Testament is not done with Paul. His story continues in the form of letters (often called epistles), which he wrote primarily to the various communities he visited during his missionary journeys. The first one we read is Romans, and we learn in the opening chapter that Paul has not yet been to Rome when he writes this letter.

> I long to see you so that I may impart to you some spiritual gift to make you strong—that is, that you and I may be mutually encouraged by each other's faith. I do not want you to be

unaware, brothers and sisters, that I planned many times to come to you (but have been prevented from doing so until now) in order that I might have a harvest among you, just as I have had among the other Gentiles. (Rom. 1:11–13)

It's appropriate that Romans is the first letter we read from Paul, because it is his theological masterpiece. Perhaps because he has not yet had the opportunity to visit the church in Rome, Paul provides a more detailed explanation of the gospel in Romans than in any of his other writings. For this reason, certain passages from Romans are among the most quoted in the Bible. Some Christians even use a standard collection of verses (often referred to as "the Romans Road") to concisely explain the good news of salvation.

When I was in seminary, I took a class dedicated to Romans. I learned so much during that term, but the most eye-opening part was when the professor (Dr. Tommy Givens) had the class read all of Romans in one sitting. I was shocked by how unfamiliar I was with much of the letter. Previously, I thought of Romans as a handbook for personal salvation, but there is so much more going on. It is deeply focused on both the history of Israel and the realities of the Jews living in the Roman Empire. It is an intricate theological argument that builds and expands with each chapter. As I read it all at once, the most famous verses from Romans suddenly came to life in new ways.

We'll slowly read through Romans over the next three weeks, but if you have time this week, read the entire thing at once. You won't regret it. And invite God to show you something new through these legendary, ancient words.

Psalms and Proverbs

I love to travel and see new places, but if you gave me the option to go anywhere in the world for a single day, I would choose to have a quiet day at home. I love my house, and I love being in it (with my wife and dog, of course) more than just about anything. When I have a day off, I even have a little song I sing sometimes that's all about how much I love being at home.

Psalm 84 is a song of praise dedicated to the house of the Lord, and verse 10 is one of my favorite verses in the Bible.

> Better is one day in your courts
> than a thousand elsewhere;
> I would rather be a doorkeeper in the house of my God
> than dwell in the tents of the wicked. (Ps. 84:10)

Think about the most beautiful place on earth. Where is that for you?

The psalmist says that a thousand days in the most perfect place on earth can't compare to one day in the house of the Lord. And that's not because God has a big, big house with lots and lots of room or a big, big table with lots and lots of food. The reason the house of the Lord is so good is because it is where he dwells. There is no better place to be than with the Lord.

Reflections

Write down a few reflections on this week's readings.

Day 190: 1 Chronicles 15:1–16:36; Acts 27:13–44; Psalm 82:1–8

Day 191: 1 Chronicles 16:37–18:17; Acts 28:1–16; Psalm 83:1–18

Day 192: 1 Chron. 19:1–22:1; Acts 28:17–31; Proverbs 16:28–17:4

Day 193: 1 Chronicles 22:2–23:32; Romans 1:1–17; Psalm 84:1–7

Day 194: 1 Chronicles 24:1–26:19; Romans 1:18–32; Psalm 84:8–12

Day 195: 1 Chronicles 26:20–27:34; Romans 2:1–16; Psalm 85:1–7

Day 196: 1 Chron. 28:1–29:30; Romans 2:17–3:8; Proverbs 17:5–14

WEEK 29

Daily Readings

	Old Testament	New Testament	Psalms / Proverbs	
Day 197	2 Chronicles 1:1–17	Romans 3:9–31	Psalm 85:8–13	☐
Day 198	2 Chronicles 2:1–5:1	Romans 4:1–15	Psalm 86:1–10	☐
Day 199	2 Chronicles 5:2–7:10	Romans 4:16–5:11	Psalm 86:11–17	☐
Day 200	2 Chronicles 7:11–9:31	Romans 5:12–21	Proverbs 17:15–24	☐
Day 201	2 Chron. 10:1–12:16	Romans 6:1–14	Psalm 87:1–7	☐
Day 202	2 Chron. 13:1–15:19	Romans 6:15–7:6	Psalm 88:1–9a	☐
Day 203	2 Chron. 16:1–18:27	Romans 7:7–25	Psalm 88:9b–18	☐

Old Testament

The first nine chapters of 2 Chronicles are dedicated to the reign of Solomon. A couple of chapters are about Solomon's great wisdom and other activities, but the vast majority of this section is focused on the temple, including its preparations, building, furnishing, and dedication. Remember that the book of Chronicles was originally the conclusion of the Hebrew Bible, so retelling Solomon's story in this way shows us that later generations clearly viewed the temple as the most significant part of his legacy.

So why is the temple so important?

When we read about Solomon building the temple in 1 Kings (week 23 of our reading plan), I told you that the temple in Jerusalem is connected to the tabernacle built by Moses back in the desert. This is the place where God dwells with his people, and that's why the temple is so important. It is the central location of the life and faith of the Jewish people, described as the place where heaven and earth overlap.

But the author of Chronicles, writing centuries later, knows that the Babylonians will destroy this temple. It will be rebuilt (as we'll soon see in Ezra and Nehemiah), but the new version won't be as epic as when it was first built by Solomon. So the extended descriptions of the temple in our readings this week are a way for the people to look back and remember their best days.

But as I said last week, this book is also designed to help readers look forward. Just as Chronicles offers a glimpse of an even greater king yet to come, it also foretells of an even greater temple in which God will dwell with them. What the Israelites don't seem to realize yet is that this king will also *be* the temple. Jesus describes himself as the new place where heaven and earth overlap and where the presence of the Lord can be found (John 2:19–22). So as you read about the temple this week, in all its grandeur and glory, let your heart and mind draw closer to Jesus.

New Testament

Romans 1–4 offers a robust overview of Paul's theological perspective. He gives a detailed explanation of the problem of sin, the righteousness of God, faith in Jesus, and how all of this connects to the law and the history of the Jews. He juxtaposes the justice and faithfulness of God to the injustice and unfaithfulness of humanity, and he makes it clear that humanity's failures are fully inclusive of both the Jews and the Gentiles.

In chapter 4, Paul uses Abraham as an example of the epitome of faith for both people groups, not just the Jews. He notes that faith was the only thing Abraham had before the law was even established, and he uses this to point his readers to faith in Jesus, who "was delivered over to death for our sins and was raised to life for our justification" (4:25). This entire opening section of the letter is a theological tour de force that would have been quite challenging to Paul's gentile readers as well as their Jewish counterparts.

In chapter 5, Paul explains how the theological argument he has been making up to this point connects to the lives of his readers. His aim is to describe the results of justification by faith, and he does so with a celebratory tone that emphasizes peace, hope, reconciliation, and the tremendous love of God. What Paul says in 5:1–11 will echo throughout the remainder of the letter and, indeed, throughout human history.

There is certainly a level of complexity to 5:1–11, but its concise and direct presentation of Paul's Christology is much clearer than that of many other portions of the letter. Through the life, death, and resurrection of Jesus, the hostility between God and humanity has come to an end. This is the work of God because of his overwhelming love and grace for us. Despite humanity's sin and injustice, we have access to peace with God through Jesus. We are justified, and this justification leads to complete reconciliation with God. The reality of this, Paul says, is reason to boast. We boast not in what we have done but in who God is and what he has done for us through Jesus. We celebrate together with hope and joy, no matter what comes our way, because of God's great reconciling love for us.

Psalms and Proverbs

I continue to be amazed at how often our weekly readings connect with one another, and this week is a perfect example. The Old Testament readings are primarily about Solomon and the temple, where God dwells in Jerusalem. The New Testament readings are from a section of Romans in which Paul explains his understanding of salvation through faith in Jesus as something that is available for all people, not just the Jews. And the final group of readings this week includes Psalm 87, which uniquely touches on both of these exact topics.

I smiled when I read Psalm 87 because the way it celebrates the city of Zion (another name for Jerusalem) reminded me of the way 2 Chronicles celebrates the temple. Not only that, but several of Israel's enemies are being given status as God's people under the phrase "This one was born in Zion" (v. 4). All five of the nations mentioned in verse 4 (Rahab is another name for Egypt) are adversaries of the Jews, yet they are being adopted into the family of God at Zion. This mirrors Paul's argument in Romans for including Gentiles alongside Jews as God's people through faith in Jesus.

One of the beautiful things about this reading plan, with multiple readings every day from different portions of the Bible, is that we get to see all the small ways in which everything is woven together. This book is a miracle.

Reflections

Write down a few reflections on this week's readings.

Day 197: 2 Chronicles 1:1–17; Romans 3:9–31; Psalm 85:8–13

Day 198: 2 Chronicles 2:1–5:1; Romans 4:1–15; Psalm 86:1–10

Day 199: 2 Chronicles 5:2–7:10; Romans 4:16–5:11; Psalm 86:11–17

Day 200: 2 Chron. 7:11–9:31; Romans 5:12–21; Proverbs 17:15–24

Day 201: 2 Chronicles 10:1–12:16; Romans 6:1–14; Psalm 87:1–7

Day 202: 2 Chronicles 13:1–15:19; Romans 6:15–7:6; Psalm 88:1–9a

_____

_____

_____

_____

_____

Day 203: 2 Chronicles 16:1–18:27; Romans 7:7–25; Psalm 88:9b–18

_____

_____

_____

_____

_____

WEEK 30

Daily Readings

	Old Testament	New Testament	Psalms / Proverbs	
Day 204	2 Chron. 18:28–21:3	Romans 8:1–17	Proverbs 17:25–18:6	☐
Day 205	2 Chron. 21:4–23:21	Romans 8:18–39	Psalm 89:1–8	☐
Day 206	2 Chron. 24:1–25:28	Romans 9:1–21	Psalm 89:9–13	☐
Day 207	2 Chron. 26:1–28:27	Romans 9:22–10:4	Psalm 89:14–18	☐
Day 208	2 Chronicles 29:1–31:1	Romans 10:5–11:10	Proverbs 18:7–16	☐
Day 209	2 Chron. 31:2–33:20	Romans 11:11–32	Psalm 89:19–29	☐
Day 210	2 Chron. 33:21–35:19	Romans 11:33–12:21	Psalm 89:30–37	☐

Old Testament

This week's Old Testament readings take place during the divided kingdom, but unlike 1–2 Kings, which bounce back and forth between the reigns of forty rulers (twenty each in the north and south), 2 Chronicles focuses entirely on the twenty kings of the Southern Kingdom.

Why do you think the Northern Kingdom gets left out?

Remember, the book of Chronicles is looking back on Israel's best king (David) while also looking forward to an even greater future king (Jesus). The rulers of the Southern Kingdom are the direct descendants of David. What happened in the Northern Kingdom isn't unimportant, but the focus of Chronicles is on the Davidic line.

These passages read like a series of character studies. The good kings "did what was right in the eyes of the LORD," while the bad kings "did evil in the eyes of the LORD." It seems rather obvious, but the legacy of each king came down to whether they honored God with their lives and leadership. Those who did (like Hezekiah) were honored when they died, but those who did not (like Jehoram) were disgraced.

> Hezekiah rested with his ancestors and was buried on the hill where the tombs of David's descendants are. All Judah and the people of Jerusalem honored him when he died. (2 Chron. 32:33)

> Jehoram was thirty-two years old when he became king, and he reigned in Jerusalem eight years. He passed away, to no one's regret, and was buried in the City of David, but not in the tombs of the kings. (2 Chron. 21:20)

As you read these passages, consider your own legacy. What do you want to be remembered for? How can you pursue doing what is right in the eyes of the Lord?

New Testament

Paul's focus on new life in Christ comes to a powerful conclusion in Romans 8, with a great deal of focus on the future hope found in Jesus. The tension we often feel between the "already and not yet" nature of God's kingdom is a topic of great joy for Paul despite the challenges of living in that tension. God's kingdom is readily available to us right here and right now, but the full glory of it (the "not yet") will not be made known until Jesus returns.

Paul's frequent use of the words *flesh* and *Spirit* creates a clear distinction between life before and after Jesus. This new life in the Spirit is not an easy one to master, but Paul keeps his eyes ahead, knowing that nothing can "separate us from the love of God that is in Christ Jesus our Lord" (8:39). As we look back on the first eight chapters of Romans, Paul has made a strong case that what God has been up to since the very beginning of creation has now been fulfilled through the life, death, and resurrection of Jesus Christ.

But there's an elephant in the room, isn't there?

What about the Jews who have rejected the gospel of Jesus?

In chapters 9–11, Paul applies everything he has said so far in the letter to the people of Israel—God's chosen people—who do not believe that Jesus is the Messiah. This matter has caused him "great sorrow and unceasing anguish" (9:2), and in these chapters it's clear that he is struggling to make sense of it all. Paul's statement in Romans 9:6 that "not all who are descended from Israel are Israel" sounds a bit odd at first, but the point he's trying to make is that being identified as one of God's people is not about being a biological descendant of Abraham who obeys the law of the Torah, but about being adopted into the family of God through faith in Jesus, who is "the culmination of the law" (10:4). So the Jews' adherence to the law was incomplete without the understanding that the goal of the law was always Jesus, and Paul uses Scripture to show that Jesus was what the Torah was always about.

In chapter 11 Paul is urging his gentile readers—just like he did earlier in the letter—not to think of themselves as better than the Jews. The metaphor of the olive tree is not intended to establish a replacement theology but to recognize the beautiful creation of something new that includes both Gentiles and Jews. The Gentiles aren't a new tree that has replaced the olive tree; they have been grafted *into* the olive tree.

Is this challenging and difficult to understand?

Absolutely.

Which is why the doxology of Romans 11:33–36 is a perfect way to conclude these three chapters. The mystery and complexity of it all leads to worship.

> Oh, the depth of the riches of the wisdom and
> knowledge of God!

How unsearchable his judgments,
and his paths beyond tracing out!
"Who has known the mind of the Lord?
Or who has been his counselor?"
"Who has ever given to God,
that God should repay them?"
For from him and through him and for him are all things.
To him be the glory forever! Amen.
(Rom. 11:33–36)

Psalms and Proverbs

At fifty-two verses, Psalm 89 is the third longest psalm in the Bible. This week we are reading the first thirty-seven verses. Next week we will read the rest. It's fitting that our reading plan divides Psalm 89 this way, because a significant shift takes place between verses 37 and 38.

Psalm 89:1–37 sings the praises of God and the covenant he established with his people. God's love and faithfulness are mentioned over and over again, and they endure forever. This covenant is everlasting, and the hope of the people is secure in the Lord. In verse 19, the Lord begins to speak about David in a series of "I" statements. It is clear that David's greatness is not of his own doing but is because of God's steadfast love and faithfulness.

And then comes the *but*.

In the reading plan, the final fifteen verses of Psalm 89 aren't until next week, but go ahead and take a peek at how this psalm concludes. Suddenly this song of praise turns into a lament. The covenant has been broken. The Israelites' enemies have crushed them. And God has allowed it to happen. We don't know the exact cause of this strife, but it's possible that this psalm was written around the time of the exile, when the people of Israel were experiencing the lowest point in their history.

This may sound odd, but I find this psalm beautiful. The tension between the joyous opening and the grief-filled conclusion feels so real to me. I can't tell you how many times I have praised God in one moment and found myself in despair the next. I love that the Bible does not gloss over the pain we experience. Instead, it gives us words to cry out to God even when we don't understand what he's doing. We know he has been faithful, and we know he will be faithful again.

Reflections

Write down a few reflections on this week's readings.

Day 204: 2 Chron. 18:28–21:3; Romans 8:1–17; Proverbs 17:25–18:6

Day 205: 2 Chronicles 21:4–23:21; Romans 8:18–39; Psalm 89:1–8

Day 206: 2 Chronicles 24:1–25:28; Romans 9:1–21; Psalm 89:9–13

_____

_____

_____

_____

_____

Day 207: 2 Chron. 26:1–28:27; Romans 9:22–10:4; Psalm 89:14–18

_____

_____

_____

_____

_____

Day 208: 2 Chron. 29:1–31:1; Romans 10:5–11:10; Proverbs 18:7–16

_____

_____

_____

_____

_____

Day 209: 2 Chron. 31:2–33:20; Romans 11:11–32; Psalm 89:19–29

_____

_____

_____

_____

_____

Day 210: 2 Chron. 33:21–35:19; Rom. 11:33–12:21; Psalm 89:30–37

WEEK 31

Daily Readings

	Old Testament	New Testament	Psalms / Proverbs	
Day 211	2 Chron. 35:20–36:23	Romans 13:1–14	Psalm 89:38–45	
Day 212	Ezra 1:1–2:67	Romans 14:1–18	Proverbs 18:17–19:2	
Day 213	Ezra 2:68–4:5	Romans 14:19–15:13	Psalm 89:46–52	
Day 214	Ezra 4:6–5:17	Romans 15:14–33	Psalm 90:1–10	
Day 215	Ezra 6:1–7:10	Romans 16:1–27	Psalm 90:11–17	
Day 216	Ezra 7:11–8:14	1 Corinthians 1:1–17	Proverbs 19:3–12	
Day 217	Ezra 8:15–9:15	1 Corinthians 1:18–2:5	Psalm 91:1–8	

Old Testament

As you might suspect, the conclusion of 2 Chronicles is slightly different from that of 2 Kings. Both books tell us about the attack of Jerusalem by King Nebuchadnezzar of Babylon. The entire city—including the temple—is destroyed, and the people of Israel are carried off into exile. But in 2 Chronicles, we get two final verses that do not appear in 2 Kings:

In the first year of Cyrus king of Persia, in order to fulfill the word of the LORD spoken by Jeremiah, the LORD moved the heart of Cyrus king of Persia to make a proclamation throughout his realm and also to put it in writing:

"This is what Cyrus king of Persia says:

"'The LORD, the God of heaven, has given me all the kingdoms of the earth and he has appointed me to build a temple for him at Jerusalem in Judah. Any of his people among you may go up, and may the Lord their God be with them.'" (2 Chron. 36:22–23)

You see, about fifty years after the destruction of Jerusalem, the Persian Empire defeats the Neo-Babylonian Empire, and King Cyrus the Great of Persia tells the Israelites they can return to their homeland to rebuild the temple. The next two books of the Old Testament, Ezra and Nehemiah, describe what happens when they return.

Zerubbabel is the leader of the first wave of returnees, whose goal is to rebuild the temple. In Ezra 1–6, we learn that this took many years thanks to opposition from their enemies as well as new leadership in Persia. Eventually, Darius the Great (three kings after Cyrus) issues a new decree allowing the Israelites to complete the temple, but it is a shell of the former one. The older priests (who remember the incredible temple Solomon built) weep loudly when they see the new one.

If this feels like a letdown, that's because it is. The glory days for the people of Israel are gone. This is a new era in which they are allowed to return home and worship the Lord, but they are doing so under the rule of a foreign king. And yet there is still a glimmer of hope. God has not forgotten them, and there are better days ahead.

New Testament

In the final few chapters of Romans, Paul weaves together many threads from throughout the letter. What he has said about humanity's relationship with God, our relationships with one another, and the overwhelming love of God as expressed through the life, death, and resurrection of Jesus all converges here. Unity is an underlying theme of this section of Romans, and we will see it repeated in many of Paul's other letters. He makes it clear that how we live in community with one another is vitally connected to our theology. What we believe about Jesus must shape how we live.

Romans 12:1 challenges readers to see their bodies as a "living sacrifice" in response to all that God has done through Jesus. Think about that. A sacrifice is something that is laid down, and in ancient Israel, the sacrifice was often an animal that was killed and laid on the altar. But Paul tells his readers to be *living* sacrifices who lay themselves down on the altar—and go on living. It is a call to be walking and talking sacrifices to the Lord. This verse is saying that our response to what God has done for us through Jesus is to give him our entire lives.

And this, Paul says, is true worship.

Worship is more than singing. It is giving our entire lives to God. It is our actions and our words. Everything we do is worship. Paul recognizes that this is countercultural, so he warns us not to "conform to the pattern of this world, but be transformed by the renewing of your mind" (12:2). Sacrificial living is not what our world values. It seems that the pattern of our world is to make much of ourselves, often at the expense of others. But God's will is not for us to make much of ourselves. He wants us to make much of Jesus by loving and serving others. When we do that, we transform the world.

Psalms and Proverbs

Psalm 90 is the one and only psalm attributed to Moses. It's a beautiful prayer that serves as a reflection on the eternal majesty of God as well as the brevity and difficulty of life. This is about as raw and honest a look at life as you can get. I find it impossible to read these words and not marvel at how big God is and how small I am. Our lives are just a speck on God's eternal timeline, yet he holds it all—past, present, and future—in his hands. The reality of this can be overwhelming, yet Moses sees it as an opportunity to invite God to give us wisdom.

> Teach us to number our days,
>> that we may gain a heart of wisdom. (Ps. 90:12)

This verse feels more like a proverb than a psalm, doesn't it? Moses knows we're only deceiving ourselves when we try to avoid thinking about how fragile and short our lives really are. Instead, the way of wisdom is to recognize that life is fleeting and to invite God to use our days for his glory.

Reflections

Write down a few reflections on this week's readings.

Day 211: 2 Chron. 35:20–36:23; Romans 13:1–14; Psalm 89:38–45

Day 212: Ezra 1:1–2:67; Romans 14:1–18; Proverbs 18:17–19:2

Day 213: Ezra 2:68–4:5; Romans 14:19–15:13; Psalm 89:46–52

Day 214: Ezra 4:6–5:17; Romans 15:14–33; Psalm 90:1–10

Day 215: Ezra 6:1–7:10; Romans 16:1–27; Psalm 90:11–17

Day 216: Ezra 7:11–8:14; 1 Corinthians 1:1–17; Proverbs 19:3–12

Day 217: Ezra 8:15–9:15; 1 Corinthians 1:18–2:5; Psalm 91:1–8

WEEK 32

Daily Readings

	Old Testament	New Testament	Psalms / Proverbs	
Day 218	Ezra 10:1–44	1 Corinthians 2:6–16	Psalm 91:9–16	
Day 219	Nehemiah 1:1–2:20	1 Corinthians 3:1–23	Psalm 92:1–15	
Day 220	Nehemiah 3:1–4:23	1 Corinthians 4:1–21	Proverbs 19:13–22	
Day 221	Nehemiah 5:1–7:3	1 Corinthians 5:1–13	Psalm 93:1–5	
Day 222	Nehemiah 7:4–8:18	1 Corinthians 6:1–20	Psalm 94:1–11	
Day 223	Nehemiah 9:1–37	1 Corinthians 7:1–16	Psalm 94:12–23	
Day 224	Nehemiah 9:38–11:21	1 Corinthians 7:17–35	Proverbs 19:23–20:4	

Old Testament

Last week we read chapter 7 of Ezra, in which Israel's story jumps forward about sixty years to the reign of a Persian king named Artaxerxes, who sends a new wave of Israelites back to Jerusalem. Included in this group is a Torah scholar and scribe named Ezra, who wants to bring about spiritual renewal. By chapter 9, the book turns its focus to the many Jews who have intermarried with other people groups and adopted their ways. This section may feel xenophobic to many modern readers, but remember that one of the key aspects of Israel's covenant with God was for them to be set apart. Time and time again, they have allowed themselves to be turned away from their allegiance to the Lord because of the influence of the people around them. Ezra sees this as a huge problem, and in our opening chapter this week, he leads the people to confession and repentance.

As we turn the page to the book of Nehemiah, the story continues without any type of introduction, and that's because Ezra and

Nehemiah were originally one book. Nehemiah is an Israelite who serves in the Persian royal court. He becomes distraught when he learns that the city of Jerusalem still lies in ruins and asks King Artaxerxes to allow him to go and fortify the city. Despite fierce opposition from their enemies surrounding Jerusalem, Nehemiah rebuilds the walls around Jerusalem.

It's a powerful story of passion and perseverance. Nehemiah saw a need, and he didn't just ask God to do something to fix it, he asked God to send him. I read this story and wonder if I would be strong enough to do the same. How often do we see a need and pray that God will do something about it, *without* offering to go ourselves. Nehemiah's story is a good reminder that God will use us if we are willing. When something breaks your heart, ask God to send you.

New Testament

1 Corinthians is the first of two letters Paul wrote to the church in Corinth, a city in Greece that he visited at the end of his second missionary journey (Acts 18). Paul spent a year and a half in Corinth, teaching about Jesus and establishing a thriving church community. He clearly cares about these people, and now he writes to them to address several issues that have arisen since his departure.

Paul's first concern is addressing the division among the believers in Corinth, who have split into quarrelling factions, each showing allegiance to a different leader (Paul, Peter, Apollos, etc.). The first four chapters of this letter are Paul's response to this issue, and even though this was written for a specific group of people two thousand years ago, it still offers great wisdom for us as we navigate similar divisions in our own church communities.

Paul's main argument is quite simple: There should be unity in Christ.

> So then, no more boasting about human leaders! All things are yours, whether Paul or Apollos or Cephas or the world or life or death or the present or the future—all are yours, and you are of Christ, and Christ is of God. (1 Cor. 3:21–23)

Everywhere I look today, I see people quoting famous pastors and church leaders. We celebrate those we agree with, but we also speak out against those we disagree with. This divisiveness isn't limited to individual leaders—it extends to entire groups. We've separated ourselves into factions—Orthodox, Catholic, Protestant—with countless subgroups and denominations that often define themselves by how they disagree with other groups of believers. 1 Corinthians reminds us that the tendency to line up behind or tear down spiritual leaders is not a new phenomenon. Since the earliest days of Christianity, there have been disagreements about what it means to faithfully follow Jesus. Paul's encouragement, at its core, is to pursue humility and unity.

Psalms and Proverbs

In Psalm 92 we find a meditation on worship that opens with a three-verse declaration about making music for the Lord.

> It is good to praise the LORD
> and make music to your name, O Most High,
> proclaiming your love in the morning
> and your faithfulness at night,
> to the music of the ten-stringed lyre
> and the melody of the harp. (Ps. 92:1–3)

Notice that verse 2 mentions both morning and night. The intention here is not to instruct readers to praise the Lord at two specific points of the day, but rather to worship him at all times. We should always be praising God.

If the *when* is always, then what is the *why*?

Verses 4–5 tell us that worship is a response to what God has done. When we see God's wondrous works and feel his great love for us, the only response that makes sense is to worship him. And if you're looking for the right words, the very next psalm (93) provides us with a simple prayer that can be used on any occasion to exalt the Lord and celebrate his glory and majesty.

How will you worship the Lord today?

Reflections

Write down a few reflections on this week's readings.

Day 218: Ezra 10:1–44; 1 Corinthians 2:6–16; Psalm 91:9–16

Day 219: Nehemiah 1:1–2:20; 1 Corinthians 3:1–23; Psalm 92:1–15

Day 220: Neh. 3:1–4:23; 1 Corinthians 4:1–21; Proverbs 19:13–22

Day 221: Nehemiah 5:1–7:3; 1 Corinthians 5:1–13; Psalm 93:1–5

Day 222: Nehemiah 7:4–8:18; 1 Corinthians 6:1–20; Psalm 94:1–11

Day 223: Nehemiah 9:1–37; 1 Corinthians 7:1–16; Psalm 94:12–23

Day 224: Neh. 9:38–11:21; 1 Cor. 7:17–35; Proverbs 19:23–20:4

WEEK 33

	Old Testament	New Testament	Psalms / Proverbs	
Day 225	Nehemiah 11:22–12:47	1 Cor. 7:36–8:13	Psalm 95:1–11	☐
Day 226	Nehemiah 13:1–31	1 Corinthians 9:1–18	Psalm 96:1–13	☐
Day 227	Esther 1:1–2:18	1 Cor. 9:19–10:13	Psalm 97:1–12	☐
Day 228	Esther 2:19–5:14	1 Cor. 10:14–11:1	Proverbs 20:5–14	☐
Day 229	Esther 6:1–8:17	1 Corinthians 11:2–34	Psalm 98:1–9	☐
Day 230	Esther 9:1–10:3	1 Corinthians 12:1–26	Psalm 99:1–9	☐
Day 231	Job 1:1–3:26	1 Cor. 12:27–13:13	Psalm 100:1–5	☐

Old Testament

This week's Old Testament readings include the book of Esther, which is one of the most fascinating stories in the Bible. The drama unfolds in a place called Susa, the capital of the Persian Empire, during the reign of King Xerxes I (486–465 BC). We know from Ezra and Nehemiah that during this timeframe several waves of Jews returned to Jerusalem (it was Xerxes's son Artaxerxes who sent Ezra back). But the two main characters of this story, Esther and her cousin Mordecai, are part of the community of Jews who have not returned.

It's a wild story. Esther becomes queen without revealing her Jewish identity. Meanwhile, one of the king's officials, a rotten and arrogant man named Haman who hates the Jews, convinces King Xerxes to issue a decree "to destroy, kill and annihilate all the Jews—young and old, women and children—on a single day" (Est. 3:13). The entire city is stunned, and Esther and Mordecai are distraught. The chapters that follow take several unexpected twists and turns. Will Haman prevail, or will Esther be able to save her people from genocide?

As you read Esther this week, notice that God is never mentioned. That may seem impossible, but it's true. But that doesn't mean God is absent from this story. At each one of the bizarre steps along the way, we can see God's hand at work. When Mordecai looks at Esther in chapter 4 and says that perhaps she has become queen "for such a time as this" (4:14), he's pointing to God's providence.

What I love most about the book of Esther is that it reminds us that God is always at work in the background. He is with us even when it doesn't feel like it. Sometimes we have to find the courage to face our fears knowing that God will be there for us when we do.

New Testament

As Paul continues to address issues in the church at Corinth, he dedicates a portion of his first letter (chs. 11–14) to worship gatherings and church community. It's here that Paul coins the phrase "the Lord's Supper," another name for communion, or the Eucharist.

> **Word Study:** *Eucharist* is a term derived from the Greek word that means "thanksgiving."

Back in week 17, we took a close look at the way Jesus instituted the Lord's Supper in Luke 22, specifically noting its Passover context and how Jesus invited his disciples to both look back and look forward. You may want to study that passage alongside Paul's instructions here in 1 Corinthians because it adds an invitation to look in another direction: within.

> So then, whoever eats the bread or drinks the cup of the Lord in an unworthy manner will be guilty of sinning against the body and blood of the Lord. Everyone ought to examine themselves before they eat of the bread and drink from the cup. For those who eat and drink without discerning the body of Christ eat and drink judgment on themselves. (1 Cor. 11:27–29)

In the Lord's Supper, we are invited to look back and remember what Jesus has done for us. We are also invited to look forward in eager anticipation of the day when Jesus will come and finish what he started by making all things new. This fragment of bread and taste of the cup are the first course of an eternal feast. And finally, we are invited to look within, or as Paul says in verse 28, to "examine ourselves" so as not to come to the table in an unworthy manner. We know that our worthiness is not found in anything we can do but in what Jesus has done for us. It's only by placing our faith in him and offering our lives to him as living sacrifices that we become worthy to share in this meal.

The next time you participate in the Lord's Supper, remember to look back, to look forward, and to look within.

Psalms and Proverbs

At just five verses, Psalm 100 is one of the simplest and shortest psalms in the Bible, but you would be wise not to skim past it too quickly. This song of gratitude and praise is so powerful and memorable that it has become an all-time favorite for many people and the foundation of countless hymns and worship songs. It's filled with action, celebration, and exuberant joy. When I read

Psalm 100 aloud, something stirs within me. If you want to memorize a psalm, this is a great place to start.

> Shout for joy to the LORD, all the earth.
>> Worship the LORD with gladness;
>> come before him with joyful songs.
> Know that the LORD is God.
>> It is he who made us, and we are his;
>> we are his people, the sheep of his pasture.
>
> Enter his gates with thanksgiving
>> and his courts with praise;
>> give thanks to him and praise his name.
> For the LORD is good and his love endures forever;
>> his faithfulness continues through all
>>> generations. (Ps. 100:1–5)

This psalm overflows with so much worship and joy that it can be easy to miss its core message: that we are God's people and his love is everlasting. This foundational truth is something to celebrate. May we never forget it.

Reflections

Write down a few reflections on this week's readings.

Day 225: Neh. 11:22–12:47; 1 Corinthians 7:36–8:13; Psalm 95:1–11

Day 226: Nehemiah 13:1–31; 1 Corinthians 9:1–18; Psalm 96:1–13

Day 227: Esther 1:1–2:18; 1 Corinthians 9:19–10:13; Psalm 97:1–12

Day 228: Esther 2:19–5:14; 1 Cor. 10:14–11:1; Proverbs 20:5–14

Day 229: Esther 6:1–8:17; 1 Corinthians 11:2–34; Psalm 98:1–9

Day 230: Esther 9:1–10:3; 1 Corinthians 12:1–26; Psalm 99:1–9

Day 231: Job 1:1–3:26; 1 Corinthians 12:27–13:13; Psalm 100:1–5

WEEK 34

Daily Readings

	Old Testament	New Testament	Psalms / Proverbs	
Day 232	Job 4:1–7:21	1 Corinthians 14:1–19	Proverbs 20:15–24	☐
Day 233	Job 8:1–10:22	1 Cor. 14:20–40	Psalm 101:1–8	☐
Day 234	Job 11:1–14:22	1 Corinthians 15:1–34	Psalm 102:1–11	☐
Day 235	Job 15:1–18:21	1 Cor. 15:35–49	Psalm 102:12–17	☐
Day 236	Job 19:1–21:34	1 Cor. 15:50–16:4	Proverbs 20:25–21:4	☐
Day 237	Job 22:1–24:25	1 Corinthians 16:5–24	Psalm 102:18–28	☐
Day 238	Job 25:1–29:25	2 Corinthians 1:1–11	Psalm 103:1–12	☐

Old Testament

The *Daily Scripture* Bible reading plan follows a mostly linear timeline with only a handful of places where the text does not move chronologically through the story of the people of Israel. But that changes in the book of Job, which tells the story of a man who has quite a bewildering experience.

Most scholars do not believe Job was an Israelite, and the Bible does not tell us one way or the other. We learn from the opening verse that he was from a land called Uz, which was probably somewhere in the Arabian Peninsula. In addition to the mystery about Job's identity and home, we don't know exactly *when* the story takes place. The lack of clarity about these key factors (who, where, when) coupled with the extreme events that take place has led many people to wonder if the book of Job is a parable instead of a true story. Either way, it offers a unique opportunity to explore divine justice and why bad things happen to good people.

The opening two chapters of Job, which we read last week, introduce us to a man who "feared God and shunned evil" (1:1). The next thing we know, God and Satan are having a debate about whether Job is truly righteous or if he only acts that way because God has blessed him. The Lord allows Satan to test Job by taking everything from him: his family, his wealth, and even his health.

The vast majority of the book of Job (chs. 3–37) revolves around a series of conversations between Job and his friends in which they debate how divine justice works and why God is allowing Job to suffer. If the readings this week are a bit challenging for you, don't lose heart. These are dense passages of Scripture that can feel quite repetitive. As your guide, I am here to remind you that the overarching point Job's friends make is that God is just and bad things happen to bad people. In their view, Job is suffering because he must have sinned against the Lord. But Job vehemently defends himself, saying he is innocent of wrongdoing. He even goes so far as to accuse God of injustice.

We won't read the climax of the story until next week, which allows us to sit with these difficult questions. Why do you think God allows good people to suffer? Do you agree with Job's friends, or do you think there's something else going on?

New Testament

In 1 Corinthians 15, Paul offers one of the New Testament's most thorough explanations of the resurrection of Jesus and the future resurrection of believers. It seems that some in the Christian community at that time were downplaying the importance of the resurrection (or denying it all together). Paul wants to correct that thinking and show just how important the resurrection is to the theology of salvation.

As you read this chapter, consider your own understanding of the resurrection. You might start by thinking about what it means to be a Christian. If you were to think about it yourself or have a conversation with someone else, how would resurrection factor into your definition of Christianity?

Many Christians focus much more on Jesus's death on the cross than they do on his resurrection. In a way, that makes sense because the cross is incredibly important. It leads us to big words like *atonement* and *justification*. We are sinners in need of a savior, and the cross represents God's willingness to sacrifice his own Son for our sins. The cross is so important that it has become the symbol of Christianity around the world. We mount it atop the steeples of our churches. We hang it on the walls of our homes. We wear it around our necks. Some of us even tattoo it on our bodies!

But hear me out: Sometimes we become so focused on the cross that we forget about the empty tomb. I'm not saying that we need to lower our view of the cross. I'm saying that we need to elevate our view of the resurrection. And Paul agrees: "And if Christ has not been raised, your faith is futile; you are still in your sins" (1 Cor. 15:17).

If Jesus had only died for us and not been raised to life, then this whole thing falls apart. The resurrection of Jesus is essential because it means that sin and death have been defeated once and for all. And it means that one day, when all is said and done, followers of Jesus will also be raised to new life in the eternal kingdom of God.

Psalms and Proverbs

Think back on all the passages we've read so far that have talked about sacrifices. A huge part of the worshiping life of the people of Israel focused on making sacrifices to atone for their sin. Yet in one of the proverbs we read this week, we're told that God loves something even more than sacrifice.

> To do what is right and just
>> is more acceptable to the Lord than sacrifice.
>> (Prov. 21:3)

What does it mean to do what is right and just?

The Hebrew word for justice is *mishpat* (pronounced "mish-pawt"). It shows up in various forms over two hundred times in the Old Testament, and it often means what we think it means. Justice is fairness. It's getting what you deserve, whether that's punishment or mercy. But it also comes up time and time again in the context of the vulnerable and marginalized. And in this proverb, there is an action attached to it. We are told to *do* justice.

This is about taking action. When we see something wrong, we should speak up. When we encounter someone who is hurting, we should help. God wants more than our sacrifices. He wants us to be the kind of people who do what is right and just.

Reflections

Write down a few reflections on this week's readings.

Day 232: Job 4:1–7:21; 1 Corinthians 14:1–19; Proverbs 20:15–24

Day 233: Job 8:1–10:22; 1 Corinthians 14:20–40; Psalm 101:1–8

Day 234: Job 11:1–14:22; 1 Corinthians 15:1–34; Psalm 102:1–11

Day 235: Job 15:1–18:21; 1 Corinthians 15:35–49; Psalm 102:12–17

Day 236: Job 19:1–21:34; 1 Cor. 15:50–16:4; Proverbs 20:25–21:4

Day 237: Job 22:1–24:25; 1 Corinthians 16:5–24; Psalm 102:18–28

Day 238: Job 25:1–29:25; 2 Corinthians 1:1–11; Psalm 103:1–12

WEEK 35

	Old Testament	New Testament	Psalms / Proverbs	
Day 239	Job 30:1–32:22	2 Corinthians 1:12–22	Psalm 103:13–22	■
Day 240	Job 33:1–34:37	2 Cor. 1:23–2:11	Proverbs 21:5–16	■
Day 241	Job 35:1–37:24	2 Corinthians 2:12–3:6	Psalm 104:1–18	■
Day 242	Job 38:1–40:2	2 Corinthians 3:7–18	Psalm 104:19–30	■
Day 243	Job 40:3–42:17	2 Corinthians 4:1–18	Psalm 104:31–35	■
Day 244	Ecclesiastes 1:1–3:22	2 Corinthians 5:1–10	Proverbs 21:17–26	■
Day 245	Ecclesiastes 4:1–6:12	2 Corinthians 5:11–6:2	Psalm 105:1–11	■

Old Testament

The strenuous back-and-forth discussion between Job and his three friends concludes in chapter 31, but then a new friend (Elihu) jumps in and offers new insight that critiques both Job and his three friends. And just when you think that this conversation will never end, something truly remarkable happens.

God shows up and speaks to Job.

> "Who is this that obscures my plans
>   with words without knowledge?
> Brace yourself like a man;
>   I will question you,
>   and you shall answer me." (Job 38:2–3)

The chapters that follow are stunning. The Lord pummels Job

with question after question, many of which seem to drip with sarcasm. God asks Job where he was when the earth was formed and if he thinks he can do things better than God can. It's clear that both Job and his friends have been looking at this situation from only one perspective, but God sees it very differently. When Job finally responds to God, he is humble and in awe.

> "I know that you can do all things;
>> no purpose of yours can be thwarted.
> You asked, 'Who is this that obscures my plans
>> without knowledge?'
>> Surely I spoke of things I did not understand,
>> things too wonderful for me to know."
>>> (Job 42:2–3)

In the end, Job is restored and goes on to live a full life. But notice that we don't get a clear explanation for the question that dominated this entire book. God's answer to why bad things happen to good people is to tell Job that he's missing the point. He can't see things the way God sees them, and neither can we. The truth is that God is God, and we are not. Although our circumstances can often become overwhelming, there is a greater plan at work beyond our understanding. The book of Job invites us to remember how small we are in the grand scheme of things and to trust God even when life doesn't make sense.

New Testament

2 Corinthians is the second letter Paul wrote to the church in Corinth, Greece. Paul first visited Corinth during his second missionary journey, which we read about in Acts 18. As we saw in 1 Corinthians, several problems had surfaced in the community of

believers in Corinth since Paul first met them, and it seems that his initial letter did not fully resolve these issues. This second letter aims to address some ongoing tensions.

In the portion of the letter we read this week, Paul makes a case for his own authority. We'll learn later in the letter that other church leaders have tarnished his reputation. While defending himself, Paul uses a unique analogy in the opening verses of chapter 3 in which he describes the community of believers in Corinth as his recommendation letter.

> You yourselves are our letter, written on our hearts, known and read by everyone. You show that you are a letter from Christ, the result of our ministry, written not with ink but with the Spirit of the living God, not on tablets of stone but on tablets of human hearts. (2 Cor. 3:2–3)

The whole thing is very meta. Paul is writing a letter in which he's talking about writing a letter. But it's a beautiful mental image, isn't it?

When we come to faith in Jesus, our lives become like letters written by him. His message goes out into the world through us. The vessel for this message is not paper or, as the verse mentions, stone (a reference to the Ten Commandments). It's our hearts. And this message is not written on our hearts with ink but with the Holy Spirit. Our hearts are the vessel, and the Spirit's work in our lives is the message.

What message is your life sending out to the world?

Psalms and Proverbs

We'll be in Psalm 104 for three days in a row this week. It's a song of worship that focuses on God as creator, so if possible, read this one outdoors. It's also a great psalm to read while finishing up the book of Job. (I know I've mentioned this a few times, but I am continually amazed at how often our readings from the Old Testament, New Testament, Psalms, and Proverbs overlap and intertwine with one another.) It's almost as if the psalmist who wrote Psalm 104 did so after dwelling on the book of Job's powerful conclusion.

Everywhere we look, there is beauty to behold. We see it when we look into the night sky filled with constellations and when we stare out into a glorious sunset. When we make our way to the mountains or the ocean or the desert, the splendor and vastness of it can be overwhelming. But to marvel at all this beauty for its own sake is to miss the opportunity to marvel at the one who created it. Creation gives us a glimpse of God's glory and power.

And in response, all we can do is worship.

All we can do is praise him.

So go outside. Find something beautiful. Open your Bible to Psalm 104, and let it be your song of praise to the one who creates all things great and small.

Reflections

Write down a few reflections on this week's readings.

Day 239: Job 30:1–32:22; 2 Corinthians 1:12–22; Psalm 103:13–22

Day 240: Job 33:1–34:37; 2 Cor. 1:23–2:11; Proverbs 21:5–16

Day 241: Job 35:1–37:24; 2 Corinthians 2:12–3:6; Psalm 104:1–18

Day 242: Job 38:1–40:2; 2 Corinthians 3:7–18; Psalm 104:19–30

Day 243: Job 40:3–42:17; 2 Corinthians 4:1–18; Psalm 104:31–35

Day 244: Ecclesiastes 1:1–3:22; 2 Cor. 5:1–10; Proverbs 21:17–26

Day 245: Ecclesiastes 4:1–6:12; 2 Cor. 5:11–6:2; Psalm 105:1–11

WEEK 36

Daily Readings

	Old Testament	New Testament	Psalms / Proverbs	
Day 246	Ecclesiastes 7:1–9:12	2 Corinthians 6:3–7:1	Psalm 105:12–22	
Day 247	Eccl. 9:13–12:14	2 Corinthians 7:2–16	Psalm 105:23–36	
Day 248	Song 1:1–4:16	2 Corinthians 8:1–15	Proverbs 21:27–22:6	
Day 249	Song 5:1–8:14	2 Corinthians 8:16–9:5	Psalm 105:37–45	
Day 250	Isaiah 1:1–2:22	2 Corinthians 9:6–15	Psalm 106:1–15	
Day 251	Isaiah 3:1–5:7	2 Corinthians 10:1–18	Psalm 106:16–31	
Day 252	Isaiah 5:8–8:10	2 Corinthians 11:1–15	Proverbs 22:7–16	

Old Testament

Alongside Proverbs and Job, Ecclesiastes is the third book categorized as wisdom literature in the Old Testament. It's a peculiar book filled with musings on life and death that can feel quite discouraging at first, but the more time you spend reading and reflecting on it, the more you realize that there's something beautiful to be found in its pages. The author recognizes that wisdom and fear of the Lord (key themes in Proverbs) are good things to pursue, but also that certain aspects of life are uncontrollable and not worth worrying about.

Word Study: The Hebrew word *hevel* is used thirty-eight times in Ecclesiastes. This is a complex word to translate. It can mean

> "vapor" or "breath" or "smoke." But in many English Bible translations, this word appears as "meaningless."

> "Meaningless! Meaningless!"
>> says the Teacher.
> "Utterly meaningless!
>> Everything is meaningless." (Eccl. 1:2)

When I read Ecclesiastes, I'm reminded that there is mystery in life. When we try to control everything, it becomes a meaningless task that leaves us grasping at vapor. The better way to live is to accept the *hevel* and remember that God is in control. At a certain point, we just need to live and enjoy life for what it is.

We're also reading Song of Songs this week. This series of poems claims to be the greatest song of all time (hence the title). It's a love song between two young lovers. Their desire for one another is intense and playful. You might find yourself blushing as you read it. When preaching through Song of Songs, many pastors explain it as an allegory for God's relationship with the people of Israel or Christ's relationship with the church. I certainly see how that interpretation can be made, but I think this book is really just a celebration of love.

New Testament

In 2 Corinthians 8–9, Paul addresses the issue of giving. Many communities in the early church offered financial support to one another. For example, when the followers of Christ in Jerusalem were struggling, those in other places sent support (see 1 Corinthians 16:1–3). Paul tells the Corinthians that the churches in Macedonia have been incredibly generous, and he challenges them to do the same. You'll notice multiple quotations from the Old Testament in these chapters, as well as several references to Jesus. Paul clearly sees generosity as an integral aspect of what it means to be one of God's people and a devoted follower of Christ.

As you read this week, consider your own relationship with money. This is a sensitive subject for many people, but the Bible does not ignore it. In fact, more than two thousand verses deal with money. What I love most about how Paul addresses the topic in these verses is that generosity is not formulaic. It's not about measuring out exactly 10 percent but about giving whatever we can with joy and gladness.

> Each of you should give what you have decided in your heart to give, not reluctantly or under compulsion, for God loves a cheerful giver. And God is able to bless you abundantly, so that in all things at all times, having all that you need, you will abound in every good work. (2 Cor. 9:7–8)

Paul wants his readers to see money as a gift from God that can be used to bless others. When we've been blessed, we need to show generosity to others. When we are in need, we need to receive generosity from others. Money does not have to be a sensitive subject when we remember that it all belongs to God and we are called to be good stewards who give generously and gladly.

Psalms and Proverbs

Psalms is the Bible's hymnbook of praise to God. You've already seen countless times that these songs aren't just celebratory anthems about God's greatness. Many of them are filled with lament and calls for repentance. Reflecting on our own sin helps us worship God because it reminds us how perfect he is in the face of our failures.

The writer of Psalm 106 praises God while recounting all the times the people of Israel have broken their covenant with him. They forgot that God delivered them from slavery in Egypt. They disobeyed God's commands. They worshiped other gods. The list goes on and on. The more we read, the more we realize just how kind and gracious God has been to his people. They don't deserve his unending love, but he lavishes it on them anyway.

When you find yourself struggling to praise God, think back on all the times you have failed him. But don't let that crush you. Remember that God still loves you. He never gives up on you. What an incredible reason to praise him.

Reflections

Write down a few reflections on this week's readings.

Day 246: Ecclesiastes 7:1–9:12; 2 Cor. 6:3–7:1; Psalm 105:12–22

Day 247: Ecclesiastes 9:13–12:14; 2 Cor. 7:2–16; Psalm 105:23–36

Day 248: Song of Songs 1:1–4:16; 2 Cor. 8:1–15; Prov. 21:27–22:6

Day 249: Song of Songs 5:1–8:14; 2 Cor. 8:16–9:5; Psalm 105:37–45

Day 250: Isaiah 1:1–2:22; 2 Corinthians 9:6–15; Psalm 106:1–15

Day 251: Isaiah 3:1–5:7; 2 Corinthians 10:1–18; Psalm 106:16–31

Day 252: Isaiah 5:8–8:10; 2 Corinthians 11:1–15; Proverbs 22:7–16

WEEK 37

	Old Testament	New Testament	Psalms / Proverbs	
Day 253	Isaiah 8:11–10:19	2 Corinthians 11:16–33	Psalm 106:32–39	
Day 254	Isaiah 10:20–13:22	2 Corinthians 12:1–10	Psalm 106:40–48	
Day 255	Isaiah 14:1–16:14	2 Corinthians 12:11–21	Psalm 107:1–9	
Day 256	Isaiah 17:1–19:25	2 Corinthians 13:1–14	Proverbs 22:17–27	
Day 257	Isaiah 20:1–23:18	Galatians 1:1–24	Psalm 107:10–22	
Day 258	Isaiah 24:1–26:21	Galatians 2:1–10	Psalm 107:23–32	
Day 259	Isaiah 27:1–28:29	Galatians 2:11–3:9	Psalm 107:33–43	

Old Testament

When we began reading the book of Isaiah at the end of last week, it marked the beginning of a new focus in our Old Testament readings: The Prophets. We have read *about* many prophets up to this point, but now we will hear directly from them. These writings span several hundred years in the history of the people of Israel, going back to the time of the Divided Kingdom and continuing through the exile as well as the eventual return of the Israelites to their homeland.

Each prophet is on a mission from God. They serve as community critics who confront the Israelites, calling on them to repent from sin and reminding them of their covenant with the Lord. They also speak truth to power, opposing kings who do evil in the sight of God. Each prophet has their own unique perspective, but they generally focus on warning the people of impending doom if they don't turn from their wicked ways. Many of the prophets mention something called "the day of the Lord," which can be either a day of judgment in which God will hold humanity accountable for their wickedness or a day of deliverance in which God will renew and restore his people once and for all and establish an eternal kingdom.

Isaiah is the first of the Major Prophets, so named because of their great length, not because they are more important than the Minor Prophets. That said, many people regard Isaiah as the most important book of prophecy in the Old Testament. Often referred to as the "fifth gospel," Isaiah is the most quoted prophet in the New Testament, and for centuries, biblical scholars have returned to its pages when seeking theological clarity.

The first thirty-nine chapters of Isaiah take place in Jerusalem during the time leading up to the Babylonian exile. Read carefully and notice how Isaiah goes back and forth between despair and hope. He describes both Assyria and Babylon as instruments God uses against the Israelites, who are being judged for their unfaithfulness. But within a chapter or two (sometimes in the same chapter), Isaiah anticipates a day when God will rescue his people and bless them beyond anything they could ever imagine. These passages are filled with references to a savior king who will come from the line of David and lead God's people in righteousness.

That's right. Hundreds of years before Jesus was born, Isaiah was telling the people of Israel that he was coming.

New Testament

Galatians is a letter Paul wrote to a community of believers in Turkey that he visited during his first missionary journey, which we read about in Acts 13–14. In it, he addresses an issue that had become hotly debated during the first century: Do gentile (non-Jewish) followers of Jesus need to convert to Judaism and follow the laws of the Torah?

The relationship between God and the people of Israel runs throughout Scripture. Although the Bible is divided into the Old and

New Testaments, the New Testament is not an entirely new story. When Jesus enters in the Gospels, it is a continuation of the same story. The New Testament writers see the life, ministry, death, and resurrection of Jesus as the long-awaited messianic fulfillment of the Hebrew Scriptures (remember what I just said about Isaiah).

The earliest followers of Jesus were Jews. And they did not stop being Jewish. They continued in the way of their faith. After his encounter with Jesus, Paul (a zealous Jewish Pharisee) became one of the leading figures of this new movement. But he believed that what Jesus had done was not only for the Jews but for *everyone*. So he started going around on missionary journeys preaching the message of Jesus to both Jews and Gentiles.

And things took off.

Paul's ministry to the Gentiles was incredibly fruitful.

But suddenly there were two groups of very different people—Jews and Gentiles—following Jesus and identifying themselves as the people of God. As you can imagine, many of the Jews were like, "Time out. This is *our* story. For generations, God has called *us* his chosen people, and we have been set apart. And now you want to let a bunch of Gentiles become part of the people of God *without* following all of our laws? No way!"

So that's the backstory of what's happening here. As this movement of Jesus that started with the Jews spreads into the gentile world, many people ask if Gentiles need to become Jews. That's clearly a conversation that is taking place in Galatia. And Paul's answer is a resounding *no*. According to him, the only thing Gentiles need in order to be identified as the people of God is faith in Jesus. That's what Galatians is all about.

Psalms and Proverbs

Many Bible translations insert a heading midway through Proverbs 22 that refers to the next set of verses as "Sayings of the Wise."

Over the next two and a half chapters, we'll find these thirty sayings. In a way, it feels like the entire book is starting over. But while these sayings may form their own little collection (proverbs within Proverbs, if you will), they still fit well within the overall focus of the book.

Verses 17–21 offer us an opportunity to remember why these proverbs are important. They teach us "to be honest and to speak the truth" (v. 21). They help us to develop deeper trust in the Lord (v. 19). But to do so, they need to be kept close in our hearts (v. 18).

That last point is something we need to dwell on. Are we applying these teachings to our hearts and letting them transform the way we live? Or do these truths from Proverbs go in one ear and out the other without making much of an impact on us? I see countless places in my own life where I have not taken these wise sayings seriously enough. I read them, but I haven't applied them to my life. Yet no matter how many times we read them, there is always something for us to reconsider. There is always room for us to grow.

Reflections

Write down a few reflections on this week's readings.

Day 253: Isaiah 8:11–10:19; 2 Cor. 11:16–33; Psalm 106:32–39

Day 254: Isaiah 10:20–13:22; 2 Cor. 12:1–10; Psalm 106:40–48

Day 255: Isaiah 14:1–16:14; 2 Corinthians 12:11–21; Psalm 107:1–9

Day 256: Isaiah 17:1–19:25; 2 Cor. 13:1–14; Proverbs 22:17–27

Day 257: Isaiah 20:1–23:18; Galatians 1:1–24; Psalm 107:10–22

Day 258: Isaiah 24:1–26:21; Galatians 2:1–10; Psalm 107:23–32

Day 259: Isaiah 27:1–28:29; Galatians 2:11–3:9; Psalm 107:33–43

WEEK 38

	Old Testament	New Testament	Psalms / Proverbs	
Day 260	Isaiah 29:1–30:18	Galatians 3:10–25	Proverbs 22:28–23:9	
Day 261	Isaiah 30:19–32:20	Galatians 3:26–4:20	Psalm 108:1–5	
Day 262	Isaiah 33:1–35:10	Galatians 4:21–5:6	Psalm 108:6–13	
Day 263	Isaiah 36:1–37:38	Galatians 5:7–26	Psalm 109:1–20	
Day 264	Isaiah 38:1–40:31	Galatians 6:1–18	Proverbs 23:10–18	
Day 265	Isaiah 41:1–42:25	Ephesians 1:1–23	Psalm 109:21–31	
Day 266	Isaiah 43:1–44:23	Ephesians 2:1–22	Psalm 110:1–7	

Old Testament

One of my favorite chapters in the book of Isaiah is one that isn't mentioned nearly as much as the others, particularly in sermons and devotionals. Isaiah 35 is just ten verses long, but in the midst of so much judgment and doom, it offers much-needed hope. Its subheading in the New International Version is "Joy of the Redeemed," and that word—*joy*—is repeated several times throughout the chapter.

Remember that Isaiah is going back and forth between pronouncing judgment on the people of Israel and offering them hope for the future. The last few chapters have been filled with prophecies about Israel's downfall and destruction. That section is quite bleak, but then chapter 35 is filled with imagery of restoration and redemption.

An arid desert suddenly springs to life.

A weak body finds strength.

The sick and hurting are healed.

These things happen because God shows up to save his people. They see his glory. Isaiah does not shy away from confronting the people with judgment, but he sees an even greater joy for their future. They are on a path to destruction, but one day they will be on the path to redemption.

> And a highway will be there;
>> it will be called the Way of Holiness;
>> it will be for those who walk on that Way.
> The unclean will not journey on it;
>> wicked fools will not go about on it.
> No lion will be there,
>> nor any ravenous beast;
>> they will not be found there.
> But only the redeemed will walk there,
>> and those the LORD has rescued will return.
> They will enter Zion with singing;
>> everlasting joy will crown their heads.
> Gladness and joy will overtake them,
>> and sorrow and sighing will flee away.
>> (Isa. 35:8–10)

New Testament

Ephesians was written to the church in Ephesus and is divided into two key sections. Chapters 1–3 focus on the gospel and who we are in Christ, while chapters 4–6 explore how the reality of what we believe about Jesus should impact the way we live. If you've been around the church for any length of time, you've likely heard sermons from Ephesians (it's a favorite among pastors), and perhaps the most-quoted verses of this letter are Ephesians 2:8–9, which I memorized as a child in Sunday school: "For it is by grace you have been saved, through faith—and this is not from yourselves, it is the gift of God—not by works, so that no one can boast."

Go back to the beginning of chapter 2 and you'll see that verses 1–3 paint a harrowing picture of what life without Jesus looks like. Simply put, it's death. But the grace of God is that he has made us "alive with Christ even when we were dead in transgressions" (v. 5). God saves us from a life of sin and death. This means that God's grace—a grace we do not deserve—is the foundation of salvation, and the vehicle by which we get there is faith in Jesus. By grace through faith.

Paul anticipates our ability to make everything about ourselves, so in verse 9 he reminds us that this is not of our own doing. We can't boast, because we did not earn our salvation. This can be challenging for many of us. We live in a world where we have to prove ourselves. We find our value in what we do. But salvation is a gift from God. It's established by his grace. And the only thing we need to do is surrender to it and have faith in Jesus.

You might need to pause here for a moment to let that sink in.

Stop trying so hard to be perfect and surrender to God's grace.

But this passage goes on. Once again, Paul anticipates that we might twist this around, so in verse 10 he says, "For we are God's handiwork, created in Christ Jesus to do good works, which God prepared in advance for us to do."

So verse 9 says our salvation is "not by works," but then verse 10 says we are "created in Christ Jesus to do good works."

What's going on here?

Isn't that a contradiction?

When you get things in the right order, it's not. We are not saved by works. We cannot earn our salvation. It is only by the grace of God that we are saved. All we are asked to do is have faith in Jesus. But when we have that faith, God gives us new life. And that new life is one in which we respond to God's grace by getting to work. We do good works *because* we are saved, not to *be* saved.

Psalms and Proverbs

I imagine that at least a few Israelites turned to Psalm 109 during the days leading up to and during the exile. In this psalm, David is angry at his enemies, and he wants God to do something about it. The first twenty verses of this chapter are intense (I would have a hard time praying this about my enemies). Yet this passage shows us that it is okay for us to go to God with our anger. It is acceptable for us to express our frustrations to God. Psalms aren't just songs of praise. They are also songs of anguish.

But once again David does not conclude his psalm until he shifts his gaze from lament to worship. In the final ten verses of Psalm 109, he still references his enemies, but his attention increasingly turns to God. David knows—much like Isaiah does—that the Lord will prove faithful and true even in life's darkest moments.

What would your version of Psalm 109 look like?

Spend a few moments this week telling God what you're angry about. I mean that. Be honest with God about what you're going through. Keep going until your heart is able to praise him.

Reflections

Write down a few reflections on this week's readings.

Day 260: Isaiah 29:1–30:18; Gal. 3:10–25; Proverbs 22:28–23:9

Day 261: Isaiah 30:19–32:20; Galatians 3:26–4:20; Psalm 108:1–5

Day 262: Isaiah 33:1–35:10; Galatians 4:21–5:6; Psalm 108:6–13

Day 263: Isaiah 36:1–37:38; Galatians 5:7–26; Psalm 109:1–20

Day 264: Isaiah 38:1–40:31; Galatians 6:1–18; Proverbs 23:10–18

Day 265: Isaiah 41:1–42:25; Ephesians 1:1–23; Psalm 109:21–31

Day 266: Isaiah 43:1–44:23; Ephesians 2:1–22; Psalm 110:1–7

WEEK 39

Daily Readings

	Old Testament	New Testament	Psalms / Proverbs	
Day 267	Isaiah 44:24–46:13	Ephesians 3:1–21	Psalm 111:1–10	
Day 268	Isaiah 47:1–49:7	Ephesians 4:1–16	Proverbs 23:19–28	
Day 269	Isaiah 49:8–51:16	Ephesians 4:17–5:7	Psalm 112:1–10	
Day 270	Isaiah 51:17–54:17	Ephesians 5:8–33	Psalm 113:1–9	
Day 271	Isaiah 55:1–57:13	Ephesians 6:1–24	Psalm 114:1–8	
Day 272	Isaiah 57:14–59:21	Philippians 1:1–26	Proverbs 23:29–24:4	
Day 273	Isaiah 60:1–62:12	Philippians 1:27–2:11	Psalm 115:1–11	

Old Testament

If the book of Isaiah were a symphony, our readings this week would bring us to the climactic crescendo of the full force of Isaiah's prophecies. Chapters 40–55 shift forward to a time after the exile, yet the people of Israel still can't seem to figure out how to remain faithful to God (we saw this play out in Ezra and Nehemiah). Despite this stubbornness, the Lord remains faithful to the covenant with his people by bringing forth a figure the text repeatedly calls "the servant" who will save the people from destruction and usher in God's eternal kingdom.

Isaiah does not describe this servant as a great warrior or hero but as one who will suffer and be rejected. He will die. One of the most powerful chapters in the Old Testament, Isaiah 53, describes this suffering. But in the final three verses we learn that this was part of God's plan for redemption all along.

Yet it was the Lord's will to crush him and cause him
to suffer,
and though the Lord makes his life an offering
for sin,
he will see his offspring and prolong his days,
and the will of the Lord will prosper in his hand.
After he has suffered,
he will see the light of life and be satisfied;
by his knowledge my righteous servant will
justify many,
and he will bear their iniquities.
Therefore I will give him a portion among the great,
and he will divide the spoils with the strong,
because he poured out his life unto death,
and was numbered with the transgressors.
For he bore the sin of many,
and made intercession for the transgressors.
(Isa. 53:10–12)

Scholars and theologians have debated Isaiah 53 for centuries, and some do not think it refers to the coming Messiah. But I find it hard to read this passage and not think about the death and resurrection of Jesus. And as we've already seen in the New Testament, the gospel writers clearly saw this connection as well. Read this chapter carefully and note the signposts that point to Jesus in every verse. Isaiah invites us to look forward to a day when we will no longer struggle to remain faithful to God, because the Suffering Servant will redeem and restore all of creation once and for all.

New Testament

Philippians is a letter Paul wrote to a community of believers in Philippi. Located along the Via Egnatia, a major road connecting the eastern provinces to Rome, Philippi played an important role in the Roman Empire. Paul's visit to the city is recorded in Acts 16. He wrote Philippians from prison, but as soon as you read the first few verses, it becomes clear that he's in a good mood, which can't be said about all his letters. Paul expresses great joy, gratitude, and confidence in what God is up to.

> I thank my God every time I remember you. In all my prayers for all of you, I always pray with joy because of your partnership in the gospel from the first day until now, being confident of this, that he who began a good work in you will carry it on to completion until the day of Christ Jesus. (Phil. 1:3–6)

Paul says becoming followers of Jesus is the *beginning* of something God is doing in their lives. It's not the end. It's an ongoing work that will be completed when Jesus returns. A few verses later (9–11), Paul offers a prayer that sheds more light on what this ongoing work will lead to: overflowing love, knowledge, wisdom, and lives that bear good fruit. In essence, Paul emphasizes that becoming a Christian is the start of a journey where God transforms their hearts, minds, and way of life into something "worthy of the gospel of Christ" (v. 27).

The big theological word Paul is talking about here is *sanctification*, which is the process of making something pure or holy. A lot of Christians think about salvation as a one-time event in which they come to faith in Jesus, but Paul describes it as an ongoing work. The longer we follow Christ (whose name appears over twenty times in the first chapter of Philippians alone), the more our lives are transformed. As we saw in Ephesians, Paul urges his readers to fully surrender their lives to Jesus. He emphasizes that being a Christian isn't just about holding correct beliefs about Jesus—it's about being continually transformed by him.

In what ways is Jesus transforming your life?

Psalms and Proverbs

What does it mean to give glory to something? This phrase is repeated throughout the Psalms in reference to worshiping, honoring, and obeying God. We are told to give him glory in response to who he is and all he has done for us. I would argue that our lives are always giving glory to something. We are always worshiping something. If someone observed your life for the past week—if they saw everything and could even read your mind— what would they say you give the most glory to?

That's uncomfortable to think about, isn't it?

One of the best ways to know what you worship is to consider how you spend your time. We give our time and attention to the things we care about. So how much of our time and attention is given to God compared with everything else? The difficult reality is that many of us give glory to a lot of things that don't deserve it. My biggest struggle is that I give far too much glory to myself. I'm always thinking about me. But then I read verses like this:

> Not to us, LORD, not to us
> > but to your name be the glory,
> > because of your love and faithfulness.
> > > (Ps. 115:1)

What a good reminder that it's not about us. Because of his love and faithfulness, God deserves the glory. Let this verse linger in your heart and mind this week. When you feel the desire to make much of yourself, whisper these words aloud and worship the only one who truly deserves the glory.

Reflections

Write down a few reflections on this week's readings.

Day 267: Isaiah 44:24–46:13; Ephesians 3:1–21; Psalm 111:1–10

Day 268: Isaiah 47:1–49:7; Ephesians 4:1–16; Proverbs 23:19–28

Day 269: Isaiah 49:8–51:16; Ephesians 4:17–5:7; Psalm 112:1–10

Day 270: Isaiah 51:17–54:17; Ephesians 5:8–33; Psalm 113:1–9

Day 271: Isaiah 55:1–57:13; Ephesians 6:1–24; Psalm 114:1–8

Day 272: Isaiah 57:14–59:21; Phil. 1:1–26; Proverbs 23:29–24:4

Day 273: Isaiah 60:1–62:12; Philippians 1:27–2:11; Psalm 115:1–11

WEEK 40

	Old Testament	New Testament	Psalms / Proverbs	
Day 274	Isaiah 63:1–65:16	Philippians 2:12–30	Psalm 115:12–18	☐
Day 275	Isaiah 65:17–66:24	Philippians 3:1–4:1	Psalm 116:1–11	☐
Day 276	Jeremiah 1:1–2:30	Philippians 4:2–23	Proverbs 24:5–14	☐
Day 277	Jeremiah 2:31–4:9	Colossians 1:1–23	Psalm 116:12–19	☐
Day 278	Jeremiah 4:10–5:31	Colossians 1:24–2:5	Psalm 117:1–2	☐
Day 279	Jeremiah 6:1–7:29	Colossians 2:6–23	Psalm 118:1–16	☐
Day 280	Jeremiah 7:30–9:16	Colossians 3:1–4:1	Proverbs 24:15–22	☐

Old Testament

After nearly four full weeks in Isaiah, we move on to Jeremiah, the second of the Major Prophets. Jeremiah was a priest commissioned by God to prophesy in Jerusalem during the final years of the Southern Kingdom leading up to the Babylonian exile in 587 BC. He confronted the people of Israel—including their kings—about their unfaithfulness to God and the covenant, and he warned them that judgment was coming in the form of the Babylonian Empire.

If all of this sounds familiar, that's because Jeremiah and Isaiah have many similarities. But one thing you'll probably notice as you read Jeremiah this week is that there is not a lot of hope found in these pages. Unlike Isaiah, who regularly reminded the people of Israel of a coming savior who would rescue them, Jeremiah rarely offers them any hope. For this reason, he is often called the Weeping Prophet.

As you read Jeremiah, make a note about why the Lord is so

displeased with his people. He gives countless examples, but I love this mental image from chapter 2:

> My people have committed two sins:
> They have forsaken me,
>   the spring of living water,
> and have dug their own cisterns,
>   broken cisterns that cannot hold water.
>   (Jer. 2:13)

The first sin is that they have neglected the covenant and forgotten everything God has done for them. They have not obeyed his commandments. That's bad enough, but on top of that, they have started to worship false gods. The Lord compares this to building broken cisterns that are unable to hold water, despite having access to an eternal spring. It's foolish and unnecessary.

How often do we do the same in our own lives? In what ways are you building broken cisterns while ignoring the living water of God?

New Testament

A friend of mine once said that reading Paul's letters is like listening to one side of a phone conversation. You can't hear what the person on the other end is saying, but you can usually figure it out based on the side you can hear. In Colossians, we're reading one of the few letters Paul wrote to a community he had never been to. The church in Colossae (modern-day Turkey) was likely started by someone named Epaphras, who Paul mentions twice in the letter.

> You learned it from Epaphras, our dear fellow servant, who is a faithful minister of Christ on our behalf, and who also told us of your love in the Spirit. (Col. 1:7–8)

Epaphras, who is one of you and a servant of Christ Jesus, sends greetings. He is always wrestling in prayer for you, that you may stand firm in all the will of God, mature and fully assured. (Col. 4:12)

It seems that Epaphras made a visit to Paul in prison and told Paul some things about the believers in Colossae that inspired him to write this letter.

So, what did Epaphras tell him?

These verses don't offer us much, but the last sentence of verse 12 gives us a hint. Epaphras is "always wrestling in prayer" for them because he wants them to "stand firm in all the will of God, mature and fully assured." This makes it sound like Epaphras was worried that believers in Colossae were struggling with staying committed to their faith.

This little hint helps us make sense of what Paul says in chapter 2, where he encourages them to remain faithful to the way of Jesus instead of the habits and customs of the world. From this one side of the conversation that we do have, it becomes clear that the Colossians' faith is being tested by the world around them.

Have you ever experienced that?

Paul's encouragement in Colossians is a helpful reminder when we face similar circumstances. As you read this letter, invite God to make you more confident in who Jesus is and who he has called you to be as his follower.

Psalms and Proverbs

At just two verses and twenty-nine words total (in the NIV), Psalm 117 is both the shortest psalm and the shortest chapter in the Bible.

> Praise the LORD, all you nations;
> extol him, all you peoples.

For great is his love toward us,
and the faithfulness of the LORD endures forever.

Praise the LORD.

The brevity of this psalm does not lessen its meaning. It is simple and direct, but it paints a remarkable picture of all people—not just the Israelites—praising God for his love and faithfulness.

Think about all we've read so far. The focus of the Old Testament is the covenantal relationship between God and the people of Israel. He established this covenant with Abraham and promised that "all peoples on earth will be blessed through you" (Gen. 12:3). This short psalm anticipates the day when that will be true. And the focus of the New Testament is Jesus, who made a way for all people to be reconciled to God through faith.

The shortest chapter in the Bible somehow tells us the whole story: God's love and faithfulness, his covenant with his people, the savior king named Jesus. It's all there. And it means that everyone must praise the Lord.

Reflections

Write down a few reflections on this week's readings.

Day 274: Isaiah 63:1–65:16; Philippians 2:12–30; Psalm 115:12–18

Day 275: Isaiah 65:17–66:24; Philippians 3:1–4:1; Psalm 116:1–11

Day 276: Jeremiah 1:1–2:30; Philippians 4:2–23; Proverbs 24:5–14

Day 277: Jeremiah 2:31–4:9; Colossians 1:1–23; Psalm 116:12–19

Day 278: Jeremiah 4:10–5:31; Colossians 1:24–2:5; Psalm 117:1–2

Day 279: Jeremiah 6:1–7:29; Colossians 2:6–23; Psalm 118:1–16

Day 280: Jer. 7:30–9:16; Colossians 3:1–4:1; Proverbs 24:15–22

WEEK 41

	Old Testament	New Testament	Psalms / Proverbs	
Day 281	Jeremiah 9:17–11:17	Colossians 4:2–18	Psalm 118:17–29	
Day 282	Jeremiah 11:18–13:27	1 Thess. 1:1–2:16	Psalm 119:1–8	
Day 283	Jeremiah 14:1–15:21	1 Thess. 2:17–3:13	Psalm 119:9–16	
Day 284	Jeremiah 16:1–17:27	1 Thess. 4:1–18	Proverbs 24:23–34	
Day 285	Jeremiah 18:1–20:18	1 Thess. 5:1–28	Psalm 119:17–24	
Day 286	Jeremiah 21:1–23:8	2 Thess. 1:1–12	Psalm 119:25–32	
Day 287	Jeremiah 23:9–25:14	2 Thess. 2:1–17	Psalm 119:33–40	

Old Testament

As you can imagine, Jeremiah's relentless prophecies of destruction and exile were not well received by the people of Israel, including their leaders. In chapter 11, God warns Jeremiah of a plot to kill him by the people of Anathoth.

Does that name sound familiar?

It is easy to miss the significance here. Most people read about the people of Anathoth's plot to kill Jeremiah and don't remember that Jeremiah is from Anathoth (Jer. 1:1). This is his hometown, and the people there are Levites (the priestly line of Aaron's descendants). So this evil plot isn't by random strangers. Jeremiah's own people—many of whom are priests—are the ones who want to kill him. God spares him this time, but a few chapters later, we read that the official in charge of the temple was so sick and tired of Jeremiah's prophecies that he ordered him to be beaten and put in prison.

How do you think Jeremiah felt about all this?

We don't have to wonder, because he tells us. Our readings this week include two passages in which Jeremiah complains to the Lord. In the first (12:1–4) he asks God why wicked people are allowed to prosper, and in the second (20:7–18) he struggles to reconcile his call as a prophet with all the hatred and persecution he is experiencing.

Your circumstances may not be as extreme as the ones Jeremiah faced, but have you ever felt like you were doing what God called you to do yet nothing seemed to be going your way? Jeremiah knew that feeling. And as in the psalms of lament from David, we see here another example of what it looks like to be honest with God and share our frustrations with him. Somehow, when we do, God allows us to see the ways he is at work even in our confusion and pain.

New Testament

Our New Testament readings this week take us through the final chapter of Colossians, all of 1 Thessalonians, and two-thirds of 2 Thessalonians. Paul first visited the city of Thessalonica during his second missionary journey (Acts 17). Considering these two letters, it seems that the Christians in Thessalonica were asking questions about when Jesus would return and what happens to their friends and family members who have died.

Like many of the Old Testament prophets, Paul refers to the eventual return of Jesus as "the day of the Lord," but he basically tells the Thessalonians that they're missing the point by worrying about it. No one knows exactly when Jesus will return, so they need to focus on standing firm in their faith and living the way Jesus taught them to live. This advice seems basic, but it's of vital importance back then and today. We often get so distracted with worrying about the future that we forget to live in the moment.

But if we focus on Jesus every day and stay faithful to him, God will work out the rest.

Regarding the question about believers who have died, Paul's words in 1 Thessalonians 4:13–18 have been used for centuries at funerals and wakes to offer encouragement to those who have lost loved ones. When Jesus returns to make all things new and redeem and restore all of creation, followers of Christ who have died will be resurrected to join the living and be with the Lord forever. There is a mystery to death, and losing a loved one is awful, but Paul offers us hope. Because of Jesus, our eternity is secure.

Psalms and Proverbs

Last week we took a close look at Psalm 117, the shortest psalm as well as the shortest chapter in the Bible. This week we turn to Psalm 119, the longest psalm and the longest chapter in the Bible. It's so long that our reading plan has us in Psalm 119 for the next four weeks. The good news is that this chapter is well structured and easy to break down into smaller sections. Psalm 119 is an acrostic poem that follows the Hebrew alphabet, which has twenty-two letters. The 176 verses are divided into twenty-two stanzas that each have eight verses. The first line of each new stanza begins with a consecutive letter in the Hebrew alphabet. The text of most Bible translations will include these Hebrew letters as headings before each stanza (e.g., א Aleph, ב Beth, ג Gimel, etc.).

It's fitting that the longest chapter in the Bible is a celebration of God's word. As you read each stanza, make a note of the different words the psalmist uses to refer to the Scriptures: law, statutes, precepts, decrees, commands, word. Reading Psalm 119 all at once may make it feel repetitive, but our reading plan has us taking it eight verses at a time, which offers the perfect opportunity to slow down and reflect on each individual stanza. Look for the ways in which each one offers new insight on the value of God's word.

I memorized Psalm 119:9–16 (the second stanza) when I was eleven years old, and it's still with me more than three decades later. These words are enduring and profound. If you find a stanza in Psalm 119 that resonates with you, I encourage you to commit it to memory.

Reflections

Write down a few reflections on this week's readings.

Day 281: Jeremiah 9:17–11:17; Colossians 4:2–18; Psalm 118:17–29

Day 282: Jeremiah 11:18–13:27; 1 Thess. 1:1–2:16; Psalm 119:1–8

Day 283: Jeremiah 14:1–15:21; 1 Thess. 2:17–3:13; Psalm 119:9–16

Day 284: Jeremiah 16:1–17:27; 1 Thess. 4:1–18; Proverbs 24:23–34

Day 285: Jeremiah 18:1–20:18; 1 Thess. 5:1–28; Psalm 119:17–24

Day 286: Jeremiah 21:1–23:8; 2 Thess. 1:1–12; Psalm 119:25–32

Day 287: Jeremiah 23:9–25:14; 2 Thess. 2:1–17; Psalm 119:33–40

WEEK 42

	Old Testament	New Testament	Psalms / Proverbs	
Day 288	Jeremiah 25:15–26:24	2 Thess. 3:1–18	Proverbs 25:1–10	☐
Day 289	Jeremiah 27:1–29:23	1 Timothy 1:1–20	Psalm 119:41–48	☐
Day 290	Jeremiah 29:24–31:14	1 Timothy 2:1–15	Psalm 119:49–56	☐
Day 291	Jeremiah 31:15–32:25	1 Timothy 3:1–16	Psalm 119:57–64	☐
Day 292	Jeremiah 32:26–34:22	1 Timothy 4:1–16	Proverbs 25:11–20	☐
Day 293	Jeremiah 35:1–37:21	1 Timothy 5:1–6:2	Psalm 119:65–72	☐
Day 294	Jeremiah 38:1–40:6	1 Timothy 6:3–21	Psalm 119:73–80	☐

Old Testament

Many church traditions do child dedications, a special ceremony in which parents commit their child to the Lord. The details differ from church to church, but in most dedications the pastor prays over the life of the child and the parents commit to raising their child as a Christian. I was on staff at a church for several years where we asked the parents to choose a "life verse" for their child, which would be read during the dedication. One of the most popular life verses—chosen by the parents of countless children—is in this week's reading.

> "For I know the plans I have for you," declares the Lord, "plans to prosper you and not to harm you, plans to give you hope and a future." (Jer. 29:11)

This is easily the most well-known verse in the book of

Jeremiah, and multiple studies and surveys place Jeremiah 29:11 as the second most read and quoted verse in the entire Bible, behind only John 3:16. Unfortunately, it's also one of the most misunderstood verses in the Bible, because its meaning becomes distorted when it is isolated from its surrounding context.

In Jeremiah 29:1, we learn that we're about to read a letter from Jeremiah "to the surviving elders among the exiles and to the priests, the prophets and all the other people Nebuchadnezzar had carried into exile from Jerusalem to Babylon" (29:1).

Did you catch that?

Jeremiah 29:11 was written to people who were taken from their homes and forced to live under the rule of a foreign power.

Out of context, it sounds like a lovely promise from God about a future filled with hope and prosperity, and that's often the way it is quoted. But in the context of this letter to the exiles, we find the fuller meaning. Prosperity looks quite different to someone living in exile, doesn't it? In an odd way, it's quite fitting that someone would choose Jeremiah 29:11 as a life verse for their child. It serves as a reminder that they will experience difficulties, just like the people of Israel did in exile. But these difficulties are not the end of the story. There is hope even in the midst of suffering.

New Testament

1 Timothy is the first of three letters written by Paul (two to Timothy and one to Titus) that are commonly referred to as the Pastoral Epistles. They deal with matters of church leadership and structure. The backstory of 1 Timothy is fairly simple. Paul learned that a group of church leaders in Ephesus was spreading false teachings, so he sent his protégé, Timothy, on a mission to confront them and restore order to the community of Christ followers. In the opening of the letter, Paul offers Timothy some encouragement for the task at hand.

As I urged you when I went into Macedonia, stay there in Ephesus so that you may command certain people not to teach false doctrines any longer or to devote themselves to myths and endless genealogies. Such things promote controversial speculations rather than advancing God's work—which is by faith. The goal of this command is love, which comes from a pure heart and a good conscience and a sincere faith. Some have departed from these and have turned to meaningless talk. They want to be teachers of the law, but they do not know what they are talking about or what they so confidently affirm. (1 Tim. 1:3–7)

In the chapters that follow, you'll read Paul's instructions to Timothy about several aspects of church life and leadership in Ephesus, but all of it will come back to the core motivation found in these verses. The main issue for Paul is that the church's primary focus has shifted from faith and love to "meaningless talk" (1:6) and far too much emphasis on matters of lesser importance.

There's an implicit invitation here for us to consider what we focus on in our own churches today. If someone visited your church this week, would they find a community that focuses on faith and love or one that is preoccupied with lesser things? There is certainly a time and place for passionate discourse about issues that matter, but when those issues become a distraction from the focus of the gospel, church leaders must recommit themselves to faith and love.

Psalms and Proverbs

The seventh stanza of Psalm 119 (verses 49–56) speaks of hope during difficult times and pairs nicely with Jeremiah 29:11. The writer of this psalm appears to be suffering, but they lean into God's word as a reminder of his love and faithfulness.

Remember your word to your servant,
 for you have given me hope.
My comfort in my suffering is this:
 Your promise preserves my life.
The arrogant mock me unmercifully,
 but I do not turn from your law.
I remember, Lord, your ancient laws,
 and I find comfort in them.
Indignation grips me because of the wicked,
 who have forsaken your law.
Your decrees are the theme of my song
 wherever I lodge.
In the night, Lord, I remember your name,
 that I may keep your law.
This has been my practice:
 I obey your precepts.

One thing I love about this psalm is that it shows that even those who love and obey God's word will experience sorrow and distress. We tend to think of troubling times as a punishment from God, but the reality is that difficult seasons are part of the natural rhythm of life. This does not mean God doesn't care for us. Just like he did for the Israelites in exile, God will remain faithful even when we go through life's darkest valleys (see Psalm 23:4). We find these promises in his Word, and we can trust them to be true.

Reflections

Write down a few reflections on this week's readings.

Day 288: Jeremiah 25:15–26:24; 2 Thess. 3:1–18; Proverbs 25:1–10

Day 289: Jeremiah 27:1–29:23; 1 Timothy 1:1–20; Psalm 119:41–48

Day 290: Jer. 29:24–31:14; 1 Timothy 2:1–15; Psalm 119:49–56

Day 291: Jeremiah 31:15–32:25; 1 Timothy 3:1–16; Psalm 119:57–64

Day 292: Jer. 32:26–34:22; 1 Timothy 4:1–16; Proverbs 25:11–20

Day 293: Jeremiah 35:1–37:21; 1 Timothy 5:1–6:2; Psalm 119:65–72

Day 294: Jeremiah 38:1–40:6; 1 Timothy 6:3–21; Psalm 119:73–80

WEEK 43

= Daily Readings =

	Old Testament	New Testament	Psalms / Proverbs	
Day 295	Jeremiah 40:7–42:22	2 Timothy 1:1–18	Psalm 119:81–88	
Day 296	Jeremiah 43:1–45:5	2 Timothy 2:1–26	Proverbs 25:21–26:2	
Day 297	Jeremiah 46:1–47:7	2 Timothy 3:1–17	Psalm 119:89–96	
Day 298	Jeremiah 48:1–49:6	2 Timothy 4:1–22	Psalm 119:97–104	
Day 299	Jeremiah 49:7–50:10	Titus 1:1–16	Psalm 119:105–112	
Day 300	Jeremiah 50:11–51:14	Titus 2:1–15	Proverbs 26:3–12	
Day 301	Jeremiah 51:15–64	Titus 3:1–15	Psalm 119:113–120	

= Old Testament =

The final chapters of Jeremiah offer more pronouncements of judgment on Israel, but then the prophet turns his attention to their enemies. You may have been wondering why God would allow the Israelite's enemies to go unpunished when they too have worshiped false gods and lived unrighteously. Jeremiah makes it clear that no one will escape God's wrath. The Egyptians, Philistines, Moabites, Ammonites, and Edomites will all be judged. Their empires will not last. Even the mighty Babylonians—whom God has used to inflict judgment on the Israelites and many of these other nations—will be put to shame.

> Therefore, hear what the Lord has planned against
> Babylon,
> what he has purposed against the land of the
> Babylonians:

The young of the flock will be dragged away;
      their pasture will be appalled at their fate.
At the sound of Babylon's capture the earth will
      tremble;
      its cry will resound among the nations.
            (Jer. 50:45–46)

Passages like these can be difficult to read, but they tell us something important about divine justice: God will not let evil go unpunished. Even when it seems like those who oppose God are in control, a day of judgment is coming. That was true in the days of the Old Testament, and it's just as true today. Jeremiah provides a glimpse of a future in which sin, death, and evil will be defeated once and for all.

New Testament

This week's New Testament readings take us through 2 Timothy and Titus, the second and third letters in the Pastoral Epistles. As a reminder from last week, 1 Timothy addressed corrupt teachers in Ephesus whose focus was on the wrong things. In 2 Timothy, Paul continues to offer wisdom about this issue by reminding Timothy to keep the focus on Scripture, particularly the teachings of Jesus. In chapter 3 we'll read a couple of verses you may already know.

All Scripture is God-breathed and is useful for teaching, rebuking, correcting and training in righteousness, so that the servant of God may be thoroughly equipped for every good work. (2 Tim. 3:16–17)

I love the mental image of Scripture being "God-breathed." Many Bible translations simply state in this verse that Scripture is "inspired by God," but the underlying Greek text literally states that Scripture is "breathed out by God." When we read the Bible, we are experiencing the very breath of God.

Paul's letter to Titus is similar to those he wrote to Timothy in that it deals with the issue of corrupt leaders in the church (this time on the island in Crete). He even mentions the same "meaningless talk" (Titus 1:10) that he wrote about in 1 Timothy. Paul urges Titus to appoint new leaders in the church who are disciplined and have good character. It's these verses that churches today often point to when electing new elders. After these instructions about leadership, Paul encourages them to teach "sound doctrine" (Titus 1:9; 2:1), which will help them transform the culture around them instead of it transforming them.

At the conclusion of the Pastoral Epistles, we can look back and see three letters filled with great wisdom for local churches. Above all, Paul encourages them to be wary of leaders who focus on the wrong things, and to instead look for leaders of wisdom and character who will help others learn from Scripture how to live with faith and love.

Psalms and Proverbs

The overwhelming focus of Proverbs is on how to live a life of wisdom, but plenty of verses talk about the antithesis, which is a life of folly. In Proverbs 26 we find a series of harsh critiques about the foolish. My favorite is found in Proverbs 26:11, which offers a graphic picture of the life of a fool.

> As a dog returns to its vomit,
>> so fools repeat their folly. (Prov. 26:11)

My apologies for asking you to dwell on this topic, but it's such a fantastic example. Ask a veterinarian and they'll tell you that there are a variety of reasons why dogs commonly do this, but the truth found in this proverb is not concerned with the scientific reasoning. It's simpler than that. Dogs get sick and then eat back up the very thing that made them sick. In the same way, many people return to the source of their sin instead of doing the wise thing by backing away from it. Only a fool would do this, yet if we're honest with ourselves, we can probably identify multiple areas of our lives in which this is exactly what we do.

Take some time this week to consider whether your actions or behaviors have drifted into foolishness instead of wisdom. What would it look like to develop new rhythms that help you back away from sin and pursue a life of wisdom?

Reflections

Write down a few reflections on this week's readings.

Day 295: Jeremiah 40:7–42:22; 2 Timothy 1:1–18; Psalm 119:81–88

Day 296: Jer. 43:1–45:5; 2 Timothy 2:1–26; Proverbs 25:21–26:2

Day 297: Jeremiah 46:1–47:7; 2 Timothy 3:1–17; Psalm 119:89–96

Day 298: Jeremiah 48:1–49:6; 2 Timothy 4:1–22; Psalm 119:97–104

Day 299: Jeremiah 49:7–50:10; Titus 1:1–16; Psalm 119:105–112

Day 300: Jeremiah 50:11–51:14; Titus 2:1–15; Proverbs 26:3–12

Day 301: Jeremiah 51:15–64; Titus 3:1–15; Psalm 119:113–120

WEEK 44

Daily Readings

	Old Testament	New Testament	Psalms / Proverbs	
Day 302	Jeremiah 52:1–34	Philemon 1–25	Psalm 119:121–128	
Day 303	Lamentations 1:1–2:6	Hebrews 1:1–14	Psalm 119:129–136	
Day 304	Lam. 2:7–3:39	Hebrews 2:1–18	Proverbs 26:13–22	
Day 305	Lam. 3:40–5:22	Hebrews 3:1–19	Psalm 119:137–144	
Day 306	Ezekiel 1:1–3:27	Hebrews 4:1–13	Psalm 119:145–152	
Day 307	Ezekiel 4:1–6:14	Hebrews 4:14–5:10	Psalm 119:153–160	
Day 308	Ezekiel 7:1–9:11	Hebrews 5:11–6:12	Proverbs 26:23–27:4	

Old Testament

The short book of Lamentations features a series of five sad poems about the destruction of Jerusalem by the Babylonians and the Israelites' subsequent exile. Even though the book does not reveal who authored it, tradition holds that it was written by Jeremiah. Now that you've read Jeremiah and understand just how sad and hopeless he can be, it's not hard to see why Lamentations is attributed to him. These pages are filled with deep lament, showing us just how devastating the events of the exile were for the people of Israel.

Despite all the pain and anguish in these poems, we find a unique and beautiful structure in Lamentations. Like Psalm 119 (which we're *still* reading), the first four chapters of Lamentations are acrostic poems that follow the Hebrew alphabet. Each of the twenty-two verses in chapters 1, 2, and 4 begins with a consecutive letter. Chapter 3 has sixty-six verses divided into twenty-two stanzas that begin with a consecutive letter, and the three verses within each stanza also begin with that same letter. Chapter 5 does not follow an acrostic pattern, but it does have twenty-two verses, making the entire book symmetrical.

This careful literary design of Lamentations is remarkable. It shows us that this book is not just an unhinged cry of lament to God but a carefully constructed set of poems intended to give voice to the Israelites' sadness. This shows us, once again, that lament has a proper place in our lives. It is okay for us to cry out to God.

But don't miss the heart of Lamentations (literally). With twenty-two verses in the pairs of opening and closing chapters, and sixty-six verses in the middle chapter, that puts Lamentations 3:33 at the center of this book. Look at what that stanza says:

> For no one is cast off
> > by the Lord forever.
> Though he brings grief, he will show compassion,
> > so great is his unfailing love.
> For he does not willingly bring affliction
> > or grief to anyone. (Lam. 3:31–33)

Perhaps this placement is a coincidence, but I find it incredible that amid so much pain and confusion, the epicenter of Lamentations is a reminder of God's faithfulness, compassion, and unfailing love. Even when our lives seem to be falling apart, we can trust that God is good.

New Testament

That's not a typo in your reading plan. We're reading the entire book of Philemon in just one day. At twenty-fives verses long, it is the shortest book of the Bible we've read so far, but it is not *the* shortest book in the Bible. Both 2 John and 3 John are shorter, and we'll read those in a few weeks. Paul wrote this letter to his friend Philemon in Colossae, and the main concern of the letter is a third man, named Onesimus. We don't get the entire backstory, but the tension is clear, and Paul worries that when Onesimus returns to Colossae that Philemon will make him a slave. Paul instead asks Philemon to welcome Onesimus as a brother in the Lord, and he offers to pay his debts. It's a short, simple, and profound letter.

When you turn the page to Hebrews, you'll be reading the most sophisticated book in the New Testament. In the early days of Christianity, the authorship of Hebrews was credited to Paul, but the content and literary style is so different from what we find in Paul's letters that most scholars now agree that someone else authored it. Whoever wrote Hebrews was deeply familiar with the storyline of ancient Israel because the book is filled with quotes and references from the Old Testament. Written to Jewish followers of Jesus, it reads a lot like a sermon because it systematically lays out a case for the superiority of Christ over everything.

Everything?

Yes, everything.

Jesus is superior to the angels (chs. 1–2). He is greater than Moses, the biggest hero of the Hebrew Bible (ch. 3). He is the source of true Sabbath rest (ch. 4). He is the great high priest (chs. 4–7). He is the fulfillment of the promise made to Abraham (ch. 6). He has established a new covenant between God and his people (chs. 8–9). He is the great sacrifice that brings forgiveness of sin to all people (ch. 10). The book of Hebrews carefully explains who Jesus is in the framework of the Jewish faith. He is the Messiah they have been longing for, and he is even better than they could have ever hoped.

Psalms and Proverbs

As we've seen over the past few weeks, Psalm 119 is an extended celebration of God's word. Remarkably, the stanzas we're reading this week have a unique connection to the book of Lamentations because they reference experiencing troubling times and being afflicted by enemies.

> Ensure your servant's well-being;
> > do not let the arrogant oppress me. (Ps. 119:122)

> Redeem me from human oppression,
> > that I may obey your precepts. (Ps. 119:134)

> Trouble and distress have come upon me,
> > but your commands give me delight.
> > > (Ps. 119:143)

> Those who devise wicked schemes are near,
> > but they are far from your law. (Ps. 119:150)

> Many are the foes who persecute me,
> > but I have not turned from your statutes.
> > > (Ps. 119:157)

Just as the central verses of Lamentations focus on God's faithfulness, compassion, and unfailing love during Jerusalem's destruction and exile, the author of Psalm 119 finds hope in God's word during times of trouble. God's word represents the way of righteousness, and those who abide by it can always find hope, even in life's darkest moments.

Reflections

Write down a few reflections on this week's readings.

Day 302: Jeremiah 52:1–34; Philemon 1–25; Psalm 119:121–128

Day 303: Lam. 1:1–2:6; Hebrews 1:1–14; Psalm 119:129–136

Day 304: Lam. 2:7–3:39; Hebrews 2:1–18; Proverbs 26:13–22

Day 305: Lam. 3:40–5:22; Hebrews 3:1–19; Psalm 119:137–144

Day 306: Ezekiel 1:1–3:27; Hebrews 4:1–13; Psalm 119:145–152

Day 307: Ezekiel 4:1–6:14; Hebrews 4:14–5:10; Psalm 119:153–160

Day 308: Ezekiel 7:1–9:11; Hebrews 5:11–6:12; Proverbs 26:23–27:4

WEEK 45

Daily Readings

	Old Testament	New Testament	Psalms / Proverbs	
Day 309	Ezekiel 10:1–12:28	Hebrews 6:13–7:10	Psalm 119:161–168	
Day 310	Ezekiel 13:1–15:8	Hebrews 7:11–28	Psalm 119:169–176	
Day 311	Ezekiel 16:1–63	Hebrews 8:1–13	Psalm 120:1–7	
Day 312	Ezekiel 17:1–18:32	Hebrews 9:1–15	Proverbs 27:5–14	
Day 313	Ezekiel 19:1–20:44	Hebrews 9:16–28	Psalm 121:1–8	
Day 314	Ezekiel 20:45–22:22	Hebrews 10:1–18	Psalm 122:1–9	
Day 315	Ezekiel 22:23–23:49	Hebrews 10:19–39	Psalm 123:1–4	

Old Testament

Last week we began reading Ezekiel, one of the most vivid books of prophecy in the Old Testament. Ezekiel lived through the Babylonians' initial attack on Jerusalem, and he prophesied from exile in Babylon. While this book has much in common with the other Major Prophets—including chapter after chapter of judgment being pronounced on Israel and the surrounding nations—it is perhaps best known for Ezekiel's intense visions and his use of rather strange and elaborate public demonstrations to illustrate his prophecies.

Notice as you read Ezekiel that he writes about being exiled in Babylon while also mentioning those who are still in Jerusalem. This can be confusing for many readers, but there is a simple explanation. The destruction of Jerusalem by the Babylonians in 587 BC was the final act of a conflict that had been going on for over a decade. King Nebuchadnezzar of Babylon first laid siege on Jerusalem ten years earlier, and Ezekiel was part of the first group of Israelites exiled at that time. Much of this book was composed during the time between the first siege and the final siege.

The chapters we're reading this week are filled with proclamations of judgment against the people of Israel who are still in Jerusalem. They're compared to a useless vine, an adulterous wife, and a prostitute (among other things). It's a lot to take in, but don't miss that God's punishment also comes with a promise of redemption.

> This is what the Sovereign LORD says: I will deal with you as you deserve, because you have despised my oath by breaking the covenant. Yet I will remember the covenant I made with you in the days of your youth, and I will establish an everlasting covenant with you. (Ezek. 16:59–60)

In one breath, God tells his people that they will get what they deserve for breaking the covenant. In the next, he offers them undeserved grace. Punishment and promise. Judgment and joy. Heartache and hope. God is fair and just, but he is also merciful and kind.

New Testament

Hebrews explains the superiority of Jesus over everything else, particularly as it relates to the faith of the people of Israel and their relationship with God. At the end of a series of comparisons that takes up the first ten chapters of the book, the focus turns to sacrifices and the covenant. After a section in which Jesus has been described as the great high priest, we read a description of the regulations from the first covenant about the annual Day of Atonement (described in detail in Leviticus 16, Jews still celebrate it today as Yom Kippur, the holiest day of the year in Judaism). Every year on this day, the high priest would enter the inner room of the tabernacle with an animal blood sacrifice "which he offered for himself and for the sins the people had committed in ignorance" (Heb. 9:7). The high priest made this sacrifice to atone for the sins of the people. The blood shed on the Day of Atonement was essential to the Israelites' relationship and covenant with God. A sacrifice had to be made.

The very next passage describes Jesus entering the tabernacle as the great high priest, but he does something different: "He did not enter by means of the blood of goats and calves; but he entered the Most Holy Place once for all by his own blood, thus obtaining eternal redemption" (Heb. 9:12).

Jesus's death on the cross was the ultimate sacrifice. His blood was shed once for all, removing the need for yearly sacrifices to atone for sins. What he did fits directly into the historical faith of the Jews, but he did so in a way that was revolutionary. So much so that the author of Hebrews calls Jesus "the mediator of a new covenant" (9:15).

Do you see how all of this is woven together?

The story we've been immersed in from the very creation of the world on the first page of Genesis has found its fulfillment and ultimate purpose in Jesus Christ.

Psalms and Proverbs

Imagine gathering with friends and family a few times a year for a communal journey to your favorite place—one big caravan, traveling together. One of my favorite things about a road trip is listening to great music, and some of my most memorable trips have included a collection of songs that everyone would sing together at the top of their lungs.

That's exactly what we find in our readings from Psalms this week. After the conclusion of Psalm 119, we come to a collection of fifteen psalms known as the Songs of Ascents. According to tradition, most of these short psalms were sung by the Israelites on their "ascent" to Jerusalem (which was built on a hill) to celebrate the three annual pilgrimage festivals of Judaism. These psalms include praise and thanksgiving, confession and repentance, and cries for help. They were likely committed to memory and sung together as the people made their journey.

We'll be reading these songs over the next few weeks, and I encourage you to choose a couple of favorites to memorize. Any of them would make a wonderful addition to your daily prayer time.

Reflections

Write down a few reflections on this week's readings.

Day 309: Ezekiel 10:1–12:28; Heb. 6:13–7:10; Psalm 119:161–168

Day 310: Ezekiel 13:1–15:8; Hebrews 7:11–28; Psalm 119:169–176

Day 311: Ezekiel 16:1–63; Hebrews 8:1–13; Psalm 120:1–7

Day 312: Ezekiel 17:1–18:32; Hebrews 9:1–15; Proverbs 27:5–14

Day 313: Ezekiel 19:1–20:44; Hebrews 9:16–28; Psalm 121:1–8

Day 314: Ezekiel 20:45–22:22; Hebrews 10:1–18; Psalm 122:1–9

Day 315: Ezekiel 22:23–23:49; Hebrews 10:19–39; Psalm 123:1–4

WEEK 46

	Old Testament	New Testament	Psalms / Proverbs	
Day 316	Ezekiel 24:1–25:17	Hebrews 11:1–16	Proverbs 27:15–22	□
Day 317	Ezekiel 26:1–27:36	Hebrews 11:17–40	Psalm 124:1–8	□
Day 318	Ezekiel 28:1–29:21	Hebrews 12:1–13	Psalm 125:1–5	□
Day 319	Ezekiel 30:1–31:18	Hebrews 12:14–29	Psalm 126:1–6	□
Day 320	Ezekiel 32:1–33:20	Hebrews 13:1–25	Proverbs 27:23–28:6	□
Day 321	Ezekiel 33:21–35:15	James 1:1–27	Psalm 127:1–5	□
Day 322	Ezekiel 36:1–37:28	James 2:1–26	Psalm 128:1–6	□

Old Testament

The bulk of this week's readings from Ezekiel are prophetic judgments against Israel's enemies. The Ammonites, Moabites, Edomites, and Philistines each receive warnings of impending doom in chapter 25, but the next seven chapters are dedicated to the nations of Tyre and Egypt. Once again, we see that the people of Israel aren't the only ones who face consequences. Anyone who does not revere God will face judgment.

Chapter 33 provides clarity on something I mentioned last week: Ezekiel was part of the first group of exiles taken to Babylon, years before the final destruction of Jerusalem. In this chapter, an Israelite arrives in Babylon and tells Ezekiel that Jerusalem has fallen, confirming that his prophecies have come true. Even though we know this is coming, it's still a devastating blow. Think back on everything the people of Israel have experienced. God has seen them through so much, but now their homeland is in ruins and the very temple where God dwells among his people has been destroyed.

Ezekiel explains that this is a consequence of their actions against God and failure to abide by the covenant, and in chapter 34 he accuses Israel's leaders of being bad shepherds. But then something startling happens.

God describes himself as a good shepherd.

He promises to rescue his sheep and return them to the good pastures of their homeland. He tells them that their future will be filled with peace, hope, and restoration. In the final chapter we read this week, Ezekiel has another one of his visions, in which he sees a valley filled with bones that come to life. God tells him that these very dry bones represent the people of Israel in exile, but that he will give them new life in their own land once again.

This is God's promise to the Israelites in exile, and I believe it's his promise to us as well. We are his people, and while we will face consequences for our unfaithfulness, God will prove to be the good shepherd who gives us a hope and a future.

New Testament

The book of Hebrews shifts at the end of chapter 10. It's noticeable because of the word *therefore* at the beginning of verse 19. Up until this point the book has been a theological juggernaut filled with beautiful language in which the writer marches through key moments in the history of God's people to show how Jesus has fulfilled and even surpassed all that they had hoped for. Now the focus turns to the readers. How are they supposed to respond to all of this?

"By faith."

This two-word phrase appears nearly two dozen times in Hebrews 11.

So what do you think it means to live by faith?

Many people see faith as believing in something we can't see. But that's not an easy way to live, is it? We like certainty.

There's a pendulum here. On one side is blind faith, where we don't allow ourselves to question anything. On the other side is the attitude that says, "I can't believe unless I can make everything add up." But the beautiful reality of living by faith lies somewhere in the tension between those two extremes. It forces us to confess that we don't have it all figured out and embrace the mystery. That requires trust, hope, and humility. That's why my working definition of faith is a deep trust in God, formed by humility, which gives us great hope.

I think the writer of Hebrews understood this. Hebrews 11 begins with this recognition that faith is, in part, belief in something we cannot see. But it does not stop there. It takes us on a journey. Verse 3 goes back to the very beginning of the story. How do we understand the creation of the world? By faith. And then the rest of the chapter retells the story of God's people. It builds and builds to chapter 12.

> Therefore, since we are surrounded by such a great cloud of witnesses, let us throw off everything that hinders and the sin that so easily entangles. And let us run with perseverance the race marked out for us, fixing our eyes on Jesus, the pioneer and perfecter of faith. For the joy set before him he endured the cross, scorning its shame, and sat down at the right hand of the throne of God. (Heb. 12:1–2)

Hebrews reminds us that we are part of a much larger story. While faith involves trusting in what we cannot see, it is far from blind, because we've seen it proven true in the lives of those who have gone before us. And the one who authors and perfects this faith is Jesus.

Psalms and Proverbs

One of the beautiful features about the book of Proverbs is its variety. Sure, it can be repetitive at times, but certain verses resonate at a deeper level than others. For me, one of those is found buried in the heart of Proverbs 27.

> As iron sharpens iron,
> so one person sharpens another. (Prov. 27:17)

The mental image here is of two pieces of iron, perhaps swords or other bladed weapons, being rubbed against one another to be made sharper. It's almost counterintuitive, isn't it? I would think that the friction of these two pieces of iron scraping against one another would cause them to dull, not sharpen. But that's what happens. Iron does not have feelings, but if it did, I have to think that this process would be painful.

The wisdom of this proverb is found in the comparison drawn in the second line, as the pieces of iron are replaced by people. We sharpen one another. But for the analogy to hold, that sharpening must come through close contact. We have to truly engage with others in order to benefit from them. This means being willing to risk some discomfort or pain in order to grow. Letting others get close to us can be difficult, especially because it opens us up to the possibility of getting hurt. But we are created for relationship, with God and with one another. It's important to have people in our lives who are close enough to help us stay sharp.

Reflections

Write down a few reflections on this week's readings.

Day 316: Ezekiel 24:1–25:17; Hebrews 11:1–16; Proverbs 27:15–22

Day 317: Ezekiel 26:1–27:36; Hebrews 11:17–40; Psalm 124:1–8

Day 318: Ezekiel 28:1–29:21; Hebrews 12:1–13; Psalm 125:1–5

Day 319: Ezekiel 30:1–31:18; Hebrews 12:14–29; Psalm 126:1–6

Day 320: Ezekiel 32:1–33:20; Heb. 13:1–25; Proverbs 27:23–28:6

Day 321: Ezekiel 33:21–35:15; James 1:1–27; Psalm 127:1–5

Day 322: Ezekiel 36:1–37:28; James 2:1–26; Psalm 128:1–6

WEEK 47

	Old Testament	New Testament	Psalms / Proverbs	
Day 323	Ezekiel 38:1–39:29	James 3:1–18	Psalm 129:1–8	▫
Day 324	Ezekiel 40:1–49	James 4:1–17	Proverbs 28:7–17	▫
Day 325	Ezekiel 41:1–42:20	James 5:1–20	Psalm 130:1–8	▫
Day 326	Ezekiel 43:1–44:31	1 Peter 1:1–2:3	Psalm 131:1–3	▫
Day 327	Ezekiel 45:1–46:24	1 Peter 2:4–25	Psalm 132:1–18	▫
Day 328	Ezekiel 47:1–48:35	1 Peter 3:1–22	Proverbs 28:18–28	▫
Day 329	Daniel 1:1–2:23	1 Peter 4:1–19	Psalm 133:1–3	▫

Old Testament

If the final chapters of Ezekiel don't excite and inspire you, I don't know what will. In chapter 40, while Ezekiel is still in exile, the Lord gives him a vision in which he is transported back to Jerusalem.

> He took me there, and I saw a man whose appearance was like bronze; he was standing in the gateway with a linen cord and a measuring rod in his hand. The man said to me, "Son of man, look carefully and listen closely and pay attention to everything I am going to show you, for that is why you have been brought here. Tell the people of Israel everything you see." (Ezek. 40:3–4)

For the next eight chapters, Ezekiel reports what he sees in the city, and it's incredible. He starts by giving detailed descriptions of the temple, which remind us of the tabernacle specifications from the book of Exodus. We know that the Babylonians burned the temple to the ground, but Ezekiel sees a magnificent new temple. Back in chapter 10, he described seeing the glory of the Lord leaving the temple, but in chapter 43, he witnesses God's glory returning to the temple. Chapter 47 contains one of my favorite moments in this vision, where Ezekiel sees water trickling out from underneath the temple. It grows and grows into a mighty river that brings new life to everything around it.

It's not just the temple that is restored but the entire city of Jerusalem. God welcomes the people of Israel back to their beloved homeland, which is divided among the twelve tribes similarly to how it was in the book of Joshua. The final verses of Ezekiel describe the new city gates, and then we learn the new name of the city.

And the name of the city from that time on will be:

THE LORD IS THERE. (Ezek. 48:35b)

This book began with the people of Israel in exile. They had lost their home. The temple was destroyed. But God gives Ezekiel a vision of what is to come. A day of redemption and hope is on the horizon. All will be restored, and the land once devastated will flow with new life. And the reason for it is quite clear. It's because God is there.

New Testament

At the end of last week, we started reading the book of James, which is commonly attributed to James the brother of Jesus (Mark 6:3). He was one of the key leaders of the early church in Jerusalem, alongside Peter and John. This is the only piece of writing from James in the New Testament, and it feels like a collection of his greatest hits. These pages are filled with short sermonettes, lessons, and extremely quotable verses in which James offers practical wisdom on what it looks like to live out your faith. He makes it clear that the only right response to the reality of what Jesus has done for us through his life, death, and resurrection is to give our lives fully to him. Take your time as you read James. Highlight the verses that stand out to you, and commit them to memory. The wisdom found in this short letter is profound and impactful.

Next, we find ourselves in 1 Peter, one of only two letters in the Bible written by the leading figure of early Christianity. Peter addresses this letter to several churches in the region of Asia Minor (modern-day Turkey). From his words, it's evident that they have been facing persecution for their faith in Jesus. You may notice that Peter refers to his readers as exiles, and even though he's writing from Rome, he calls it Babylon. Peter clearly wants to make a connection between the followers of Jesus living in the Roman Empire and the exiled Jews who lived in Babylon centuries earlier.

Think about that. In both cases, God's people are trying to figure out how to live faithfully in a world that opposes their beliefs. And in many ways, that's true for us as well. A life of faithfulness is just as countercultural today as it was then. But we are called to persevere and continue to pursue the way of Jesus no matter what.

Psalms and Proverbs

We're still in the Songs of Ascents this week, which you'll remember are a collection of fifteen psalms sung by the Israelites on their "ascent" to Jerusalem for the annual pilgrimage festivals. One of my favorites is Psalm 130, which offers a unique perspective on forgiveness.

Out of the depths I cry to you, Lord;
    Lord, hear my voice.
Let your ears be attentive
    to my cry for mercy.

If you, Lord, kept a record of sins,
    Lord, who could stand?
But with you there is forgiveness,
    so that we can, with reverence, serve you.
        (Ps. 130:1–4)

Did anything stand out to you in those verses?

The first two establish this psalm as a cry for mercy, and the second two are a celebration of God's forgiveness. But do you notice what the psalmist says this forgiveness leads to?

Reverence and service.

When we truly understand God's forgiveness of our sins, the right response is not for us to pat ourselves on the back and feel relieved but to humbly offer our lives to him through service. Forgiveness is not an excuse to go on sinning; it is an invitation to give our lives more fully to the one who forgives.

Reflections

Write down a few reflections on this week's readings.

Day 323: Ezekiel 38:1–39:29; James 3:1–18; Psalm 129:1–8

Day 324: Ezekiel 40:1–49; James 4:1–17; Proverbs 28:7–17

Day 325: Ezekiel 41:1–42:20; James 5:1–20; Psalm 130:1–8

Day 326: Ezekiel 43:1–44:31; 1 Peter 1:1–2:3; Psalm 131:1–3

Day 327: Ezekiel 45:1–46:24; 1 Peter 2:4–25; Psalm 132:1–18

Day 328: Ezekiel 47:1–48:35; 1 Peter 3:1–22; Proverbs 28:18–28

_____

_____

_____

_____

_____

_____

Day 329: Daniel 1:1–2:23; 1 Peter 4:1–19; Psalm 133:1–3

_____

_____

_____

_____

_____

_____

Week 48

	Old Testament	New Testament	Psalms / Proverbs	
Day 330	Daniel 2:24–3:12	1 Peter 5:1–14	Psalm 134:1–3	☐
Day 331	Daniel 3:13–4:18	2 Peter 1:1–21	Psalm 135:1–12	☐
Day 332	Daniel 4:19–5:16	2 Peter 2:1–22	Proverbs 29:1–9	☐
Day 333	Daniel 5:17–6:28	2 Peter 3:1–18	Psalm 135:13–21	☐
Day 334	Daniel 7:1–8:14	1 John 1:1–2:11	Psalm 136:1–12	☐
Day 335	Daniel 8:15–9:19	1 John 2:12–27	Psalm 136:13–26	☐
Day 336	Daniel 9:20–11:1	1 John 2:28–3:10	Proverbs 29:10–18	☐

Old Testament

The book of Daniel takes place shortly after Babylon's initial attack on Jerusalem (just like Ezekiel) and follows Daniel and his three friends—Hananiah, Mishael, and Azariah—as they are carried into exile and placed in the service of King Nebuchadnezzar. You may not recognize the Hebrew names of these three friends because they are given new names by the chief official in Babylon: Shadrach, Meshach, and Abednego. Daniel is also given a new name, Belteshazzar, which is what the king calls him throughout the book.

The book of Daniel is widely known for two incredible stories in which God protects Daniel and his friends from certain death. In chapter 3, King Nebuchadnezzar becomes incensed when Shadrach, Meshach, and Abednego refuse to bow down and worship a massive golden idol, so he has them thrown into a blazing furnace. In chapter 6, Daniel refuses to stop praying to the Lord and King Darius has him thrown into a lions' den. In both circumstances, God sends an angel of protection to prevent certain death, and the kings respond by worshiping the Lord. The faithfulness of God's people in the face of intense pressure and persecution leads to his continuing provision and protection.

But these two stories are only a small part of the book of Daniel. There are also several apocalyptic visions and dreams throughout the book that often draw comparisons to Revelation, the final book of the New Testament. These visions are filled with imagery about beasts and wars and coming kingdoms, all of which can be quite confusing, even when we read the interpretations offered within the text. I wish I could offer a simple explanation for these visions, but the truth is that biblical scholars have debated their meaning ever since these texts were written. There seems to be a connection between the beasts described in Daniel and several of the empires that followed the Babylonians, including the Persians, Greeks, and Romans. But not everything found in these pages has a clear meaning.

What is clear, however, is that God's people are called to remain faithful in the midst of great tribulation. Even when we don't fully understand what is happening in the world around us, our priority should always be to honor and obey God. When we do this, we can trust that our lives are in God's hands.

New Testament

2 Peter has a distinctly different tone than 1 Peter. It's much more direct, with a level of intensity and harshness that we don't often find in the New Testament. Perhaps that's because Peter knows that his death is imminent and that he will not be writing any more letters to his fellow followers of Christ.

I think it is right to refresh your memory as long as I live in the tent of this body, because I know that I will soon put it aside, as our Lord Jesus Christ has made clear to me. And I will make every effort to see that after my departure you will always be able to remember these things. (2 Pet. 1:13–15)

In his final words, Peter focuses on a few key topics. First, he encourages his readers to live a godly life so that they may be effective witnesses for Jesus (1:3–11). Second, he reminds them that what they have been taught about Jesus is not a bunch of "cleverly devised stories" (v. 16) but eyewitness accounts of his life and ministry that have been affirmed by God himself (1:16–21). In chapters 2–3, Peter issues a stern warning against false teachers who seek to corrupt the truth of the gospel and confuse everyone about the return of Jesus (he even compares them to the dog from Proverbs 26 that we examined a few weeks ago!). He also reassures his readers that Jesus will return.

But do not forget this one thing, dear friends: With the Lord a day is like a thousand years, and a thousand years are like a day. The Lord is not slow in keeping his promise, as some understand slowness. Instead he is patient with you, not wanting anyone to perish, but everyone to come to repentance. (2 Pet. 3:8–9)

Peter has a lot to say but little time to say it (I particularly love how he squeezes in a quick commendation of Paul's letters just before he says goodbye). One of the greatest figures in the early church uses his last letter to encourage believers to commit themselves to the way of Jesus and continue to wait eagerly for his return. I believe, if given the chance, he would say the same thing to us today.

Psalms and Proverbs

The theme of Psalm 136 is hard to miss. While this psalm recounts the glory of God through creation, as well as his faithfulness to the people of Israel through many difficult trials, each of the twenty-six verses of this song of praise ends with the same refrain: "His love endures forever."

And what does the reality of God's love require of us?

That we give thanks.

> Give thanks to the LORD, for he is good.
>> *His love endures forever.*
> Give thanks to the God of gods.
>> *His love endures forever.*
> Give thanks to the Lord of lords:
>> *His love endures forever.* . . .
>
> Give thanks to the God of heaven:
>> *His love endures forever.* (Ps. 136:1–3, 26)

Don't overthink this. When you look at the stars at night or marvel at the sunrise, remember God's love and give thanks. When you look back on your life and see God's faithfulness even through the darkest of times, remember God's love and give thanks. When you have a reason to celebrate in the best of times, remember God's love and give thanks.

His love endures forever, so give thanks.

Reflections

Write down a few reflections on this week's readings.

Day 330: Daniel 2:24–3:12; 1 Peter 5:1–14; Psalm 134:1–3

Day 331: Daniel 3:13–4:18; 2 Peter 1:1–21; Psalm 135:1–12

Day 332: Daniel 4:19–5:16; 2 Peter 2:1–22; Proverbs 29:1–9

Day 333: Daniel 5:17–6:28; 2 Peter 3:1–18; Psalm 135:13–21

Day 334: Daniel 7:1–8:14; 1 John 1:1–2:11; Psalm 136:1–12

Day 335: Daniel 8:15–9:19; 1 John 2:12–27; Psalm 136:13–26

Day 336: Daniel 9:20–11:1; 1 John 2:28–3:10; Proverbs 29:10–18

WEEK 49

	Old Testament	New Testament	Psalms / Proverbs	
Day 337	Daniel 11:2–35	1 John 3:11–4:6	Psalm 137:1–9	
Day 338	Daniel 11:36–12:13	1 John 4:7–21	Psalm 138:1–8	
Day 339	Hosea 1:1–2:23	1 John 5:1–21	Psalm 139:1–10	
Day 340	Hosea 3:1–5:15	2 John 1–13	Proverbs 29:19–27	
Day 341	Hosea 6:1–7:16	3 John 1–14	Psalm 139:11–16	
Day 342	Hosea 8:1–9:17	Jude 1–25	Psalm 139:17–24	
Day 343	Hosea 10:1–11:11	Revelation 1:1–20	Psalm 140:1–5	

Old Testament

After the conclusion of Daniel, we come to the final section of the Old Testament. This series of twelve prophetic books is collectively known as the Minor Prophets, and they were written over the span of several hundred years from before, during, and after the exile. The term *minor* only means these writings are shorter than the Major Prophets, not less important (it took us nearly four weeks to read through the book of Isaiah, but we will read all the Minor Prophets in that same amount of time). In the Hebrew Bible, these writings are grouped together as one book called The Twelve, but in the Christian Old Testament, they are separated as individual books.

What we find in the twelve Minor Prophets is similar to what we read in the Major Prophets: warnings and declarations of judgment, calls for repentance and renewed commitment to the covenant, and promises of future deliverance and hope.

Hosea is the first book in the Minor Prophets. Hosea prophesied during the reign of Jeroboam II in the northern kingdom of Israel (remember that they divided into two kingdoms after the reign of Solomon). Jeroboam II was an evil man who did not honor God. Hosea prophesied that God's judgment would come through Assyria, and not long after Jeroboam II's reign, the Assyrian Empire attacked the Northern Kingdom and destroyed it.

Don't miss the peculiar way that God instructs Hosea to use his own family in his work as a prophet. His wife, Gomer, is described as a promiscuous woman (1:2) and an adulteress (3:1). Hosea's children's names are Jezreel, Lo-Ruhamah, and Lo-Ammi. Jezreel was the site of a massacre (2 Kings 9–10). Lo-Ruhamah means "not loved." Lo-Ammi means "not my people." These key relationships in Hosea's life are symbolic of God's fraught relationship with the people of Israel. But when Hosea reconciles with Gomer in chapter 3, we also see a glimpse of God's steadfast love for his people despite their unfaithfulness. There is always hope for the people of God.

New Testament

After reading two letters from Peter, we come to three letters from John. John was a common name when the New Testament was being written, and multiple Johns are mentioned in connection with the early church, which makes the identity of the author less than certain. But the vocabulary, style, and overall outlook of these letters is similar to those of the gospel of John, so it stands to reason that they were written by the same person.

In these letters, John offers pastoral wisdom to his readers about a variety of issues. As we've already seen in the letters of Paul, James, and Peter, the explosive growth of the early church led to quite a bit of confusion and disagreement. Some leaders had begun teaching things about Jesus that were untrue (for example,

John addresses the false notion that Jesus was just a spiritual being without a physical body in 1 John 4). John writes to address these issues and encourage everyone to persevere in truth and love. His focus on love is so prominent that the word is used more than fifty times in these three letters. For John, love is the main thing. God is love, he says, and God's people should love one another.

The last letter before the New Testament's epic conclusion in Revelation is called Jude. This short letter is commonly attributed to a brother of Jesus named Judah. Jude also confronts corrupt teachers and encourages followers of Jesus to persevere in their faith.

What we read in these short letters at the end of the New Testament gives us additional insight about the difficulties of the early church, but it also invites us to consider the voices speaking into our own lives. If John and Jude were around today, I imagine they would offer some of these same warnings about false teachers and the need to stay focused on what really matters. It's easy to be distracted by charismatic voices with big ideas, but we need to persevere as people of love who are committed to the core truths of the gospel.

Psalms and Proverbs

Psalm 139 is one of the most commonly quoted psalms, and I think that's because it has a beautiful way of illustrating the unlimited power, knowledge, and presence of God. The first eighteen verses of this psalm are a celebration of God's majesty and creativity. The author, King David, is overwhelmed.

> Such knowledge is too wonderful for me,
>   too lofty for me to attain. (Ps. 139:6)

As he continues to consider who God is and what he's capable of, David's natural response is worship.

I praise you because I am fearfully and
  wonderfully made;
  your works are wonderful,
  I know that full well. (Ps. 139:14)

And when all is said and done, David surrenders his own heart and life to God.

Search me, God, and know my heart;
  test me and know my anxious thoughts.
See if there is any offensive way in me,
  and lead me in the way everlasting.
    (Ps. 139:23–24)

It can be overwhelming to recognize just how great and powerful God is. Many people run and hide from this, but David shows us that the only right response to the awesome reality of God's power is worship and surrender.

Reflections

Write down a few reflections on this week's readings.

Day 337: Daniel 11:2–35; 1 John 3:11–4:6; Psalm 137:1–9

Day 338: Daniel 11:36–12:13; 1 John 4:7–21; Psalm 138:1–8

Day 339: Hosea 1:1–2:23; 1 John 5:1–21; Psalm 139:1–10

Day 340: Hosea 3:1–5:15; 2 John 1–13; Proverbs 29:19–27

Day 341: Hosea 6:1–7:16; 3 John 1–14; Psalm 139:11–16

Day 342: Hosea 8:1–9:17; Jude 1–25; Psalm 139:17–24

Day 343: Hosea 10:1–11:11; Revelation 1:1–20; Psalm 140:1–5

WEEK 50

Daily Readings

	Old Testament	New Testament	Psalms / Proverbs	
Day 344	Hosea 11:12–14:9	Revelation 2:1–17	Proverbs 30:1–10	
Day 345	Joel 1:1–2:17	Revelation 2:18–3:6	Psalm 140:6–13	
Day 346	Joel 2:18–3:21	Revelation 3:7–22	Psalm 141:1–10	
Day 347	Amos 1:1–2:16	Revelation 4:1–11	Psalm 142:1–7	
Day 348	Amos 3:1–4:13	Revelation 5:1–14	Proverbs 30:11–23	
Day 349	Amos 5:1–27	Revelation 6:1–17	Psalm 143:1–12	
Day 350	Amos 6:1–7:17	Revelation 7:1–17	Psalm 144:1–8	

Old Testament

The second book in the Minor Prophets is Joel. We don't know exactly when this book was written, because the text itself does not mention specific people or events that can help us narrow it down. Regardless of whether Joel wrote these prophecies before, during, or after the exile, we can be certain that his mission was to call on God's people to repent from their wicked ways and return to the Lord.

You'll notice multiple references to the "day of the Lord" in Joel. This is a common theme in the prophets that is used to refer to one of two things: (1) a day of judgment in which the Lord holds people accountable for their sin or (2) a day of restoration when the Lord redeems and renews all things. Some prophets lean more heavily into one of these versions of the day of the Lord than the other, but Joel gives us a glimpse of both. In the first two chapters, it's seen as a day of judgment in the form of a violent plague of locusts. But in the final chapter, we see a day when Jerusalem flourishes once again and flows with new life (much like the conclusion of Ezekiel).

Next comes Amos, who prophesied during the reign of King Jeroboam II in the Northern Kingdom (making him a contemporary of Hosea). The first two chapters of Amos sound a lot like the other prophecies we've read. He proclaims judgment on the people of Israel as well as on their enemies. But then Amos digs a little bit deeper, and in the middle chapters of this book we find some interesting accusations from God that illuminate why he's so disappointed in them.

In Amos 4, the people of Israel are chastised for not returning to the Lord even after all the different ways he has punished them (famine, drought, plagues, etc.). They are so stubborn that they can't even recognize their sins when faced with terrible consequences. In chapter 5, Amos tells the people that their offerings and sacrifices don't mean anything to God if the rest of their lives are filled with evil. He essentially calls them hypocrites and tells them that they need to be people of justice and righteousness if they want God to bless them.

Amos offers a good reminder that how we live matters. We can't become complacent or prideful if we want God to bless us. We can't simply go through the motions on Sundays and live however we want the rest of the week. We are called to wake up every day and give everything we have to the Lord. He is worth nothing less.

New Testament

Revelation is one of the most complex books in the Bible. It was written by John in a literary style or genre known as apocalyptic literature, which was common in the ancient world.

It's important to know that ancient apocalyptic literature was filled with prophetic symbolism, allusions, and numerology. It is prophecy, yes, but it's a type of prophecy that has layer upon layer of meaning that needs to be studied and unraveled to be fully understood.

Revelation can feel overwhelming and confusing if you don't first understand the type of book you're reading. And it's difficult to make sense of even when you do! It's tempting to read this book and think that the end of the world is going to look exactly as described in these pages—and many people have interpreted it literally over the years—but the true beauty of Revelation is found beneath the surface of the text.

The first three chapters of Revelation read a lot like many of the letters we've just finished. John writes brief messages to seven churches, encouraging them to remain faithful to Jesus at all costs. Once again, it seems clear that many of the followers of Jesus were getting discouraged and wondering when Jesus would return. John's answer is to describe a vision.

It starts in the throne room of heaven, where John sees humans and creatures gathered in worship. It's a remarkable image, and as you read this passage, you may be reminded of various hymns and worship songs that have been crafted using the very words from these pages. The next thing we know, John is weeping because the Lord is holding a scroll that is sealed, yet there is no one worthy enough to break the seals and open it. The next scene is one of my favorite moments in the Bible.

Then one of the elders said to me, "Do not weep! See, the Lion of the tribe of Judah, the Root of David, has triumphed. He is able to open the scroll and its seven seals."

Then I saw a Lamb, looking as if it had been slain, standing at the center of the throne, encircled by the four living creatures and the elders. (Rev. 5:5–6)

Don't miss this. John is told that a lion can open the scroll, but when he turns to look at this lion, he sees a sacrificial lamb. The Lion of Judah (Gen. 49:9) and the Root of David (Isa. 11:10) are other names for "the Lamb of God, who takes away the sin of the world" (John 1:29). This is Jesus. He is the lion and the lamb, and he is the only one worthy to open the scroll. As everyone in the throne room falls down to worship him, I find myself joining them.

In a loud voice they were saying:

> "Worthy is the Lamb, who was slain,
>> to receive power and wealth and wisdom and
>>> strength
>> and honor and glory and praise!" (Rev. 5:12)

Psalms and Proverbs

How many times have you wished God would just show up and help you out of a difficult situation? We've probably all been there, but how do we express those things to God? David wrote psalms 140–144 during a time of distress. As you read through these passages, you'll hear him ask God for mercy, deliverance, safety, justice, refuge, freedom, rescue, and more.

David is able to talk openly and honestly with God when he's struggling, and we should do that too. I read these chapters and find comfort in the fact that the Bible is filled with psalms of lament. Hard times are a normal part of life, and God is okay with us questioning him and crying out for help. But if you read these psalms carefully, you'll notice that David's complaints to God are filled with reverence, awe, and faith. He cries out, yes, but he does so from a place of trust. He never stops worshiping God even when he protests.

The next time you need comfort during a tough time, open your Bible to one of these psalms and pray these words to God. Cry out to him for help, but do so with a heart full of praise.

Reflections

Write down a few reflections on this week's readings.

Day 344: Hosea 11:12–14:9; Revelation 2:1–17; Proverbs 30:1–10

Day 345: Joel 1:1–2:17; Revelation 2:18–3:6; Psalm 140:6–13

Day 346: Joel 2:18–3:21; Revelation 3:7–22; Psalm 141:1–10

Day 347: Amos 1:1–2:16; Revelation 4:1–11; Psalm 142:1–7

Day 348: Amos 3:1–4:13; Revelation 5:1–14; Proverbs 30:11–23

Day 349: Amos 5:1–27; Revelation 6:1–17; Psalm 143:1–12

Day 350: Amos 6:1–7:17; Revelation 7:1–17; Psalm 144:1–8

WEEK 51

Daily Readings

	Old Testament	New Testament	Psalms / Proverbs	
Day 351	Amos 8:1–9:15	Revelation 8:1–9:12	Psalm 144:9–15	☐
Day 352	Obadiah 1–21	Revelation 9:13–10:11	Proverbs 30:24–33	☐
Day 353	Jonah 1:1–4:11	Revelation 11:1–19	Psalm 145:1–7	☐
Day 354	Micah 1:1–4:13	Revelation 12:1–13:1a	Psalm 145:8–13a	☐
Day 355	Micah 5:1–7:20	Revelation 13:1b–18	Psalm 145:13b–21	☐
Day 356	Nahum 1:1–3:19	Revelation 14:1–13	Proverbs 31:1–9	☐
Day 357	Habakkuk 1:1–3:19	Revelation 14:14–15:8	Psalm 146:1–10	☐

Old Testament

This week we're reading six books from the Minor Prophets: the conclusion of Amos, followed by the complete books of Obadiah, Jonah, Micah, Nahum, and Habakkuk. With so much here to explore, it was hard to decide what to share with you this week, but I kept coming back to one verse.

> He has shown you, O mortal, what is good.
> > And what does the Lord require of you?
> To act justly and to love mercy
> > and to walk humbly with your God. (Mic. 6:8)

Picture yourself in a courtroom.

God is the judge. The prophet Micah is the prosecutor. And the people of Israel are the defendants.

That's what is happening here in the sixth chapter of Micah, where one of the most famous verses in the Bible appears in the middle of a courtroom drama where the prophet Micah is putting the people of Israel on trial. The verses leading up to Micah 6:8 feel like an interrogation. God wants to know why the people of Israel are complaining and why they have turned their backs on him. He then reminds them of how he has repeatedly showed kindness and faithfulness to them (when he mentions what happened "from Shittim to Gilgal" in verse 5, that's when the Israelites crossed the Jordan River and entered the promised land).

When the people of Israel respond to God by talking about offerings and sacrifices—the methods they have always used to make things right with God—he tells them he wants something else.

Act justly. Love mercy. Walk humbly with your God.

God tells his people that he wants them to remember all he has done for them, and the response he is looking for is not for them to go through the motions of religion but to live differently. The pursuit of justice and mercy and humility is what God wants to see in the lives of his people.

This is God's message to the Israelites through the prophet Micah, but it's also his message to us. When we understand the reality of what God has done for us, our only right response is to offer our lives to God as doers of justice, lovers of mercy, and people of humility who walk with God.

What does it look like for you to do justice?

What does it look like for you to love mercy?

What does it look like for you to walk humbly with your God?

When we look back on our lives and see all the times God has been faithful to us, it should make us want to live differently.

New Testament

The complexity of Revelation is on full display in this week's readings as we see what happens when the seven seals of the scroll are opened, followed by the sounding of seven trumpets by the angels. Woven throughout these chapters are John's visions of armies, wars, plagues, beasts, earthquakes, and more. Each one is filled with symbolism, numbers, and Old Testament references.

Remember that this book is a piece of apocalyptic literature with multiple layers of prophetic meaning. I would need to write another book the size of this one to fully explore and explain what's going on in these pages, and even then, some of it would be incredibly difficult to understand. Perhaps this is why many people have opted to interpret Revelation literally. The text is so challenging to make sense of that it's easier to convince ourselves that everything will happen exactly as described than it is to wrestle with its symbolism.

I've said this in previous weeks, but it bears repeating here: Not everything in the Bible was designed to be read plainly. There is so much nuance in the pages of Scripture, and just because something is not literally true doesn't mean it's not filled with truth (e.g., the parables of Jesus). To interpret what we read in Revelation symbolically does not mean we aren't taking it seriously. Quite the opposite, in fact.

So how do you go about that?

How do you find clarity about what this book is trying to tell us?

Revelation is one of the books that needs to be read with a good study Bible or commentary close by. Most of us need some help from biblical scholars to better understand what John is doing in these pages. As we near the end of our journey through the Bible, you may need to just get through the reading this week and keep moving, but perhaps a deeper study of Revelation is something to explore in a couple of weeks when this reading plan comes to an end.

Psalms and Proverbs

Have you noticed how often the Bible tells us to care for the most vulnerable members of society? Every time I do a read-through of the Bible, I am reminded just how much God cares about the poor, widows, orphans, and oppressed. In the final chapter of Proverbs, we are told not only to care for these people but to speak up for them as well.

> Speak up for those who cannot speak for themselves,
>> for the rights of all who are destitute.
> Speak up and judge fairly;
>> defend the rights of the poor and needy.
> (Prov. 31:8–9)

I love the saying "Actions speak louder than words" because it reminds me that I need to follow through on the things I say. But in this case, words become actions. To speak up for someone is a form of taking action.

In many places in our society, "the least of these" do not have a voice. They are unable to stand up for themselves and be heard. In those circumstances, the wisdom of the Bible tells us to speak up on their behalf and defend their rights. We are called to be people who show compassion and kindness to the poor and needy, but we're also called to use our voices to help them when they need it most.

Reflections

Write down a few reflections on this week's readings.

Day 351: Amos 8:1–9:15; Revelation 8:1–9:12; Psalm 144:9–15

_____

_____

_____

_____

_____

_____

Day 352: Obadiah 1–21; Revelation 9:13–10:11; Proverbs 30:24–33

Day 353: Jonah 1:1–4:11; Revelation 11:1–19; Psalm 145:1–7

Day 354: Micah 1:1–4:13; Revelation 12:1–13:1a; Psalm 145:8–13a

Day 355: Micah 5:1–7:20; Revelation 13:1b–18; Psalm 145:13b–21

Day 356: Nahum 1:1–3:19; Revelation 14:1–13; Proverbs 31:1–9

Day 357: Hab. 1:1–3:19; Revelation 14:14–15:8; Psalm 146:1–10

WEEK 52

	Old Testament	New Testament	Psalms / Proverbs	
Day 358	Zephaniah 1:1–3:20	Revelation 16:1–21	Psalm 147:1–11	☐
Day 359	Haggai 1:1–2:23	Revelation 17:1–18	Psalm 147:12–20	☐
Day 360	Zechariah 1:1–4:14	Revelation 18:1–17a	Proverbs 31:10–20	☐
Day 361	Zechariah 5:1–8:23	Rev. 18:17b–19:10	Psalm 148:1–6	☐
Day 362	Zechariah 9:1–11:17	Revelation 19:11–21	Psalm 148:7–14	☐
Day 363	Zechariah 12:1–14:21	Revelation 20:1–15	Psalm 149:1–9	☐
Day 364	Malachi 1:1–2:16	Revelation 21:1–27	Proverbs 31:21–31	☐
Day 365	Malachi 2:17–4:6	Revelation 22:1–21	Psalm 150:1–6	☐

Old Testament

The final four books of the Minor Prophets—and the Old Testament as a whole—are Zephaniah, Haggai, Zechariah, and Malachi. Zephaniah was written prior to the exile and contains similar prophetic language about "the day of the LORD" as found in many of the other prophetic books. But the final three books jump forward to a time *after* the exile. The book of Haggai overlaps with the book of Ezra, and we learn that it was Haggai who prophesied that the Lord wanted the temple to be rebuilt. This prompted Zerubbabel (who we read about in Ezra 1–6) to return to Jerusalem and begin construction.

Just like Ezra flows straight into Nehemiah (they were originally one book); Haggai connects directly to the book of Zechariah, named after another prophet who worked alongside Haggai. Zechariah is divided into two distinct sections. The first section, chapters 1–8, is filled with visions and dreams that contain some of the same elements we've been reading about in Revelation (John did this on purpose, so make a note every time you see a similarity). The second section, chapters 9–14, is more traditional prophecy. But what unifies these two portions of Zechariah is that they are filled with references to the coming kingdom of God and the Messiah, many of which are directly fulfilled by Jesus.

In the final book of the Old Testament, the prophet Malachi confronts Israel one last time for breaking the covenant. After issuing severe warnings against sin and idolatry, he begs them to remember the law of Moses and remain faithful to God, who promises that "for you who revere my name, the sun of righteousness will rise with healing in its rays" (Mal. 4:2).

I find it truly moving that after everything we've read, the Old Testament ends with hope on the horizon like a morning sunrise.

New Testament

In the closing chapters of Revelation, things get worse before ultimately getting better. In chapter 16, John describes a vision in which angels pour out the contents of seven bowls that bring a series of plagues across the earth, reminding us of the plagues in Exodus. In this chapter we read of Armageddon, which is not an event but the name of a location where the armies of the beast gather for a battle against the Lord. The description of the downfall of Babylon in chapters 17–18 is arguably the most complex section of Revelation. Most biblical scholars agree that this is not a reference to the Babylonian Empire that destroyed Jerusalem and carried the Israelites into exile in 587 BC but a representation of all evil structures and empires in the world that oppose the kingdom of God. In chapters 19–20 we read about a final battle at Armageddon, where John sees Jesus leading an army from heaven to victory over the armies of the beast, followed by the final judgment.

In the final two chapters of Revelation, John has a vision in which God comes to dwell once again with his people in a new Jerusalem. He makes all things new and eradicates pain, suffering, and death once and for all. God and Jesus—referred to as "the Lamb"—are enthroned in the city, and a river of life flows from the throne. At the end of chapter 22, the Lord promises that he is coming soon.

This is how the Bible ends. It's a radical vision of war and death and all kinds of madness, but when the dust settles, the final victory belongs to the Lord. While these pages are just as complex and symbolic as the rest of Revelation, they reveal a central truth: The story we are all part of has a conclusion—and it is glorious. Jesus will return. God will redeem and restore all things. The brokenness of this world will end. No matter what we face today, the promise of the future is that the kingdom of God will reign forever.

Amen. Come, Lord Jesus.

Psalms and Proverbs

The final passage of Proverbs is an acrostic poem (each of the twenty-two verses begins with a new letter from the Hebrew alphabet) that describes a "wife of noble character" (31:10). It's a brilliant conclusion because it describes what someone's life would look like if they took all the wisdom from Proverbs and lived by it. Verse by verse, it describes her life as overflowing with goodness that spreads into the world around her. And it's not just an example, it's an invitation for us to follow her lead. When we choose the way of wisdom, God's goodness will overflow in our lives and the lives of others.

It seems only fitting that the final few chapters of Psalms are an anthem of praise to the Lord. The word *praise* occurs more than thirty-five times in the four psalms we're reading this week.

Over the past year, we have read a wide range of poems, prayers, and songs that have reflected on almost every aspect of human existence, including a great deal of lament over life's sadness and pain. And what we find as the foundation of all these psalms, even the saddest ones, is worship. Psalms reminds us that God alone is worthy of our praise, and no matter what our circumstances may be, a song of praise should always be on our lips.

> Let everything that has breath praise the Lord.
>
> Praise the Lord. (Ps. 150:6)

Reflections

Write down a few reflections on this week's readings.

Day 358: Zephaniah 1:1–3:20; Revelation 16:1–21; Psalm 147:1–11

Day 359: Haggai 1:1–2:23; Revelation 17:1–18; Psalm 147:12–20

Day 360: Zec. 1:1–4:14; Revelation 18:1–17a; Proverbs 31:10–20

Day 361: Zec. 5:1–8:23; Revelation 18:17b–19:10; Psalm 148:1–6

Day 362: Zechariah 9:1–11:17; Revelation 19:11–21; Psalm 148:7–14

Day 363: Zechariah 12:1–14:21; Revelation 20:1–15; Psalm 149:1–9

Day 364: Malachi 1:1–2:16; Revelation 21:1–27; Proverbs 31:21–31

Day 365: Malachi 2:17–4:6; Revelation 22:1–21; Psalm 150:1–6

CONCLUSION

We made it.

How does it feel?

Whether you completed this reading plan in fifty-two weeks (my guess is that some of you did it even faster than that) or it's taken you a bit longer (which is absolutely fine), I hope this has been as meaningful an experience for you as it has been for me.

All the way back in the introduction, I said that God has a way of meeting us through his Word in incredible and unexpected ways. And you know what? That was true for me *so many times* as I wrote this book. I've read the entire Bible several times in my life, but I still discovered something new every week as I worked my way through the text and wrote the weekly reading guides.

You see, the Bible always has something new to teach us. Whether you've read it one time or a hundred, there is more to discover and learn. So after you take a few moments to celebrate the completion of this journey through the Bible, I want to encourage you to make a plan to start again. If you keep returning to God's Word, he will keep showing you something new.

Your word, Lord, is eternal; it stands firm in the heavens. (Ps. 119:89)

ACKNOWLEDGMENTS

Writing this book was not my idea. In fact, I was really struggling to come up with *any* good book ideas when I met with my friend and editor, Dale Williams, last year to do some brainstorming. I knew I wanted my next book to go deeper than where I had gone in *Bible Translations for Everyone*, and that I wanted to lean into my work as both a pastor and a professor, but I couldn't figure out what that should look like. In that meeting, Dale suggested that I think about how I would approach writing a book that would guide readers through the Bible over the course of a year.

As soon as he suggested it, something clicked.

I knew this was it.

Thank you, Dale, for being my guide. And to everyone at Zondervan Reflective and HarperCollins Christian Publishing–especially Emily Voss and Kim Tanner–thank you for your encouragement, kindness, and support.

My wife has been by my side every step of the way with this book. She's the one I called as soon as Dale gave me the idea, and she helped me figure out the best way to approach the weekly structure. She was my first reader and my biggest encourager . . . and she even designed the cover! I love you, Becca. I cannot thank you enough.

I don't know anyone who loves Scripture more than my mom, and her devotion to it is contagious. I learned to love the Bible from her, and I am so grateful that she and my dad made God's Word a priority for our family. Mom and Dad, thank you for your endless love and support. I am so grateful for you.

Many of the entries I wrote for this book were adapted from

past sermons and class lectures that I first wrote during my time at Brookside Church, Core Community Church, First Baptist Nashville, Crievewood Baptist Church, and Belmont University. When I think about these places, there are countless names and faces that come to mind of people who made a deep impact on my life and my understanding of God's Word. My love and thanks to all of you.

My life is abundantly blessed by an incredible community of family and friends. I count among these friends the global network of people who watch my videos and support my ministry. Thank you all. This book is for you.

THE READING PLAN

Week 4

- [ ] **Day 22:** Genesis 43:1–44:34; Matthew 15:10–39; Psalm 13:1–6
- [ ] **Day 23:** Genesis 45:1–47:12; Matthew 16:1–20; Psalm 14:1–7
- [ ] **Day 24:** Genesis 47:13–48:22; Matthew 16:21–17:13; Proverbs 3:1–10
- [ ] **Day 25:** Genesis 49:1–50:26; Matthew 17:14–18:9; Psalm 15:1–5
- [ ] **Day 26:** Exodus 1:1–3:22; Matthew 18:10–35; Psalm 16:1–11
- [ ] **Day 27:** Exodus 4:1–6:12; Matthew 19:1–15; Psalm 17:1–5
- [ ] **Day 28:** Exodus 6:13–8:32; Matthew 19:16–30; Proverbs 3:11–20

Week 5

- [ ] **Day 29:** Exodus 9:1–10:29; Matthew 20:1–19; Psalm 17:6–12
- [ ] **Day 30:** Exodus 11:1–12:51; Matthew 20:20–34; Psalm 17:13–15
- [ ] **Day 31:** Exodus 13:1–14:31; Matthew 21:1–17; Psalm 18:1–6
- [ ] **Day 32:** Exodus 15:1–16:36; Matthew 21:18–32; Proverbs 3:21–35
- [ ] **Day 33:** Exodus 17:1–18:27; Matthew 21:33–22:14; Psalm 18:7–15
- [ ] **Day 34:** Exodus 19:1–20:26; Matthew 22:15–46; Psalm 18:16–24
- [ ] **Day 35:** Exodus 21:1–22:31; Matthew 23:1–39; Psalm 18:25–36

Week 6

- [ ] **Day 36:** Exodus 23:1–24:18; Matthew 24:1–31; Proverbs 4:1–9
- [ ] **Day 37:** Exodus 25:1–26:37; Matthew 24:32–25:13; Psalm 18:37–42
- [ ] **Day 38:** Exodus 27:1–28:43; Matthew 25:14–46; Psalm 18:43–50
- [ ] **Day 39:** Exodus 29:1–30:38; Matthew 26:1–30; Psalm 19:1–6
- [ ] **Day 40:** Exodus 31:1–33:6; Matthew 26:31–46; Proverbs 4:10–19
- [ ] **Day 41:** Exodus 33:7–34:35; Matthew 26:47–68; Psalm 19:7–14
- [ ] **Day 42:** Exodus 35:1–36:38; Matthew 26:69–27:10; Psalm 20:1–9

Week 7

- [ ] **Day 43:** Exodus 37:1–38:31; Matthew 27:11–44; Psalm 21:1–7
- [ ] **Day 44:** Exodus 39:1–40:38; Matthew 27:45–66; Proverbs 4:20–27
- [ ] **Day 45:** Leviticus 1:1–3:17; Matthew 28:1–20; Psalm 21:8–13
- [ ] **Day 46:** Leviticus 4:1–5:13; Mark 1:1–28; Psalm 22:1–11
- [ ] **Day 47:** Leviticus 5:14–7:10; Mark 1:29–2:17; Psalm 22:12–21
- [ ] **Day 48:** Leviticus 7:11–8:36; Mark 2:18–3:30; Proverbs 5:1–14
- [ ] **Day 49:** Leviticus 9:1–10:20; Mark 3:31–4:29; Psalm 22:22–31

Week 8

- [ ] **Day 50:** Leviticus 11:1–12:8; Mark 4:30–5:20; Psalm 23:1–6
- [ ] **Day 51:** Leviticus 13:1–59; Mark 5:21–6:6a; Psalm 24:1–10
- [ ] **Day 52:** Leviticus 14:1–57; Mark 6:6b–29; Proverbs 5:15–23
- [ ] **Day 53:** Leviticus 15:1–16:34; Mark 6:30–56; Psalm 25:1–7
- [ ] **Day 54:** Leviticus 17:1–18:30; Mark 7:1–30; Psalm 25:8–15
- [ ] **Day 55:** Leviticus 19:1–20:27; Mark 7:31–8:13; Psalm 25:16–22
- [ ] **Day 56:** Leviticus 21:1–22:33; Mark 8:14–9:1; Proverbs 6:1–11

Week 9

- [ ] **Day 57:** Leviticus 23:1–24:23; Mark 9:2–32; Psalm 26:1–12
- [ ] **Day 58:** Leviticus 25:1–26:13; Mark 9:33–10:12; Psalm 27:1–6
- [ ] **Day 59:** Leviticus 26:14–27:34; Mark 10:13–31; Psalm 27:7–14
- [ ] **Day 60:** Numbers 1:1–2:9; Mark 10:32–52; Proverbs 6:12–19
- [ ] **Day 61:** Numbers 2:10–3:51; Mark 11:1–25; Psalm 28:1–9
- [ ] **Day 62:** Numbers 4:1–5:10; Mark 11:27–12:12; Psalm 29:1–11
- [ ] **Day 63:** Numbers 5:11–6:27; Mark 12:13–27; Psalm 30:1–7

Week 10

- [ ] **Day 64:** Numbers 7:1–65; Mark 12:28–44; Proverbs 6:20–29
- [ ] **Day 65:** Numbers 7:66–9:14; Mark 13:1–31; Psalm 30:8–12
- [ ] **Day 66:** Numbers 9:15–11:3; Mark 13:32–14:16; Psalm 31:1–8
- [ ] **Day 67:** Numbers 11:4–13:25; Mark 14:17–42; Psalm 31:9–18
- [ ] **Day 68:** Numbers 13:26–14:45; Mark 14:43–72; Proverbs 6:30–35
- [ ] **Day 69:** Numbers 15:1–16:35; Mark 15:1–32; Psalm 31:19–24
- [ ] **Day 70:** Numbers 16:36–18:32; Mark 15:33–47; Psalm 32:1–11

Week 11

- [ ] **Day 71:** Numbers 19:1–21:3; Mark 16:1–20; Psalm 33:1–11
- [ ] **Day 72:** Numbers 21:4–22:20; Luke 1:1–25; Proverbs 7:1–5
- [ ] **Day 73:** Numbers 22:21–23:26; Luke 1:26–38; Psalm 33:12–22
- [ ] **Day 74:** Numbers 23:27–26:11; Luke 1:39–56; Psalm 34:1–10
- [ ] **Day 75:** Numbers 26:12–27:11; Luke 1:57–80; Psalm 34:11–22
- [ ] **Day 76:** Numbers 27:12–29:11; Luke 2:1–20; Proverbs 7:6–20
- [ ] **Day 77:** Numbers 29:12–31:24; Luke 2:21–40; Psalm 35:1–10

Week 12

- [ ] **Day 78:** Numbers 31:25–32:42; Luke 2:41–52; Psalm 35:11–18
- [ ] **Day 79:** Numbers 33:1–34:29; Luke 3:1–22; Psalm 35:19–28
- [ ] **Day 80:** Numbers 35:1–36:13; Luke 3:23–4:13; Proverbs 7:21–27
- [ ] **Day 81:** Deuteronomy 1:1–2:23; Luke 4:14–37; Psalm 36:1–12
- [ ] **Day 82:** Deuteronomy 2:24–4:14; Luke 4:38–5:16; Psalm 37:1–9
- [ ] **Day 83:** Deuteronomy 4:15–5:33; Luke 5:17–32; Psalm 37:10–20
- [ ] **Day 84:** Deuteronomy 6:1–8:20; Luke 5:33–6:11; Proverbs 8:1–11

Week 13

- [ ] **Day 85:** Deuteronomy 9:1–10:22; Luke 6:12–36; Psalm 37:21–31
- [ ] **Day 86:** Deuteronomy 11:1–12:32; Luke 6:37–7:10; Psalm 37:32–40
- [ ] **Day 87:** Deuteronomy 13:1–14:29; Luke 7:11–35; Psalm 38:1–12
- [ ] **Day 88:** Deuteronomy 15:1–16:20; Luke 7:36–50; Proverbs 8:12–21
- [ ] **Day 89:** Deuteronomy 16:21–18:22; Luke 8:1–18; Psalm 38:13–22
- [ ] **Day 90:** Deuteronomy 19:1–20:20; Luke 8:19–39; Psalm 39:1–13
- [ ] **Day 91:** Deuteronomy 21:1–22:30; Luke 8:40–9:9; Psalm 40:1–8

Week 14

- [ ] **Day 92:** Deuteronomy 23:1–25:19; Luke 9:10–27; Proverbs 8:22–31
- [ ] **Day 93:** Deuteronomy 26:1–28:14; Luke 9:28–56; Psalm 40:9–17
- [ ] **Day 94:** Deuteronomy 28:15–68; Luke 9:57–10:24; Psalm 41:1–6
- [ ] **Day 95:** Deuteronomy 29:1–30:10; Luke 10:25–11:4; Psalm 41:7–13
- [ ] **Day 96:** Deuteronomy 30:11–31:29; Luke 11:5–32; Proverbs 8:32–36
- [ ] **Day 97:** Deuteronomy 31:30–32:52; Luke 11:33–54; Psalm 42:1–6a
- [ ] **Day 98:** Deuteronomy 33:1–34:12; Luke 12:1–34; Psalm 42:6b–11

Week 15

- [ ] **Day 99:** Joshua 1:1–2:24; Luke 12:35–59; Psalm 43:1–5
- [ ] **Day 100:** Joshua 3:1–5:12; Luke 13:1–30; Proverbs 9:1–12
- [ ] **Day 101:** Joshua 5:13–7:26; Luke 13:31–14:14; Psalm 44:1–12
- [ ] **Day 102:** Joshua 8:1–9:15; Luke 14:15–35; Psalm 44:13–26
- [ ] **Day 103:** Joshua 9:16–10:43; Luke 15:1–32; Psalm 45:1–9
- [ ] **Day 104:** Joshua 11:1–12:24; Luke 16:1–18; Proverbs 9:13–18
- [ ] **Day 105:** Joshua 13:1–14:15; Luke 16:19–17:10; Psalm 45:10–17

Week 16

- [ ] **Day 106:** Joshua 15:1–16:10; Luke 17:11–37; Psalm 46:1–11
- [ ] **Day 107:** Joshua 17:1–18:28; Luke 18:1–30; Psalm 47:1–9
- [ ] **Day 108:** Joshua 19:1–21:19; Luke 18:31–19:10; Proverbs 10:1–10
- [ ] **Day 109:** Joshua 21:20–22:34; Luke 19:11–44; Psalm 48:1–8
- [ ] **Day 110:** Joshua 23:1–24:33; Luke 19:45–20:26; Psalm 48:9–14
- [ ] **Day 111:** Judges 1:1–2:5; Luke 20:27–21:4; Psalm 49:1–20
- [ ] **Day 112:** Judges 2:6–3:31; Luke 21:5–38; Proverbs 10:11–20

Week 17

- [ ] **Day 113:** Judges 4:1–5:31; Luke 22:1–38; Psalm 50:1–15
- [ ] **Day 114:** Judges 6:1–7:8a; Luke 22:39–62; Psalm 50:16–23
- [ ] **Day 115:** Judges 7:8b–8:35; Luke 22:63–23:25; Psalm 51:1–9
- [ ] **Day 116:** Judges 9:1–57; Luke 23:26–56; Proverbs 10:21–30
- [ ] **Day 117:** Judges 10:1–11:40; Luke 24:1–35; Psalm 51:10–19
- [ ] **Day 118:** Judges 12:1–13:25; Luke 24:36–53; Psalm 52:1–9
- [ ] **Day 119:** Judges 14:1–15:20; John 1:1–28; Psalm 53:1–6

Week 18

- [ ] **Day 120:** Judges 16:1–17:13; John 1:29–51; Proverbs 10:31–11:8
- [ ] **Day 121:** Judges 18:1–19:30; John 2:1–25; Psalm 54:1–7
- [ ] **Day 122:** Judges 20:1–21:25; John 3:1–21; Psalm 55:1–11
- [ ] **Day 123:** Ruth 1:1–2:23; John 3:22–36; Psalm 55:12–23
- [ ] **Day 124:** Ruth 3:1–4:22; John 4:1–26; Proverbs 11:9–18
- [ ] **Day 125:** 1 Samuel 1:1–2:26; John 4:27–42; Psalm 56:1–13
- [ ] **Day 126:** 1 Samuel 2:27–4:22; John 4:43–5:15; Psalm 57:1–6

Week 19

- [ ] **Day 127:** 1 Samuel 5:1–7:17; John 5:16–30; Psalm 57:7–11
- [ ] **Day 128:** 1 Samuel 8:1–10:8; John 5:31–47; Proverbs 11:19–28
- [ ] **Day 129:** 1 Samuel 10:9–12:25; John 6:1–24; Psalm 58:1–11
- [ ] **Day 130:** 1 Samuel 13:1–14:23; John 6:25–59; Psalm 59:1–8
- [ ] **Day 131:** 1 Samuel 14:24–15:35; John 6:60–7:13; Psalm 59:9–17
- [ ] **Day 132:** 1 Samuel 16:1–17:37; John 7:14–44; Proverbs 11:29–12:7
- [ ] **Day 133:** 1 Samuel 17:38–18:30; John 7:45–8:11; Psalm 60:1–4

Week 20

- [ ] **Day 134:** 1 Samuel 19:1–20:42; John 8:12–30; Psalm 60:5–12
- [ ] **Day 135:** 1 Samuel 21:1–23:29; John 8:31–59; Psalm 61:1–8
- [ ] **Day 136:** 1 Samuel 24:1–25:44; John 9:1–34; Proverbs 12:8–17
- [ ] **Day 137:** 1 Samuel 26:1–28:25; John 9:35–10:21; Psalm 62:1–12
- [ ] **Day 138:** 1 Samuel 29:1–31:13; John 10:22–42; Psalm 63:1–11
- [ ] **Day 139:** 2 Samuel 1:1–2:7; John 11:1–44; Psalm 64:1–10
- [ ] **Day 140:** 2 Samuel 2:8–3:21; John 11:45–12:11; Proverbs 12:18–27

Week 21

- [ ] **Day 141:** 2 Samuel 3:22–5:5; John 12:12–36; Psalm 65:1–13
- [ ] **Day 142:** 2 Samuel 5:6–6:23; John 12:37–13:17; Psalm 66:1–12
- [ ] **Day 143:** 2 Samuel 7:1–8:18; John 13:18–38; Psalm 66:13–20
- [ ] **Day 144:** 2 Samuel 9:1–10:19; John 14:1–31; Proverbs 12:28–13:9
- [ ] **Day 145:** 2 Samuel 11:1–12:31; John 15:1–16:4; Psalm 67:1–7
- [ ] **Day 146:** 2 Samuel 13:1–39; John 16:5–17:5; Psalm 68:1–6
- [ ] **Day 147:** 2 Samuel 14:1–15:12; John 17:6–26; Psalm 68:7–14

Week 22

- [ ] **Day 148:** 2 Samuel 15:13–16:14; John 18:1–24; Proverbs 13:10–19
- [ ] **Day 149:** 2 Samuel 16:15–18:18; John 18:25–40; Psalm 68:15–20
- [ ] **Day 150:** 2 Samuel 18:19–19:43; John 19:1–27; Psalm 68:21–27
- [ ] **Day 151:** 2 Samuel 20:1–21:22; John 19:28–20:9; Psalm 68:28–35
- [ ] **Day 152:** 2 Samuel 22:1–23:7; John 20:10–31; Proverbs 13:20–14:4
- [ ] **Day 153:** 2 Samuel 23:8–24:25; John 21:1–25; Psalm 69:1–12
- [ ] **Day 154:** 1 Kings 1:1–2:12; Acts 1:1–22; Psalm 69:13–28

Week 23

- [ ] **Day 155:** 1 Kings 2:13–3:15; Acts 1:23–2:21; Psalm 69:29–36
- [ ] **Day 156:** 1 Kings 3:16–5:18; Acts 2:22–47; Proverbs 14:5–14
- [ ] **Day 157:** 1 Kings 6:1–7:22; Acts 3:1–26; Psalm 70:1–5
- [ ] **Day 158:** 1 Kings 7:23–8:21; Acts 4:1–22; Psalm 71:1–8
- [ ] **Day 159:** 1 Kings 8:22–9:9; Acts 4:23–5:11; Psalm 71:9–18
- [ ] **Day 160:** 1 Kings 9:10–11:13; Acts 5:12–42; Proverbs 14:15–24
- [ ] **Day 161:** 1 Kings 11:14–12:24; Acts 6:1–7:19; Psalm 71:19–24

Week 24

- [ ] **Day 162:** 1 Kings 12:25–14:20; Acts 7:20–43; Psalm 72:1–20
- [ ] **Day 163:** 1 Kings 14:21–16:7; Acts 7:44–8:3; Psalm 73:1–14
- [ ] **Day 164:** 1 Kings 16:8–18:15; Acts 8:4–40; Proverbs 14:25–35
- [ ] **Day 165:** 1 Kings 18:16–19:21; Acts 9:1–31; Psalm 73:15–28
- [ ] **Day 166:** 1 Kings 20:1–21:29; Acts 9:32–10:23a; Psalm 74:1–9
- [ ] **Day 167:** 1 Kings 22:1–53; Acts 10:23b–11:18; Psalm 74:10–17
- [ ] **Day 168:** 2 Kings 1:1–2:25; Acts 11:19–12:19a; Proverbs 15:1–10

Week 25

- [ ] **Day 169:** 2 Kings 3:1–4:37; Acts 12:19b–13:12; Psalm 74:18–23
- [ ] **Day 170:** 2 Kings 4:38–6:23; Acts 13:13–41; Psalm 75:1–10
- [ ] **Day 171:** 2 Kings 6:24–8:15; Acts 13:42–14:7; Psalm 76:1–12
- [ ] **Day 172:** 2 Kings 8:16–9:37; Acts 14:8–28; Proverbs 15:11–20
- [ ] **Day 173:** 2 Kings 10:1–11:21; Acts 15:1–21; Psalm 77:1–9
- [ ] **Day 174:** 2 Kings 12:1–14:22; Acts 15:22–41; Psalm 77:10–20
- [ ] **Day 175:** 2 Kings 14:23–15:38; Acts 16:1–15; Psalm 78:1–8

Week 26

- [ ] **Day 176:** 2 Kings 16:1–17:41; Acts 16:16–40; Proverbs 15:21–30
- [ ] **Day 177:** 2 Kings 18:1–19:13; Acts 17:1–21; Psalm 78:9–16
- [ ] **Day 178:** 2 Kings 19:14–20:21; Acts 17:22–18:8; Psalm 78:17–31
- [ ] **Day 179:** 2 Kings 21:1–22:20; Acts 18:9–19:13; Psalm 78:32–39
- [ ] **Day 180:** 2 Kings 23:1–24:7; Acts 19:14–41; Proverbs 15:31–16:7
- [ ] **Day 181:** 2 Kings 24:8–25:30; Acts 20:1–38; Psalm 78:40–55
- [ ] **Day 182:** 1 Chronicles 1:1–2:17; Acts 21:1–26; Psalm 78:56–72

Week 27

- [ ] **Day 183:** 1 Chronicles 2:18–4:8; Acts 21:27–22:21; Psalm 79:1–13
- [ ] **Day 184:** 1 Chronicles 4:9–5:26; Acts 22:22–23:11; Proverbs 16:8–17
- [ ] **Day 185:** 1 Chronicles 6:1–81; Acts 23:12–35; Psalm 80:1–7
- [ ] **Day 186:** 1 Chronicles 7:1–9:1a; Acts 24:1–27; Psalm 80:8–19
- [ ] **Day 187:** 1 Chronicles 9:1b–10:14; Acts 25:1–22; Psalm 81:1–7
- [ ] **Day 188:** 1 Chronicles 11:1–12:22; Acts 25:23–26:23; Proverbs 16:18–27
- [ ] **Day 189:** 1 Chronicles 12:23–14:17; Acts 26:24–27:12; Psalm 81:8–16

Week 28

- ☐ **Day 190:** 1 Chronicles 15:1–16:36; Acts 27:13–44; Psalm 82:1–8
- ☐ **Day 191:** 1 Chronicles 16:37–18:17; Acts 28:1–16; Psalm 83:1–18
- ☐ **Day 192:** 1 Chronicles 19:1–22:1; Acts 28:17–31; Proverbs 16:28–17:4
- ☐ **Day 193:** 1 Chronicles 22:2–23:32; Romans 1:1–17; Psalm 84:1–7
- ☐ **Day 194:** 1 Chronicles 24:1–26:19; Romans 1:18–32; Psalm 84:8–12
- ☐ **Day 195:** 1 Chronicles 26:20–27:34; Romans 2:1–16; Psalm 85:1–7
- ☐ **Day 196:** 1 Chronicles 28:1–29:30; Romans 2:17–3:8; Proverbs 17:5–14

Week 29

- ☐ **Day 197:** 2 Chronicles 1:1–17; Romans 3:9–31; Psalm 85:8–13
- ☐ **Day 198:** 2 Chronicles 2:1–5:1; Romans 4:1–15; Psalm 86:1–10
- ☐ **Day 199:** 2 Chronicles 5:2–7:10; Romans 4:16–5:11; Psalm 86:11–17
- ☐ **Day 200:** 2 Chronicles 7:11–9:31; Romans 5:12–21; Proverbs 17:15–24
- ☐ **Day 201:** 2 Chronicles 10:1–12:16; Romans 6:1–14; Psalm 87:1–7
- ☐ **Day 202:** 2 Chronicles 13:1–15:19; Romans 6:15–7:6; Psalm 88:1–9a
- ☐ **Day 203:** 2 Chronicles 16:1–18:27; Romans 7:7–25; Psalm 88:9b–18

Week 30

- ☐ **Day 204:** 2 Chron. 18:28–21:3; Romans 8:1–17; Proverbs 17:25–18:6
- ☐ **Day 205:** 2 Chronicles 21:4–23:21; Romans 8:18–39; Psalm 89:1–8
- ☐ **Day 206:** 2 Chronicles 24:1–25:28; Romans 9:1–21; Psalm 89:9–13
- ☐ **Day 207:** 2 Chronicles 26:1–28:27; Romans 9:22–10:4; Psalm 89:14–18
- ☐ **Day 208:** 2 Chron. 29:1–31:1; Romans 10:5–11:10; Proverbs 18:7–16
- ☐ **Day 209:** 2 Chronicles 31:2–33:20; Romans 11:11–32; Psalm 89:19–29
- ☐ **Day 210:** 2 Chron. 33:21–35:19; Romans 11:33–12:21; Psalm 89:30–37

Week 31

- [ ] **Day 211:** 2 Chronicles 35:20–36:23; Romans 13:1–14; Psalm 89:38–45
- [ ] **Day 212:** Ezra 1:1–2:67; Romans 14:1–18; Proverbs 18:17–19:2
- [ ] **Day 213:** Ezra 2:68–4:5; Romans 14:19–15:13; Psalm 89:46–52
- [ ] **Day 214:** Ezra 4:6–5:17; Romans 15:14–33; Psalm 90:1–10
- [ ] **Day 215:** Ezra 6:1–7:10; Romans 16:1–27; Psalm 90:11–17
- [ ] **Day 216:** Ezra 7:11–8:14; 1 Corinthians 1:1–17; Proverbs 19:3–12
- [ ] **Day 217:** Ezra 8:15–9:15; 1 Corinthians 1:18–2:5; Psalm 91:1–8

Week 32

- [ ] **Day 218:** Ezra 10:1–44; 1 Corinthians 2:6–16; Psalm 91:9–16
- [ ] **Day 219:** Nehemiah 1:1–2:20; 1 Corinthians 3:1–23; Psalm 92:1–15
- [ ] **Day 220:** Nehemiah 3:1–4:23; 1 Corinthians 4:1–21; Proverbs 19:13–22
- [ ] **Day 221:** Nehemiah 5:1–7:3; 1 Corinthians 5:1–13; Psalm 93:1–5
- [ ] **Day 222:** Nehemiah 7:4–8:18; 1 Corinthians 6:1–20; Psalm 94:1–11
- [ ] **Day 223:** Nehemiah 9:1–37; 1 Corinthians 7:1–16; Psalm 94:12–23
- [ ] **Day 224:** Neh. 9:38–11:21; 1 Corinthians 7:17–35; Proverbs 19:23–20:4

Week 33

- [ ] **Day 225:** Neh. 11:22–12:47; 1 Corinthians 7:36–8:13; Psalm 95:1–11
- [ ] **Day 226:** Nehemiah 13:1–31; 1 Corinthians 9:1–18; Psalm 96:1–13
- [ ] **Day 227:** Esther 1:1–2:18; 1 Corinthians 9:19–10:13; Psalm 97:1–12
- [ ] **Day 228:** Esther 2:19–5:14; 1 Cor. 10:14–11:1; Proverbs 20:5–14
- [ ] **Day 229:** Esther 6:1–8:17; 1 Corinthians 11:2–34; Psalm 98:1–9
- [ ] **Day 230:** Esther 9:1–10:3; 1 Corinthians 12:1–26; Psalm 99:1–9
- [ ] **Day 231:** Job 1:1–3:26; 1 Corinthians 12:27–13:13; Psalm 100:1–5

Week 34

- [ ] **Day 232:** Job 4:1–7:21; 1 Corinthians 14:1–19; Proverbs 20:15–24
- [ ] **Day 233:** Job 8:1–10:22; 1 Corinthians 14:20–40; Psalm 101:1–8
- [ ] **Day 234:** Job 11:1–14:22; 1 Corinthians 15:1–34; Psalm 102:1–11
- [ ] **Day 235:** Job 15:1–18:21; 1 Corinthians 15:35–49; Psalm 102:12–17
- [ ] **Day 236:** Job 19:1–21:34; 1 Cor. 15:50–16:4; Proverbs 20:25–21:4
- [ ] **Day 237:** Job 22:1–24:25; 1 Corinthians 16:5–24; Psalm 102:18–28
- [ ] **Day 238:** Job 25:1–29:25; 2 Corinthians 1:1–11; Psalm 103:1–12

Week 35

- [ ] **Day 239:** Job 30:1–32:22; 2 Corinthians 1:12–22; Psalm 103:13–22
- [ ] **Day 240:** Job 33:1–34:37; 2 Corinthians 1:23–2:11; Proverbs 21:5–16
- [ ] **Day 241:** Job 35:1–37:24; 2 Corinthians 2:12–3:6; Psalm 104:1–18
- [ ] **Day 242:** Job 38:1–40:2; 2 Corinthians 3:7–18; Psalm 104:19–30
- [ ] **Day 243:** Job 40:3–42:17; 2 Corinthians 4:1–18; Psalm 104:31–35
- [ ] **Day 244:** Ecclesiastes 1:1–3:22; 2 Cor. 5:1–10; Proverbs 21:17–26
- [ ] **Day 245:** Ecclesiastes 4:1–6:12; 2 Cor. 5:11–6:2; Psalm 105:1–11

Week 36

- [ ] **Day 246:** Ecclesiastes 7:1–9:12; 2 Cor. 6:3–7:1; Psalm 105:12–22
- [ ] **Day 247:** Ecclesiastes 9:13–12:14; 2 Cor. 7:2–16; Psalm 105:23–36
- [ ] **Day 248:** Song of Songs 1:1–4:16; 2 Cor. 8:1–15; Proverbs 21:27–22:6
- [ ] **Day 249:** Song of Songs 5:1–8:14; 2 Cor. 8:16–9:5; Psalm 105:37–45
- [ ] **Day 250:** Isaiah 1:1–2:22; 2 Corinthians 9:6–15; Psalm 106:1–15
- [ ] **Day 251:** Isaiah 3:1–5:7; 2 Corinthians 10:1–18; Psalm 106:16–31
- [ ] **Day 252:** Isaiah 5:8–8:10; 2 Corinthians 11:1–15; Proverbs 22:7–16

Week 37

- [ ] **Day 253:** Isaiah 8:11–10:19; 2 Corinthians 11:16–33; Psalm 106:32–39
- [ ] **Day 254:** Isaiah 10:20–13:22; 2 Corinthians 12:1–10; Psalm 106:40–48
- [ ] **Day 255:** Isaiah 14:1–16:14; 2 Corinthians 12:11–21; Psalm 107:1–9
- [ ] **Day 256:** Isaiah 17:1–19:25; 2 Corinthians 13:1–14; Proverbs 22:17–27
- [ ] **Day 257:** Isaiah 20:1–23:18; Galatians 1:1–24; Psalm 107:10–22
- [ ] **Day 258:** Isaiah 24:1–26:21; Galatians 2:1–10; Psalm 107:23–32
- [ ] **Day 259:** Isaiah 27:1–28:29; Galatians 2:11–3:9; Psalm 107:33–43

Week 38

- [ ] **Day 260:** Isaiah 29:1–30:18; Galatians 3:10–25; Proverbs 22:28–23:9
- [ ] **Day 261:** Isaiah 30:19–32:20; Galatians 3:26–4:20; Psalm 108:1–5
- [ ] **Day 262:** Isaiah 33:1–35:10; Galatians 4:21–5:6; Psalm 108:6–13
- [ ] **Day 263:** Isaiah 36:1–37:38; Galatians 5:7–26; Psalm 109:1–20
- [ ] **Day 264:** Isaiah 38:1–40:31; Galatians 6:1–18; Proverbs 23:10–18
- [ ] **Day 265:** Isaiah 41:1–42:25; Ephesians 1:1–23; Psalm 109:21–31
- [ ] **Day 266:** Isaiah 43:1–44:23; Ephesians 2:1–22; Psalm 110:1–7

Week 39

- [ ] **Day 267:** Isaiah 44:24–46:13; Ephesians 3:1–21; Psalm 111:1–10
- [ ] **Day 268:** Isaiah 47:1–49:7; Ephesians 4:1–16; Proverbs 23:19–28
- [ ] **Day 269:** Isaiah 49:8–51:16; Ephesians 4:17–5:7; Psalm 112:1–10
- [ ] **Day 270:** Isaiah 51:17–54:17; Ephesians 5:8–33; Psalm 113:1–9
- [ ] **Day 271:** Isaiah 55:1–57:13; Ephesians 6:1–24; Psalm 114:1–8
- [ ] **Day 272:** Isaiah 57:14–59:21; Philippians 1:1–26; Proverbs 23:29–24:4
- [ ] **Day 273:** Isaiah 60:1–62:12; Philippians 1:27–2:11; Psalm 115:1–11

Week 40

- [ ] **Day 274:** Isaiah 63:1–65:16; Philippians 2:12–30; Psalm 115:12–18
- [ ] **Day 275:** Isaiah 65:17–66:24; Philippians 3:1–4:1; Psalm 116:1–11
- [ ] **Day 276:** Jeremiah 1:1–2:30; Philippians 4:2–23; Proverbs 24:5–14
- [ ] **Day 277:** Jeremiah 2:31–4:9; Colossians 1:1–23; Psalm 116:12–19
- [ ] **Day 278:** Jeremiah 4:10–5:31; Colossians 1:24–2:5; Psalm 117:1–2
- [ ] **Day 279:** Jeremiah 6:1–7:29; Colossians 2:6–23; Psalm 118:1–16
- [ ] **Day 280:** Jeremiah 7:30–9:16; Colossians 3:1–4:1; Proverbs 24:15–22

Week 41

- [ ] **Day 281:** Jeremiah 9:17–11:17; Colossians 4:2–18; Psalm 118:17–29
- [ ] **Day 282:** Jeremiah 11:18–13:27; 1 Thess. 1:1–2:16; Psalm 119:1–8
- [ ] **Day 283:** Jeremiah 14:1–15:21; 1 Thess. 2:17–3:13; Psalm 119:9–16
- [ ] **Day 284:** Jeremiah 16:1–17:27; 1 Thess. 4:1–18; Proverbs 24:23–34
- [ ] **Day 285:** Jeremiah 18:1–20:18; 1 Thess. 5:1–28; Psalm 119:17–24
- [ ] **Day 286:** Jeremiah 21:1–23:8; 2 Thess. 1:1–12; Psalm 119:25–32
- [ ] **Day 287:** Jeremiah 23:9–25:14; 2 Thess. 2:1–17; Psalm 119:33–40

Week 42

- [ ] **Day 288:** Jeremiah 25:15–26:24; 2 Thess. 3:1–18; Proverbs 25:1–10
- [ ] **Day 289:** Jeremiah 27:1–29:23; 1 Timothy 1:1–20; Psalm 119:41–48
- [ ] **Day 290:** Jeremiah 29:24–31:14; 1 Timothy 2:1–15; Psalm 119:49–56
- [ ] **Day 291:** Jeremiah 31:15–32:25; 1 Timothy 3:1–16; Psalm 119:57–64
- [ ] **Day 292:** Jeremiah 32:26–34:22; 1 Timothy 4:1–16; Proverbs 25:11–20
- [ ] **Day 293:** Jeremiah 35:1–37:21; 1 Timothy 5:1–6:2; Psalm 119:65–72
- [ ] **Day 294:** Jeremiah 38:1–40:6; 1 Timothy 6:3–21; Psalm 119:73–80

Week 43

- [ ] **Day 295:** Jeremiah 40:7–42:22; 2 Timothy 1:1–18; Psalm 119:81–88
- [ ] **Day 296:** Jeremiah 43:1–45:5; 2 Timothy 2:1–26; Proverbs 25:21–26:2
- [ ] **Day 297:** Jeremiah 46:1–47:7; 2 Timothy 3:1–17; Psalm 119:89–96
- [ ] **Day 298:** Jeremiah 48:1–49:6; 2 Timothy 4:1–22; Psalm 119:97–104
- [ ] **Day 299:** Jeremiah 49:7–50:10; Titus 1:1–16; Psalm 119:105–112
- [ ] **Day 300:** Jeremiah 50:11–51:14; Titus 2:1–15; Proverbs 26:3–12
- [ ] **Day 301:** Jeremiah 51:15–64; Titus 3:1–15; Psalm 119:113–120

Week 44

- [ ] **Day 302:** Jeremiah 52:1–34; Philemon 1–25; Psalm 119:121–128
- [ ] **Day 303:** Lamentations 1:1–2:6; Hebrews 1:1–14; Psalm 119:129–136
- [ ] **Day 304:** Lamentations 2:7–3:39; Hebrews 2:1–18; Proverbs 26:13–22
- [ ] **Day 305:** Lam. 3:40–5:22; Hebrews 3:1–19; Psalm 119:137–144
- [ ] **Day 306:** Ezekiel 1:1–3:27; Hebrews 4:1–13; Psalm 119:145–152
- [ ] **Day 307:** Ezekiel 4:1–6:14; Hebrews 4:14–5:10; Psalm 119:153–160
- [ ] **Day 308:** Ezekiel 7:1–9:11; Hebrews 5:11–6:12; Proverbs 26:23–27:4

Week 45

- [ ] **Day 309:** Ezekiel 10:1–12:28; Hebrews 6:13–7:10; Psalm 119:161–168
- [ ] **Day 310:** Ezekiel 13:1–15:8; Hebrews 7:11–28; Psalm 119:169–176
- [ ] **Day 311:** Ezekiel 16:1–63; Hebrews 8:1–13; Psalm 120:1–7
- [ ] **Day 312:** Ezekiel 17:1–18:32; Hebrews 9:1–15; Proverbs 27:5–14
- [ ] **Day 313:** Ezekiel 19:1–20:44; Hebrews 9:16–28; Psalm 121:1–8
- [ ] **Day 314:** Ezekiel 20:45–22:22; Hebrews 10:1–18; Psalm 122:1–9
- [ ] **Day 315:** Ezekiel 22:23–23:49; Hebrews 10:19–39; Psalm 123:1–4

Week 46

- [ ] **Day 316:** Ezekiel 24:1–25:17; Hebrews 11:1–16; Proverbs 27:15–22
- [ ] **Day 317:** Ezekiel 26:1–27:36; Hebrews 11:17–40; Psalm 124:1–8
- [ ] **Day 318:** Ezekiel 28:1–29:21; Hebrews 12:1–13; Psalm 125:1–5
- [ ] **Day 319:** Ezekiel 30:1–31:18; Hebrews 12:14–29; Psalm 126:1–6
- [ ] **Day 320:** Ezekiel 32:1–33:20; Hebrews 13:1–25; Proverbs 27:23–28:6
- [ ] **Day 321:** Ezekiel 33:21–35:15; James 1:1–27; Psalm 127:1–5
- [ ] **Day 322:** Ezekiel 36:1–37:28; James 2:1–26; Psalm 128:1–6

Week 47

- [ ] **Day 323:** Ezekiel 38:1–39:29; James 3:1–18; Psalm 129:1–8
- [ ] **Day 324:** Ezekiel 40:1–49; James 4:1–17; Proverbs 28:7–17
- [ ] **Day 325:** Ezekiel 41:1–42:20; James 5:1–20; Psalm 130:1–8
- [ ] **Day 326:** Ezekiel 43:1–44:31; 1 Peter 1:1–2:3; Psalm 131:1–3
- [ ] **Day 327:** Ezekiel 45:1–46:24; 1 Peter 2:4–25; Psalm 132:1–18
- [ ] **Day 328:** Ezekiel 47:1–48:35; 1 Peter 3:1–22; Proverbs 28:18–28
- [ ] **Day 329:** Daniel 1:1–2:23; 1 Peter 4:1–19; Psalm 133:1–3

Week 48

- [ ] **Day 330:** Daniel 2:24–3:12; 1 Peter 5:1–14; Psalm 134:1–3
- [ ] **Day 331:** Daniel 3:13–4:18; 2 Peter 1:1–21; Psalm 135:1–12
- [ ] **Day 332:** Daniel 4:19–5:16; 2 Peter 2:1–22; Proverbs 29:1–9
- [ ] **Day 333:** Daniel 5:17–6:28; 2 Peter 3:1–18; Psalm 135:13–21
- [ ] **Day 334:** Daniel 7:1–8:14; 1 John 1:1–2:11; Psalm 136:1–12
- [ ] **Day 335:** Daniel 8:15–9:19; 1 John 2:12–27; Psalm 136:13–26
- [ ] **Day 336:** Daniel 9:20–11:1; 1 John 2:28–3:10; Proverbs 29:10–18

Week 49

- [ ] **Day 337:** Daniel 11:2–35; 1 John 3:11–4:6; Psalm 137:1–9
- [ ] **Day 338:** Daniel 11:36–12:13; 1 John 4:7–21; Psalm 138:1–8
- [ ] **Day 339:** Hosea 1:1–2:23; 1 John 5:1–21; Psalm 139:1–10
- [ ] **Day 340:** Hosea 3:1–5:15; 2 John 1–13; Proverbs 29:19–27
- [ ] **Day 341:** Hosea 6:1–7:16; 3 John 1–14; Psalm 139:11–16
- [ ] **Day 342:** Hosea 8:1–9:17; Jude 1–25; Psalm 139:17–24
- [ ] **Day 343:** Hosea 10:1–11:11; Revelation 1:1–20; Psalm 140:1–5

Week 50

- [ ] **Day 344:** Hosea 11:12–14:9; Revelation 2:1–17; Proverbs 30:1–10
- [ ] **Day 345:** Joel 1:1–2:17; Revelation 2:18–3:6; Psalm 140:6–13
- [ ] **Day 346:** Joel 2:18–3:21; Revelation 3:7–22; Psalm 141:1–10
- [ ] **Day 347:** Amos 1:1–2:16; Revelation 4:1–11; Psalm 142:1–7
- [ ] **Day 348:** Amos 3:1–4:13; Revelation 5:1–14; Proverbs 30:11–23
- [ ] **Day 349:** Amos 5:1–27; Revelation 6:1–17; Psalm 143:1–12
- [ ] **Day 350:** Amos 6:1–7:17; Revelation 7:1–17; Psalm 144:1–8

Week 51

- [ ] **Day 351:** Amos 8:1–9:15; Revelation 8:1–9:12; Psalm 144:9–15
- [ ] **Day 352:** Obadiah 1–21; Revelation 9:13–10:11; Proverbs 30:24–33
- [ ] **Day 353:** Jonah 1:1–4:11; Revelation 11:1–19; Psalm 145:1–7
- [ ] **Day 354:** Micah 1:1–4:13; Revelation 12:1–13:1a; Psalm 145:8–13a
- [ ] **Day 355:** Micah 5:1–7:20; Revelation 13:1b–18; Psalm 145:13b–21
- [ ] **Day 356:** Nahum 1:1–3:19; Revelation 14:1–13; Proverbs 31:1–9
- [ ] **Day 357:** Habakkuk 1:1–3:19; Revelation 14:14–15:8; Psalm 146:1–10

Week 52

Bible Translations for Everyone

A Guide to Finding a Bible That's Right for You

Navigate the complex world of Bible translations with Tim Wildsmith.

Have you ever wondered why there are so many translations of the Bible? It can be overwhelming and challenging to make sense of the differences, similarities, strengths, and weakness of each. With over four hundred English translations to choose from, how do you know one is right for you? This book is here to help. Chapter by chapter, it tells the story of many different versions of the Bible, including information about their historical context, the people who translated them, and what makes them unique.

Bible Translations for Everyone contains:

- An introduction to how Bible translations work
- The fascinating history of early English Bibles like Tyndale and Wycliffe
- The textual basis, translation philosophy, strengths, and weaknesses of each popular English translation, including The New King James Version, The New International Version, The English Standard Version, and more
- Translation comparisons
- Timelines and charts

After reading this book, you will understand the essentials of each translation and be able to make an informed decision about which ones are right for you.

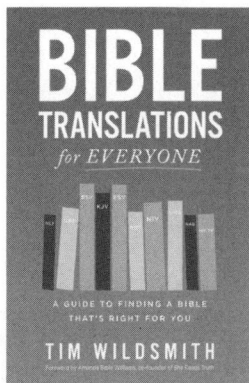

Available in stores and online!

ZONDERVAN®
.com